C 170 929 00 DF

KU-734-991

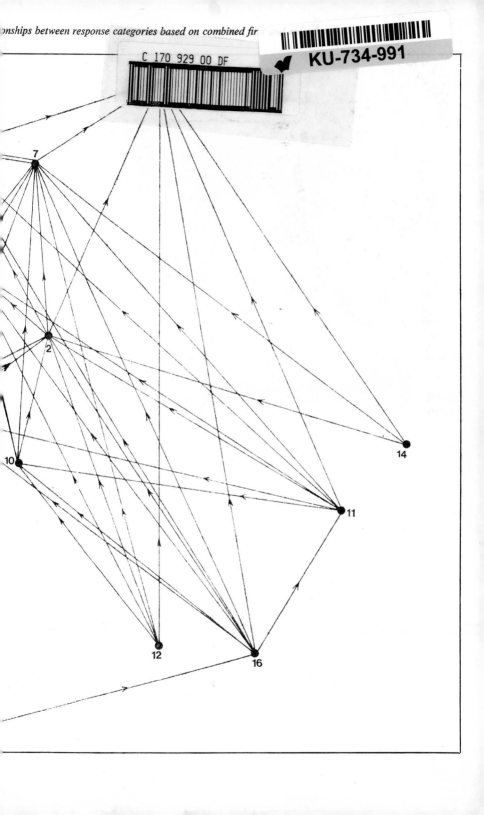

STAGES AND TRANSITION IN CONCEPTUAL DEVELOPMENT

An Experimental Study

Stages and Transition in Conceptual Development

An Experimental Study

J G Wallace
School of Education, University of Warwick

NFER

*Published by the National Foundation for Educational Research
in England and Wales*
Registered Office: The Mere, Upton Park, Slough, Bucks, SL1 2DQ
London Office: 79 Wimpole Street, London, W1M 8EA
*Book Publishing Division: 2 Jennings Buildings, Thames Avenue,
Windsor, Berks, SL4 1QS*
First Published 1972
© *J. G. Wallace, 1972*
SBN 901225 60 6

Cover design by
PETER GAULD, FSIA
Printed in Great Britain by
KING, THORNE & STACE LTD., SCHOOL ROAD, HOVE, SUSSEX BN3 5JE

170929

155
. A13

CONTENTS

TABLES

FIGURES

ACKNOWLEDGEMENTS

THE WORK REPORTED IN the present volume has benefited greatly from the advice of Mr. M. A. Brimer of the School of Education, University of Bristol. In particular, I am grateful for permission to use his method of analysis of qualitative data.

I would like to thank Miss M. Morton and Mrs. M. McKay for their assistance in the collection and processing of the data and Mr. R. H. Thomason for his invaluable help in producing the necessary computer programs.

Finally, I would like to thank the Headmistresses of Ashton Vale Infants' School, Henleaze Infants' School, Romney Avenue Infants' School and South Street Infants' School for agreeing to provide children to act as subjects and for enduring the inevitable disruption of school routine.

INTRODUCTION

IN 1965 THE WRITER produced a survey of the research literature on the subject of conceptualization in the period 1955-63. Under the title of *Concept Growth and the Education of the Child* this work has gained fairly wide currency in Britain and beyond. The scope of the survey was defined by the view that studies dealing with consistency in action over changing situations can be regarded as falling within the province of conceptual behaviour. Its primary objective was to highlight problems and methods for possible incorporation in an experimental programme dealing with conceptualization as an aspect of intellectual development in children. Appropriately enough the aim of the present volume is to report the results of the writer accepting his own recommendations and attempting an experimental attack on some of the issues pinpointed in the survey.

Despite a rise in the number of specialist journals in the field, the explosive increase in the number of psychological research papers meriting publication has inevitably resulted in an attenuation of the amount of space which can be allotted to each research report. The resulting emphasis on brevity, however, has had a deleterious effect. It has led to the according of a minimal amount of space, or even none at all, to dealing with the rationale underlying research studies and to indicating how they fit into the total picture of work in the area concerned. It has, also, encouraged the fragmentation of integrated research reports into numerous 'paper length' articles. As these often appear in several different journals, and due to variations in publication lag become available out of their logical sequence, it is extremely difficult to obtain a coherent picture of the implications of the research in question. More particularly, this piecemeal presentation destroys the continuity which is necessary to permit the reader to derive maximum benefit by following the development of the work from its inception with the choice of a problem, through the ups and downs which accompany the phases of design and practical execution, to the processing of data, the discussion of results and the planning of future action. Since all too few opportunities for contact with integrated research reports arise at the present time it is intended that this account will swell the number available by offering a detailed and complete description of the development of an experimental approach to a number of intractable problems in the area of intellectual development. No attempt will be made to benefit from hindsight by refurbishing the account of the reasoning behind the design of the experiments in the light of research reports which have appeared in the interim since their execution. Such more recent material will only play a part in the discussion of the experimental results and in the consideration of future directions for research in the area.

The survey of research on conceptualization in the period up to 1963 presented an exceedingly gloomy picture of the contribution of past work on this theme. The few features of the research scene which provided grounds for a more optimistic prognosis were largely to be attributed to the work of the Geneva school. In particular, the prominence of Piaget's work has had the laudable result of highlighting the major methodological and theoretical issues involved in the study of concept formation. Both his protagonists and his critics are compelled to descend to fundamentals and to squarely tackle crucial but intractable problems which it is all too tempting to avoid. On the methodological plane criticism of the dependence of the clinical method on a highly verbal approach has initiated a search for viable non-verbal alternatives, while the shortcomings of the cross-sectional nature of Piaget's developmental studies has resulted in a reappraisal of the merits of the longitudinal approach. Another refractory problem in this area which is now receiving the attention which it merits stems from the subjective method of allotting children's responses to categories adopted by the Geneva group. Is it possible to devise an objective approach to the task of detecting similarities and differences in detailed, qualitative data?

Fundamental theoretical issues have, also, been brought sharply into focus. They pose basic questions which clamour for an answer if we are to gain real understanding of conceptualization. Are stages characteristic of the course of conceptual development? If they exist must they be gone through in an invariable order? What is the nature of the transition rule underlying the course of development? Is it possible to achieve acceleration of the process of conceptual growth, and, if so, what limits does maturation impose upon it? Can we obviate the use of over-simplified, blanket terms such as abstraction and generalization by producing a convincing detailed analysis of the process of conceptualization? What is the effect of variations in cultural milieu on the course of concept formation? How is conceptualization related to perception?

Since no single study could hope to make a worthwhile contribution to all of these areas, it was decided as a first step in the design of the experimental investigation to be reported that it would focus on four important problems. Two of these are methodological, namely the question of the relative merits of the verbal and non-verbal approaches and the need for an objective method of analysing qualitative data, while the others are of a theoretical nature. The latter comprise the age-old issues of stages and the task of determining the possibility of accelerating the course of conceptual development.

With the selection of the broad problem areas complete, the task of deciding on the specific topics to be tackled and methods to be adopted became of prime importance. An essential preliminary to informed decision making in this context was a review of the existing work on these themes. Even the relatively generous limits of the present research report will not permit a detailed account of the relevant literature. The next chapter will, accordingly, present only the results of the preliminary appraisal which were of major importance in determining the nature of the experimental investigation.

CHAPTER ONE

Background to the Problems to be Investigated

The Verbal and Non-Verbal Approaches to the Investigation of Concept Formation—I

PIAGET'S METHODS of obtaining data have, like his theoretical formulations, altered to some extent with the passage of time. A consistent feature of the clinical method over the years, however, has been its extreme dependence on verbalization. The child is questioned by the experimenter, makes verbal responses and is asked for an explanation of them. These features have been retained by those of Piaget's followers who, like Vinh-Bang (1957), Laurendeau and Pinard (1962), have altered other aspects of the clinical method in the cause of standardization. Piaget maintains that the nature of the questions and the order of their presentation are adapted to the child's level of comprehension. The genuineness and consistency of his responses are tested by modifying the questions and the experimental conditions, while caution is exercised to avoid imposing on the child a point of view which is foreign to him.

Despite these protestations, Piaget has frequently been attacked for his use of verbally posed problems and for his reliance upon interpretation of verbal responses in his approach to the study of concept formation. His critics maintain that by making frequent use of verbal stimuli the experimenter becomes involved simultaneously with the problems of the conceptual process and the equally difficult questions posed by the relationship between language and conceptualization. The ensuing confusion considerably reduces the possibility of arriving at results of value. The child presumably responds to the 'meanings' which he attributes to the experimenter's words. What these 'meanings' are we do not know, we know only that they are intimately related to the events and circumstances surrounding the child's original learning of them. The verbal method may, therefore, only serve to conceal the effective stimulus for the subject's response.

Criticism of the verbal method was carried even further by Braine (1962). He asserted that it would seem to be intrinsically impossible to study how a concept develops with methods which employ verbal cues to evoke the concept. For, if the child understands the verbal cue, he must already have developed the concept. If he responds more or less appropriately, it is certain that he has the concept; but, if he fails to do so, very little is learned. The course of development of the concept remains obscure, and no light is thrown on the variation with age in the learning and generalization processes upon which the development of the concept depends.

Acceptance of the truth of these criticisms leaves only one constructive line of action open, the application of non-verbal methods to the study of conceptualization. Braine, to his credit, has not shirked this task.

His starting point was provided by the work of Piaget, Inhelder and Szeminska (1948) on the development of the concepts of length and measurement. Children who have the notion of transitivity of length are capable of making inferences of the type $A >$ (is longer than) B. $B > C : \supset A > C$ and $A <$ (is shorter than) B. $B < C : \supset A < C$. Braine (1959) proceeded to conduct an experiment which sparked off a controversy on the age at which this ability is first exhibited. He employed a non-verbal procedure in which children were first trained to find sweets under the longer (or shorter) of two sticks. After the training phase came a series of transitivity trials in which, for example, two sticks, A and C, intended not to be perceptibly different in length, were presented. The children were shown that A was longer than a measuring stick B, and then that B was longer than C. The measuring stick was removed and the child was asked to find the sweet. If he looked for it under stick A this was regarded as evidence of a transitive inference. Braine's results indicated that the average age at which children become capable of making such an inference is probably around five years.

This conclusion was strongly attacked by Smedslund (1963b) on two grounds. In an experiment using verbally posed transitivity problems he discovered that the average age at which children reveal a grasp of transitivity of length lies near eight years. In addition to providing this contradictory evidence, he was critical of Braine's non-verbal procedure. He contended that it permits the children to make correct responses based on empirical non-transitive hypotheses rather than on a transitive inference. A child, for example, directly applying his training to depend on relative length might succeed by simply responding to the stick which is longer than the measuring stick. ($A > B$ means $A > C$). This approach would permit him to disregard the comparison with the other stick. In support of this criticism he adduced results obtained with a group of five-year-old children who were trained by a non-verbal procedure to find sweets near the longer member of pairs of sticks and then confronted with a number of pseudomeasurement trials. In these problems a pair of sticks of exactly the same length were used. A measuring stick, which was shorter than both of them, was applied to only one of the sticks. Smedslund contended that children with a grasp of transitivity of length would realize that no conclusion could be reached on the basis of a single measurement and would be reduced to responding on a perceptual comparison basis. With sticks of equal length this would yield an approximate 50–50 proportion of responses to eack stick. Subjects employing a non-transitive hypothesis would be content with the single comparison and would respond to the stick which it indicated was the longer without considering the lack of information about the other stick. All of the five-year-olds tested appeared to adopt the latter approach.

Braine's (1964) rejoinder was, also, twofold. He argued that the nature of Smedslund's verbal procedure prevented his younger subjects from understanding what was required of them and his results cannot, therefore, claim to reveal the earliest age at which the average child grasps the transitivity of length. The evidence derived from the non-verbal pseudomeasurement trials is, also, of questionable validity. The child could simply be responding to the measured stick on the grounds that the experimenter, having said that he would help him, then pointed to only one of the comparison sticks. Although Smedslund does not state so explicitly, it appears that the subjects were reinforced for choosing the measured stick. Having achieved one success in this fashion the children naturally continued to respond to the stick to which the gesture was made on subsequent trials. This basis for response was not available in Braine's transitivity trials where both sticks were measured. An additional possibility is that children with a firm grasp of transitivity may conclude that the measured stick is longer by guessing the missing premise, i.e. they assume that there is no point in presenting A > B unless B > C. These arguments, and additional ambiguous features highlighted in a later joint paper (Smedslund, 1965), clearly indicated that no definitive answer to the question of the relative incidence of genuine transitivity of length and non-transitive hypotheses in the non-verbal test performance of five-year-olds can be derived by the use of single comparison pseudomeasurement trials.

Two main reasons motivated the decision to provide an account of the Smedslund-Braine controversy. The points made by Smedslund in his methodological analysis of the pitfalls of the non-verbal approach are not restricted to transitivity of length but are relevant to the study of concrete transitivity in general and of other concepts such as classification, conservation, and, indeed, the whole area of concrete intelligence. In addition, this debate provides the only available example to date of the complex and detailed nature of the arguments adduced when the relative merits of the verbal and non-verbal approaches to a specific problem area are thrashed out.

The summary presented above terminated with the contributions published in 1965, the year in which the writer was planning his experimental study. At that juncture Smedslund and Braine were agreed on the necessity for abandoning pseudomeasurement as a method but neither had offered an alternative approach to the problem of non-transitive hypotheses. It appeared that any future experimental procedure to be acceptable would have to be consistent with two constraints. It must involve the application of the measuring rod to both uprights on each trial since this would prevent attention to the measured object being an additional basis for responses and it must, also, facilitate the detection of children who are employing non-transitive hypotheses. Attempts to produce experimental procedures satisfying these conditions have been made by Smedslund and the writer in the period since 1965. Description and discussion of the outcome of these ventures will be deferred, however, to Chapter Five which will be devoted to further treatment of the verbal versus non-verbal approach issue.

In the above account of the transitivity of length controversy we have seen the verbal approach to the study of conceptual development ranged against the non-verbal approach, Genevan revisionism opposed by American neo-behaviourism. A study by Wohlwill (1960a) methodologically undoubtedly belongs to the latter tradition but it, also, stems from a degree of cross-pollination since, although trained in the USA Wohlwill elected to use a post-doctoral fellowship to allow him to work with Piaget and Inhelder in Geneva. One of the results of this sojourn was an investigation, using non-verbal methods, of the developmental process by which the young child arrives at an abstract concept of number. The study and Wohlwill's later work have had a considerable methodological influence on the present investigation. It will not be accorded an extended treatment at the present juncture, however, since it was discussed at considerable length in the survey (Wallace, 1965, pp 72–78). Particular features of Wohlwill's methods and results will be mentioned at appropriate points in the chapters which follow.

The work of Braine, Smedslund and Wohlwill constitute the most seminal studies in the period up to 1965 unequivocally directed at throwing light on the feasibility of employing non-verbal methods in the investigation of conceptual development. The paucity of direct studies of the problem prompted the expansion of the review to encompass marginally related studies or to broach the fundamental problem of the relationship between language and thought. This temptation was resisted not because of any lack of conviction of the importance of such work but due to the danger of clouding the clear cut methodological issue of the relative merits of the verbal and non-verbal approaches by raising theoretical questions which, though undoubtedly important, were at best of tangential relevance to the main object of the investigation.

The question of stages in conceptual development

The question of the existence of stages in the development of conceptualization has attracted a great deal of attention from researchers and yet, to a large extent, remains as baffling as ever. It represents one particular aspect of an ever-present and fundamental psychological problem. Although it has usually been argued that development is continuous and without discrete shifts, men seem always to have felt a need to impose segmentation on the complicated course of human development. Terms such as 'stage' or 'level' are employed to aid in the division of behaviour into units, which are suitable for precise description, and to facilitate understanding of the speed and fluidity of change in children.

A variety of uses have been made of the term 'stage' in the literature on child development. It has, for example, been employed as an alternative method of expressing a child's age. This usage constitutes the main reason for the rejection of the notion of stages characteristic of most of the protagonists of learning theory who have turned their attention to developmental studies. They regard it as a superfluous term which is rendered redundant by plotting the course of behavioural development against chronological age.

Some indication of the complexity of the relationship between 'stages and ages', as depicted in accounts of psychological development, is provided by Osterrieth (1956). An analysis of 18 systems of stages, emanating from both Europe and America, produced a total of 61 different chronological periods which were cited as stages. Each year from birth to 24 years was considered to mark the beginning or end of a stage. The greatest amount of agreement centred on the first year of life, which was regarded as a distinct stage in only seven of the 18 systems examined.

The terminology of stages is also used in the description of observations. An expression such as 'He's at the teething stage' can be reduced to 'He's teething' without any loss of meaning. The need for segmentation of behaviour may be satisfied by employing 'stages' in this way, but they are just as redundant in this context as those in which they are substitutes for age.

These psychologically meaningless usages of the term 'stage' do not currently hold sway in the area of conceptualization. It is Piaget's outline of the stages of development which is the centre of controversy and he regards a stage not as a conventional analytical device for dealing with behaviour but rather as a natural transition revealed by new modes of behaviour and theoretically attributed to the emergence of a new intellectual level of operational structures. Piaget's account of intellectual development has elicited reactions on both the theoretical and practical levels. On the one hand there is criticism based on a purely theoretical examination of his viewpoint, and, on the other, support for his position and criticism of it founded on experimental replication of his studies or attempts at applying his principles to new aspects of concept formation. Two questions highlighting the issues in the areas of methods and aims which appeared to be of paramount importance were selected as guidelines in reviewing the considerable volume of literature generated by these activities. What were the methodological weaknesses of Piaget's approach and how far had the replication studies avoided reproducing them? What constituted realistic aims for future research in the light of the current status of the concept of developmental stages?

Piaget has been castigated for his failure to conform to the accepted canons of research procedure as exemplified in his adoption of unstandardized methods of inquiry and in the absence of statistical procedures from his data analyses. It was criticism of his standpoint on two other fundamental methodological issues, however, which exerted the greatest influence on the design of the present investigation. Piaget's studies, with the exception of his minute observations of the development of his own children, have always been cross-sectional and, as a result, this has been the dominant approach in recent conceptual research. Its limitations as a method for the study of development are clearly revealed by the type of results obtained. Broad, normative development trends are reported and little or no attention is paid to individual differences. In the case of Piaget's scheme of stages it is simply assumed that with the passage of time individual children will successively attain the levels of performance detected by testing groups of older children. There is, however, no guarantee that the development of any single individual follows the normative course since no one has been followed up over a period of time and no effort has been made to get to grips with the nuances of cognitive change. Cross-sectional studies by their very nature can never throw light on the development with increasing age of an individual child's ability to conceptualize or, for that matter, on the equally crucial issue of the relationship between various types of experience and training and conceptualization at a subsequent point of time. The appropriate method for tackling these and related questions is obviously the longitudinal approach. Despite widespread recognition of this fact, however (Piaget [1956 b] himself suggested the adoption of longitudinal methods), longitudinal studies have to date found many advocates but few executors.

As already indicated, Piaget has frequently been attacked for his use of verbally posed problems and for his reliance upon interpretation of verbal responses. The question of the relative merits of verbally and non-verbally posed problems has already been discussed at some length and it is the issues raised by the task of analysing verbal responses which must now be considered. Piaget (1926) discussed the dangers involved in detecting the cognitive, developmental implications of children's verbalizations but there is little evidence in his practice that he has coped successfully with them. In particular, he appears to have failed to resist the supreme temptation of capitalizing on the ambiguity of verbal responses to derive support for his preconceptions. For example, although verbatim protocols for a number of subjects are usually presented in his work on intellectual development, there is little indication that Piaget followed a systematic inductive strategy in moving from this data to the formulation of his theory of stages. On the contrary, there is a case for viewing the children's verbalizations cited as simply illustrations of the appropriateness of a preconceived theory.

A suggested solution to the problem of inferring cognitive structures from verbalizations has already been encountered in dealing with the Smedslund-Braine controversy. This is, of course, to circumvent the difficulty by employing non-verbal problems which elicit nonverbal responses. Some of the issues raised by this suggestion have already been dealt with but there are additional factors which must be taken into consideration. If a non-verbal approach is adopted the possibility must be borne in mind that by ceasing to demand appropriate use of even a minimal concept-related vocabulary a child's stage of intellectual development may be overestimated on the basis of responses of a lower conceptual or non-conceptual level.

The use of non-verbal responses would appear to diminish the possible influence of the experimenter's preconceptions since there is less need for subjective interpretation of the data. Much of this objectivity may, however, be apparent rather than real. Preconceived ideas may exert an equally powerful influence in a non-verbal experiment at the earlier stage of design rather than in the interpretation of the data. The nature of the apparatus by means of which the problem is presented to the child, may, for example, produce bias by limiting the range of possible responses.

The goal of completely removing bias emanating from the predilections of the experimenter from the results of a study is, of its very nature, unattainable. The necessity for imposing structure upon the situation even to a minimal degree in the work of design and in the interpretation of the data obtained makes this certain. It is clear, however, that the ultimate degree of objectivity attainable by refinement of methods has not yet been achieved. In the case of the interpretation of responses the outstanding requirement is an objective method which would allow the data to determine their own patterns and groupings and, for example, to confirm or deny the existence of stages without the necessity for the researcher to adopt any preconceived scheme as a guide. Although it appears highly unlikely that a technique could be devised which would render it unnecessary for the investigator to make any subjective decisions about the categorizing of data, it should be possible to cut such decisions to an absolute minimum; for example, a judgement as to whether responses are the same or different.

The replication studies, to their credit, abandoned Piaget's practice of using different subjects for each test, adopted standardized methods of inquiry to a greater or lesser degree, and employed statistical procedures in their data analyses. On the debit side, however, they almost all retained the cross-sectional approach and reliance upon interpretation of verbal responses. The typical method employed involved scrutinizing the subjects' protocols to see how far the data could be categorized on the basis of Piaget's stages and to what extent additional categories were required. Objectivity was achieved by having each set of protocols processed by a number of independent assessors and then comparing their ratings. An encouragingly high level of agreement was usually obtained. When this initial categorization had been completed, it was then possible to check whether certain groupings occurred with others more often than would be expected by chance.

The degree of objectivity obtained with this procedure was, of necessity, limited since the assessors already had Piaget's developmental scheme in mind as a structural framework when they began the task of categorization. The freedom available to them in their interpretation of the data was, thus, drastically diminished from the outset. The vast majority of researchers appeared to be undisturbed by the bias introduced by the adoption of a preconceived scheme as a guide. Smedslund (1964), however, showed some signs of disquiet with this type of approach when he expressed the belief that it should be possible to devise a set of completely objective rules for interpreting verbal responses, based exclusively on a pattern of direct judgements. A more direct and general plea for action was made by Dienes (1959) who stressed the pressing need for a statistical technique which would make it possible to find those patterns or groupings of responses which are essentially determined by a set of qualitative data, without invoking a preconceived theoretical bias in any particular direction. The appearance of such an analytical instrument would certainly provide renewed hope of the attainment of definitive answers to the questions of the existence of developmental stages in general and the validity of Piaget's theory in particular.

From this consideration of the Piaget replication studies two methodological requirements emerged as paramount for future work. Since the cross-sectional approach had clearly contributed all that could reasonably be expected of it, longitudinal studies had to be undertaken if further progress was to be made. Secondly, although the goal of complete objectivity in the interpretation of subjects' responses is unattainable, strenuous efforts should be made to devise new methods which would rely as little as possible on the operation of subjective judgement.

So much for methods. What of ends as distinct from means? What were realistic aims for future research in the light of the status of the concept of stages as revealed in the results of the Piaget replication studies? As Flavell (1963) has pointed out, there are two distinct angles of approach to the term 'stage'. It can be used to indicate an over-all state in a sequence of over-all states which are said to characterize a person undergoing ontogenetic development. This gives rise to statements of the type, 'Child A is at stage X'. It can, also, be employed to designate a level or step in a sequence of levels or steps with respect to a particular psychological process of acquisition and change. Piaget, for example, postulates three main stages in the formation of the concept of conservation of number. The evidence from the replication studies was considered from each of these viewpoints in turn.

The results provide little support for the view that stages

characterize the development of persons. On the contrary they present a picture of inconsistency in individual performance. Inconsistency is rife when, to use Smedslund's (1964) terms, inference patterns are held constant and goal objects and percepts are varied and, also, when inference patterns and goal objects are held constant and only percepts are varied. The percept is a process depending on the momentary stimulus-inputs, the goal object is what the subject is instructed to attain, and the inference pattern is formed by the set of premises and the conclusion. Transitivity and conservation are inference patterns, length and quantity are goal objects, and the stimulus situations as apprehended by the subject, are percepts. Annett (1959) stresses that it is wrong to suggest that stages should be characteristic of individuals since this implies that all problems of conceptual thinking are equally difficult. The existence of developmental stages can still be asserted, however, on the grounds that concepts develop through the same stages without all being at the same stage simultaneously. To determine the validity of this line of argument it was necessary to consider the evidence on the question of whether or not stages are characteristic of the process of acquisition of particular concepts.

The picture presented by the evidence on this issue is no less complex than that on the question of stages and individual development. This is hardly surprising as it is inevitably based on the same individual performance data since the process of acquisition must take place in a person just as the over-all state of the person is necessarily a cross-section or intersect of a series of co-occurring processes. The similarity in complexity to the stages and individual development issue is continued in that there are several levels at which the question can be tackled. For example, the process of attainment of transitivity of length and conservation of number can be compared or those of conservation of quantity and conservation of number or, narrowing the field still further, conservation of quantity with plasticine and conservation of quantity with a rubber band. The breadth of definition of a 'particular concept' adopted determines the level of approach. They are all alike, however, in that they entail grappling with evidence of inconsistency in individual performance.

In addition to the complex features which it shares with the problem of stages in individual development, the issue of stages in the process of acquisition of concepts presents further difficulties which are entirely its own. These are largely of a methodological nature. It would be true to say that almost none of the data available from the

Piaget replication studies are completely relevant to the stages in acquisition issue. This stems from the fact that they are cross-sectional in approach while it poses questions which are of an essentially longitudinal nature. For example, 'Do individuals pass through the same stages in acquiring concepts when the inference pattern, goal object and percepts vary, when the goal object and percepts vary, when only the percepts vary, or when all three are held constant?' (Smedslund, 1964). Cross-sectional studies can at best result in the identification of what appear to be normative sequences of stages in the process of acquisition of concepts. They have no bearing on the possibility that the routes by which individuals acquire concepts may vary, yet this is the crucial point if questions such as those cited above are to be answered.

Although the shortcomings of the cross-sectional approach are obvious, the mounting of longitudinal studies of this problem is far from being an easy task. The difficulties are particularly evident if Piaget's criterion that the sequence of stages must be fixed is adopted.

This leaves no room whatsoever for individual variations and, consequently, it is essential that a longitudinal study should commence before any of the subjects have had experience likely to initiate the process of concept acquisition being investigated. Failure to achieve this would make it impossible to reach firm conclusions since observed variations in the course of acquisition may indicate individual variations inimical to Piaget's hypothesis or may simply be due to the fact that some subjects have already passed through the initial stages of acquisition before the commencement of the study. Ensuring complete naiveté on the part of the subjects at the outset presents a well-nigh impossible task. Although steps may be taken to ensure that children have had no direct experience with a concept as represented in the test situation to be used, there can be no certainty that the process of acquisition has not been initiated by experiences in day to day life. Selecting children on the basis of a 'zero' performance on a pre-test of the concept is no solution to this difficulty since differential outside experience continues during the follow-up period. Nor is the exercise of control over such outside activities the answer since to a large extent we do not know what kinds of real life experiences are relevant to the conceptual areas being studied.

The task of devising a viable method of tackling the problem of stages on the basis of the confused mass of inconsistency and difficulty outlined above is such a daunting one that there is a strong temptation to discard the concept of stages in conceptual development altogether. There are, however, two less radical alternatives to this drastic step. The first of these is exemplified in the work of Smedslund (1964). This involves the retention of the Piagetian view of stages with its emphasis on rigidly predictable developmental sequences and the generality of application of logical structure, and its disregard for individual differences. The goal of research conducted from this point of view is to definitively establish the truth or otherwise of Piaget's scheme by progressively refining methods until all variation in the data due to extraneous factors has been removed. This approach has much in common with Braine's (1964) endeavours to determine the earliest ages at which processes can be unequivocally elicited by devising test situations which present the relevant cues in the simplest possible manner and remove ambiguities of presentation. Like Braine's work it, also, poses some awkward questions. Is it practically feasible? Smedslund (1964), for example, maintained that the next objective of research should be to study the relationships between the various concrete inference patterns utilizing a single goal object and a single set of percepts. It would seem to be extremely difficult, if not impossible, however, to retain identical stimulus situations while varying the inference pattern under consideration.

In general, those who adopt this approach seem doomed to resort to narrower and narrower situations and a greater and greater degree of specificity in a desire to avoid the influence of factors considered irrelevant and in pursuit of the chimera of exact relations. The only hope of achieving their objective would appear to lie in studying the course of acquisition by a single individual of a single inference pattern as represented in a single goal object and a single set of percepts. Conclusions on the question of stages reached on this basis would be of such specificity as to be of little utility. In addition, the task of determining the extent to which these conclusions could be generalized to the myriad other possible situations of this straitened type would take several millenia.

The account of the alternative course of action must, of necessity, be of a more speculative nature since none of the studies prior to the present one have attempted to follow it. It involves a readjustment of aims in the direction of greater flexibility rather than more rigorous control. This is not to say that methodological issues are disregarded. It is, for example, perfectly compatible with the recourse to longitudinal studies and the search for more objective methods of judging responses advocated above. The increase in flexibility lies in the acceptance of the inevitability of inconsistencies and individual variations in subjects' responses and in a consequent adjustment in the criteria employed in identifying developmental stages. As far as the stages and individuals issue is concerned this approach entails rejection of the aim of assigning particular individuals to single stages characterizing their performance across all situations and based on hypothesized underlying structures with the constraints on the order of acquisition of inference patterns which this involves. The typical procedure adopted consists of obtaining profiles of the qualitative performance of a group of individuals on a substantial number of conceptual tasks each presented by means of a variety of sets of percepts. The profiles are then compared and if a number of children show a substantial degree of agreement in the qualitative features of their performance they are assigned to the same stage. The decision as to when the degree of agreement is sufficiently substantial to justify positing a stage is based on objective statistical procedures involving the use of predetermined significance levels. Subjective judgement is required in determining whether individual subjects' responses are the same or different. Longitudinal studies may reveal a sequence of such broadly defined stages through which the majority of children seem to pass. It may, also, be possible to discern different sequences, or sequences of different stages, in the development of minority groups of children and to attempt to discover some of the factors underlying such variations.

A similar rejection of the pursuit of exact relations and acceptance of inconsistent performance characterizes the approach to the problem of stages in the process of acquisition of concepts. The same basic procedure outlined above is adopted but the performance of a number of individuals on a particular conceptual task is compared rather than profiles of individual performance on a number of tasks. Similarity in the quality of response made by a number of subjects is regarded as indicative of a stage in the process of acquisition of the concept. The adoption of the longitudinal approach may again reveal a normative sequence of such stages and minority group variations.

Can any firm general conclusions be reached about the existence of stages in the process of concept formation by means of the method outlined above? It is true that the results obtained in a study of a particular concept must necessarily be highly specific. It is, also, certain that, as already indicated, it would be impossible to contemplate carrying out similar studies covering the processes of acquisition of all inference patterns as represented by all goal objects and all conceivable sets of percepts. The compromise suggested by Flavell (1963) appears to be eminently reasonable in this context. He maintains that a less time-consuming and far more practical way of catching hold of some of the developmental reality at the process level would be to follow a case-study method. This would involve looking for the expression and exemplification of *general* developmental principles in a few carefully selected *individual* processes. The guiding question would be: 'What are the general sorts of things which are likely to happen in any development, as indicated by a very intensive study of what happens in a few, test case processes?' The intensive study envisaged would be essentially longitudinal and the processes selected for study would have to have a measure of developmental richness, that is, produce a sufficient amount of variation in individual performance to enable the detection of stages, if they exist. Piaget's work provides a multitude of tasks which satisfy this condition.

There was no difficulty in discerning the salient features which emerged from the review of the Piaget replication studies and their import for future research on the problem of stages. In summary, on the methodological plane there appeared to be an undeniable case for the adoption of the longitudinal approach and the necessity of devising more objective methods of processing subjects' responses. As far as aims were concerned, if the concept of stages in conceptual development was not to be rejected altogether, it seemed clear that criteria should be adopted for the determination of stages which made some allowance for the inevitably inconsistent nature of individuals' performance.

Can the course of conceptual development be accelerated?

Kessen (1962) made an important distinction between the study of developmental states or stages in themselves and the study of the rules of transition, the mechanism or processes which govern the child's movement from state to state through the ontogenetic sequence. The most natural angle of approach to the problem of acceleration is to pose the more fundamental question of the nature of the transition rule in conceptual development and then to design the procedure intended to produce acceleration in accordance with the best answer obtained. Unfortunately no clear-cut answer is available since no accepted body of theory exists from which a transition rule can be derived to guide attempts to accelerate the process of concept formation. In this situation the approach adopted in the present study was to seek points of consensus in the theoretical literature which are of relevance to the problem of acceler҉. full description of the course of this search is provided in Wall҈ (1967) but a brief account of the results can be presented here.

Generally accepted as above contention is the fact that maturation is a necessary, although not a sufficient, condition for conceptual development, and, thus, sets upper limits to the possibilities of acceleration. What these limits are remains to be determined. This principle is, however, of minimal assistance in the practical task of devising acceleration techniques.

The prominence accorded to conceptual conflict appeared to be a potentially much more useful lead. It plays a fundamental part, for example, in Berlyne's (1965) neo-associationist account of the dynamics of directed thinking or problem solving and it is equally prominent, if less explicitly stated, in Piaget's (1960a) formulations. In Berlyne's view directed thinking can certainly be initiated and guided by the sources of motivation that are familiar from other areas of psychology. These include, for example, hunger, fear of pain, desire for wealth, and social ambition. He, also, believes that there may be certain additional sources of motivation which possess particularly close ties with thinking and work in conjunction with these other factors. This hypothesis is founded on a consideration of exploratory behaviour, the type of nonsymbolic behaviour which is most closely related to directed thinking. Recent research on the motivation of exploratory behaviour (Berlyne, 1960a) has revealed that the probability and direction of specific exploratory responses can apparently be influenced by many properties of external stimulation, as well as by many intraorganismic variables. The paramount determinants appear to be a group of stimulus properties commonly referred to by such words as 'novelty', 'surprisingness', 'incongruity', 'complexity' and 'indistinctness'. Berlyne (1965) proposes the term 'collative' as an epithet to denote all of these stimulus properties collectively, since they all depend on collation or comparison of information from different stimulus elements, whether they be elements belonging to the present and the past or elements which are simultaneously present in different parts of one stimulus field.

The second feature of collative stimulus properties is that they can all be regarded as entailing conflict. This is defined by Berlyne (1965) as the simultaneous instigation of incompatible responses and is said to occur whenever there are stimulus conditions which are associated with incompatible responses. When a subject is beset by discrepant items of information, responses corresponding to each of them will presumably be instigated, but these responses must necessarily compete with one another. A subject is placed in a condition of uncertainty whenever he is exposed to a situation that might, in the light of previous experience, be followed by any of a number of mutually exclusive stimulus events, each having its probability. In such circumstances, mutually incompatible responses, corresponding to these possible impending stimulus events, must be held in readiness.

It is evident that conflict, thus conceived, is not something that the subject is either in or not in. He will always have some degree of conflict, at least while he is awake. He will invariably be surrounded by stimulus objects each of which is associated with at least one response, verbal, locomotor, or manual, and he will not be able to perform all of these responses at once. But the degree of conflict will vary from moment to moment. Most of the time, it will be quite moderate, but there are times when it will be intense. When a subject has a high level of conflict owing to collative properties of his external environment, there will be a high degree of objective uncertainty about which of the instigated responses will actually be performed.

It is Berlyne's contention that the motivational qualities of collative stimulus properties revealed in studies of exploratory behaviour are equally relevant to the area of directed thinking. The human nervous system is so made that symbolic representations of stimulus patterns are apt to linger after they have left the stimulus field and to prolong any disturbance to which the stimulus patterns gave rise. Conflict due to discrepant or inconsistent relations among symbolic processes can presumably be reduced only by modifying symbolic structures and injecting new information into them. This extension or reorganization of symbolic structures is what is referred to as 'acquisition of knowledge' in everyday speech. A state of high drive induced by conflict traceable to disharmonious symbolic processes constitutes 'epistemic curiosity'. This is a condition that can be relieved by the acquisition of knowledge and which, therefore, leads to epistemic behaviour including directed thinking.

The kind of conflict which affects directed thinking and other forms of epistemic behaviour most directly will be 'conceptual conflict'. This is conflict between incompatible symbolic response patterns in the shape of beliefs, attitudes, thoughts and ideas. It is Berlyne's hypothesis that conceptual conflict will be the principal, but not necessarily the only, factor producing epistemic curiosity. Of the various ways in which responses can become incompatible, he believes that innate antagonism plays only a small part in covert symbolic behaviour and that most conceptual conflict by far must depend on learned antagonism. Two symbolic response patterns will be incompatible when each is associated with the inhibition of the other. The inhibitory bonds may result directly from symbolic learning, including directed thinking processes belonging to the past. In other cases, an incompatibility between symbolic responses will be a by-product of an incompatibility between motor and other non-symbolic (for example, affective) responses associated with the stimulus patterns that the symbolic responses represent. The degree of conceptual conflict, like degree of conflict in general, is assumed to increase with the number of competing responses, the degree to which they approach equality in strength and their total absolute strength.

Conceptual conflict is, also, an integral part of Piaget's theory of intellectual development. He believes that the crucial feature of intellectual development is the progressive construction within the individual of structures which are able to maintain stability and a balance when confronted with the demands of the environment. Piaget employs the term 'equilibrium', borrowed from the physical sciences, to describe this stability. These structures constitute equilibrium states which are organized systems of internalized actions whose attributes as systems can be described in terms of equilibrium. Piaget maintains that the course of development is determined by equilibration, a continuous process which gives rise to a succession of essentially discontinuous equilibrium states. Although the equilibration process itself is regarded as being the same throughout the course of development, the equilibrium states are not. Each represents a higher degree of equilibrium than the one which precedes it in the course of development. This hierarchy is specified in terms of four main dimensions along which the states vary. These are, respectively, the size of their field of application, the spatio-temporal distances which the actions of the system traverse in the course of their operation, the extent to which the objects on which the actions bear change their value when new objects are centred, and the system's capacity to compensate or cancel disturbances which tend to alter the existing state of equilibrium.

What of the process of equilibration itself which underlies the successive appearance of organized systems exhibiting greater and greater degrees of equilibrium as assessed on these dimensions? It has its origins in the child's active interactions with his environment and, in particular, in the operations of the complementary processes of assimilation and accommodation. Every cognitive encounter with an environmental object necessarily involves the child in some kind of

B

cognitive structuring or restructuring of that object in accord with the nature of his existing intellectual organization. He must assimilate it to his existing intellectual structure. At the same time it is clear that he will encounter objects which due to novel features cannot be assimilated and, thus, necessitate changes in his intellectual structure to accommodate them. The process of accommodation is, then, structural adaptation initiated by the unprecedented demands which the environment makes on the child from time to time.

Although assimilation and accommodation are described separately, in operation they are indissociable. As Piaget (1954) expresses it, 'accommodation of mental structures to reality implies the existence of assimilating schemata apart from which any structure would be impossible. Inversely, the formation of schemata through assimilation entails the utilization of external realities to which the former accommodate, however crudely'. Equilibration is the process of bringing the inseparable functional invariants, assimilation and accommodation, into balanced co-ordination. The sequence of different equilibrium states which results represents the various forms which this co-ordination takes during ontogenesis and provides the basis for Piaget's well-known system of developmental stages.

The function of the processes of assimilation and accommodation appears to be to resolve problems raised by interaction with the environment and belonging to types which Berlyne would regard as among the potential sources of conceptual conflict. Piaget (1957b, 1960a) provides a further example of conceptual conflict in action, at a more specific level, in the succession of centrations on the two dimensions of the situation which is an essential feature of his account of the part played by equilibration in the appearance of conservation of quantity. This is based on a sequence of four strategies which, he maintains, successively, dominate the child's behaviour. The variations in the strategies are described in terms of two kinds of qualities or variables which from the observer's point of view vary inversely one to the other and which are features of all arrangements where the problem of conservation appears. In the classic conservation of quantity experiment, for example, the ball of clay which is changed into a sausage shape increases in length. This constitutes the first variable A. On the other hand it becomes thinner and this provides the second variable B which is modified inversely as the first.

In the first strategy the child consistently deals with only one of these characteristics, A, and totally ignores the other, B. He says, for example, that the clay ball has got longer and consequently there is more clay. Its thinness is ignored. With the adoption of the second strategy a series of repeated centrations on one characteristic is eventually followed by a centration on the other characteristic. This substitution does not result in conservation but simply yields the opposite non-conservation error. Behaviour consisting of a whole series of alternations between A and B centration is, also, characteristic of the second strategy. These centrations are always successive and isolated from one another and never co-ordinated. When the child deals with A he forgets his previous centration on B and *vice versa*. The beginnings of co-ordination of A and B appear with the third strategy. The child is able to fleetingly apprehend both characteristics within a single cognitive act and when confronted with a new problem hesitates before deciding to respond on the basis of one or other of them. He is, also, able to appreciate the complementary nature of the changes in A and B when the changes made are comparatively slight. The fourth and final strategy is based on a full appreciation of the inverse relationship of the two characteristics, A and B, regardless of the nature of the transformations which they undergo. It indicates a grasp of the necessary nature of conservation.

In view of the important function which it performs in both neo-associationist and Piagetian theory, an attempt to foster conceptual conflict appeared to be an appropriate goal for any acceleration technique. The search for further points of consensus led to consideration of the merits of direct training accompanied by external reinforcement as a feature of a treatment calculated to accelerate conceptual development. This approach involves placing the child in a situation in which he is invited to make judgements on the basis of his current appreciation of the principle to be learned and then providing him with feedback on the accuracy of his responses or permitting him to check their accuracy for himself. In the case of conservation of weight, for example, the child is first shown on a beam balance that two balls of plasticine are equal in weight. One of the balls is deformed and he is asked to predict the outcome of re-weighing them. The accuracy of his response is then demonstrated on the balance.

There can be no doubt that protagonists of neo-associationist theory would advocate the inclusion of direct training using external reinforcement in an acceleration programme since learning on the basis of experience is the fundamental principle in their account of conceptual development. The position with regard to Genevan theory is a much more complex one. Piaget (1957b, 1960a) maintains that the logical structures fundamental to intellectual activity neither stem completely from hereditary mechanisms nor from discoveries made by experience with objects or by social transmission nor from a contribution of two or three of these single factors which are distinct although always interdependent. They depend in a more basic fashion on the process of equilibration, which he regards as being more general than the others. It governs their interaction and their individual functioning and, also, has its own unique part to play in the explanation of the course of intellectual development.

Piaget's conception of equilibration as a general meta-process governing the interaction and action of maturation and physical and social learning, and guiding them towards the production of a stable balanced state in the individual's transactions with his environment, is comparatively unexceptionable, although Zazzo (1960) has argued against the erection of a system of relationships into a distinct factor. The major focus of controversy is the special developmental function assigned to equilibration. The nature of this unique contribution is most clearly revealed in the construction of the logical structures which, Piaget believes, constitutes the only area in which complete equilibration is ever attained. The particular example which Piaget (1957b, 1960a) uses is the development of conservation. He maintains that it cannot be explained by maturation or learning on the basis of external reinforcement or social transmission.

As Piaget regards learning on the basis of external reinforcement as an insufficient explanation of the formation of stable intellectual structures, it is tempting to reach the facile conclusion that he would deny the usefulness of direct training accompanied by external reinforcement in accelerating conceptual development. This temptation must be resisted since there is evidence that such a conclusion would be based on a gross over-simplification of his viewpoint. Piaget does not assert that equilibration should replace learning on the basis of external reinforcement as the transition rule in intellectual development but rather that equilibration is a necessary addition or complement to it. He advocates a search for the laws common to both of them and their amalgamation as learning 'in the wider sense'. This interpretation of his position is supported by the fact that he rebuked Smedslund (Piaget, 1959, p.183) for implying in an article (Smedslund, 1959) that Piaget wished to substitute equilibration for learning. He also stated that the only question is that of the nature of the relationship existing between them.

A fairly clear indication of Piaget's views on this subject, and also on the part which direct training using external reinforcement might play in accelerating intellectual development, is provided in his discussion (Piaget, 1959) of the results of Smedslund's (1959) attempts to accelerate the development of conservation of weight by this technique. Piaget makes a distinction between the acquisition of content and structure in intellectual development. The former is the province of learning on the basis of external reinforcement and involves the type of appreciation of the physical facts of a situation imparted by Smedslund's demonstration on a beam balance that deformation of pieces of plasticine does not alter their weight. The latter consists of the active formation and reorganization by the subject of the logical structures necessary to cope with the content derived from experience and is, of course, identified with equilibration. In the case of 'spontaneous' development, learning and equilibration together lead to the acquisition of physical content and logical structure concurrently. An acceleration sequence of the type employed by Smedslund imposes knowledge of content before a corresponding development of logical structure. This results in a 'short-circuit' between form and content and necessitates retrospective structural reorganization. It would thus seem to be a reasonable deduction from Piaget's expressed views that he would agree with the inclusion of direct training using external reinforcement in a treatment aimed at accelerating intellectual development on two conditions: firstly, that it was not regarded as a sufficient feature, and secondly, that due attention was also given to features such as the encouragement of conceptual conflict, which would be likely to lead subjects to engage in structural reorganization and which would thus be conducive to the operation of the process of equilibration.

Having derived what meagre guidelines were available from theoretical work, further assistance in tackling the task of acceleration was sought at an empirical level in the results of studies in which an attempt to accelerate conceptual development had been made. A full discussion of these studies is presented in Wallace (1967) and only the features which influenced the form of the present study will be dealt with here.

Despite the widespread lack of success characteristic of attempts made to accelerate conceptual development in the period up to 1965, the results of the studies reviewed did provide some useful leads. Most importantly they afforded empirical support, albeit a meagre amount, for the possible efficacy of acceleration treatments including a combination of externally reinforced practice on the principle to be inculcated and efforts aimed at inducing appropriate conceptual conflict and, thus, catering for the acquisition of both content and structure. In the case of the study of number conservation carried out by Wohlwill and Lowe (1962), for example, the relevant treatment took the form of a mixed sequence, a third of which was devoted to direct training on the conservation principle with external reinforcement. These trials involved determining the number of stars in a row before and immediately after their spatial arrangement in terms of length of row had been changed. If the child made an incorrect response on the conservation phase of the trial he was instructed to count the stars in the row. Although it was not an explicit objective of Wohlwill and Lowe, the remaining two-thirds of the sequence took a form which seemed to be conducive to appropriate conceptual conflict. In these trials the experimenter either added or subtracted a star at the end of a row before diminishing or increasing its length. This series of actions placed the child in a situation in which both the operations of addition and subtraction and the perceptual deformations provided a basis for his response but the specific responses which they prompted on each trial were diametrically opposed—a fair recipe for the production of conflict. The mixed sequence proved to be the most successful of the three acceleration techniques employed by Wohlwill and Lowe but, even so, it did not give rise to a post-test performance which was significantly superior to that of the control group.

A series of experiments on conservation of substance and weight conducted by Smedslund (1959, 1961, 1963) also proved of considerable interest in tackling the task of designing acceleration treatments. His results indicated the failure of treatments based solely on direct, externally reinforced practice and a degree of success with an approach consisting entirely of efforts aimed at inculcating appropriate conceptual conflict but with no external reinforcement. In the case of conservation of weight the latter approach involved showing the child two plasticine balls at the outset of the experiment and informing him that they were the same amount. Conflict was induced by simultaneously deforming a ball, and adding to or subtracting from it or the other ball. The experimenter took care to remain completely neutral and indifferent in attitude to all of the child's responses to his questions. Thus, Smedslund believed that the children, as far as could be ascertained, received no systematic and unambiguous external reinforcement.

On the basis of the outcome of his own and other studies Smedslund denied direct reinforced practice a place in any acceleration technique on the grounds of its failure and the danger that any acquisitions produced by this approach may prove to be 'pseudo-concepts' founded entirely on simple response learning. The shortcomings of exclusive reliance on direct, externally reinforced practice do not, however, rule out the possibility of this technique playing an important role in facilitating development when used in concert with another technique, such as the 'conflict' approach. It is, of course, true that Smedslund produced acceleration by employing only trials of the 'conflict' type. The degree of success achieved, however, would suggest the existence of a major gap in the technique. In every experiment carried out the percentage of successful subjects was less than fifty. In designing the present study it was, therefore, concluded that the incorporation of trials aimed at the acquisition of content might well provide the missing ingredient.

In addition to rejecting the use of direct externally reinforced practice, Smedslund stressed the exclusion from his conflict-producing treatment of any external reinforcement in the shape of knowledge of results. This point of view is open to attack since Smedslund (1961) stated that in the case of conservation, for example, the aim of the 'conflict' treatment was to emphasize the consistency of the addition-subtraction schema and the ambiguity and contradiction of the perceptual mode of operation. It is hard to believe that the use of external reinforcement, in the shape of informing the children of the appropriateness or otherwise of their judgement, would not be likely to assist in the attainment of these objectives.

Two additional suggestions made in previous studies influenced the construction of the acceleration programmes used in the present investigation. In discussing the results of their experiment Wohlwill and Lowe (1962) suggested that future work on the problem of acceleration should involve the use of a set of learning experiences covering a wide variety of situations, and in line with Harlow's emphasis on generalized experience as a prerequisite for the learning of broad concepts. In their view it is plausible to suppose that it is precisely such generalized experience, obtained in everyday activities, which is the basis for the seemingly spontaneous appearance of conservation in the child.

The second suggestion which was adopted was the use of a more protracted series of practice sessions in order to obtain more definite results. When making this proposal in the discussion of his own experiments Smedslund (1963) suggested two weeks as a possible duration of training. This represented a very marked increase on the customary length of acceleration treatments adopted in studies in the period up to 1965.

The review of studies concerned with the acceleration of conceptual development was not entirely devoted to work within the broad Piagetian framework and to neo-associationist theory and research. Russian psychologists have expended a great deal of effort in investigating the processes underlying the learning of new ideas and concepts in the school setting. An uncritical, doctrinaire adherence to Pavlovian reflexology, the Russian penchant for obscurantism in the production of research reports and the 'noise' created by translation, greatly diminish the value of these studies but, in spite of the obstacles, the work of Gal'perin and Leon'tev of Moscow University on the facilitation of concept formation exercised a considerable influence on the design of the present study.

The rationale for Gal'perin's (1961) method of attack on the problem of acceleration is founded on his account of the development of the processes on which concept formation is based. He believes that the primary source of these internal processes or thought actions is external action and that a description of their development should be couched in terms of changes in four relatively independent features or 'parameters'. The first of these is the level of the process. There are three such levels corresponding to degree of interiorization. The initial, or material, level commences with preliminary orientation to the conditions and requirements to which the process must respond. The child then performs on external objects the actions which are eventually to be internalized, or works with other material which constitutes a concrete representation of the process. The second level is that of the spoken word. The process is freed from dependence on objects or other concrete props but is carried out in the form of a series of remarks which, of necessity, are made aloud. Finally this audible speech form of the process is transmuted into an internal series of thought actions and takes the form of the individual talking to himself. This verbal thinking, as a result of abbreviations and complete assimilation, attains a final form which is hard to follow by introspection.

Abbreviation and assimilation constitute two more of the dimensions of developmental change. The internal processes are gradually shortened. This progressive contraction is seen, for example, in the fact that a child, who initially in counting two groups of objects counts the objects in each group and then counts the objects again one by one in the two groups together, subsequently performs this act of summation by adding the total number of objects in the second group directly to the number of objects in the first group. At any stage in its contraction a process can manifest a different degree of assimilation. This is defined in terms of the extent to which the process becomes the property of the individual. For example, under the guidance of his teacher, the child may effect the summation by adding the number of objects in one group to the number in the other but does not employ this method of his own accord, using the method of counting them one by one which has been better assimilated by him.

Finally, the fourth parameter of change is the degree of generalization. This is determined by how far a process elaborated by the child on one type of material in one set of conditions can be transferred by him to other materials in other conditions.

As already indicated, all of the parameters are relatively independent of each other. A process may be generalized, abbreviated and well assimilated but may be carried out only on a physical level in the presence of material objects or their concrete representations. Alternatively, a process may occur entirely in the form of verbal thinking but only be applied to a particular object without any appreciable degree of generalization.

The import of Gal'perin's account of the development of the processes underlying concept formation emerges more clearly from a consideration of his practical attempts to accelerate conceptualization. The reports of this section of his work available in translation are largely concerned with the formation of relatively simple geometrical concepts such as those of a perpendicular, a line, an angle, the bisector of an angle, and adjacent and supplementary adjacent angles.[1] The general method adopted begins with an examination of the components from which the concept in question is built up in order to distinguish those which are necessary and sufficient to determine whether a particular phenomenon is to be included in the concept under consideration. These essential criteria are listed and numbered in a column on a card and, thereafter, they constitute the material or concrete form of the process to be inculcated. They enable the components of the concept to be considered objectively, and the actions of the subject in applying them to the experimental tasks to be controlled.

At the outset the subject is informed that the list comprises the essential features of the concept and he is instructed in how to apply each of these components to each part of the material, i.e. to all the conditions of a problem and to all the elements of the figure by means of which it is presented. Only when all of the components are present will the phenomenon be included among the examplars of the

[1]OBUKHOVA (1966) has attempted to accelerate the appearance of conservation in 5- and 6-year-old children by means of a technique based on Gal'perin's principles. The approach is very different from that adopted in the present study since it is based on the use of measurement. The procedure is said to be very successful but detailed data are not available.

concept. The decision as to the nature of the material to which the conceptual definition is to be applied is guided by the desire to develop a concept which may be generalized to a certain extent. Gal'perin (1961, pp. 250–1) believes that, for this purpose, it is not sufficient merely to vary the material since variation over a range of one or more forms selected at random does not afford adequate generalization. What is required is a systematic variation in a definite order of the basic forms of the material to each of which a clear, unchanging definition of the new concept must be applied. By presenting a variety of problems of this type, in which the conditions stipulated by the definition may be completely or incompletely fulfilled and the verbal set of stipulated conditions, consequently, may or may not agree with the diagram presented, the essential features of the concept are, also, highlighted.

The sequence of problems employed by Gal'perin in his acceleration studies are in conformity with these principles. When, in the course of a sequence, a subject has reached a point at which he appears to have thoroughly assimilated the list of essential features of the concept, the card is first turned over and then later removed. The subject is, thus compelled to recite aloud from memory the components which he has been shown and to indicate aloud whether each of them corresponds to the figure under consideration. Finally, the same process is carried out in the same order, but the subject is urged to speak 'to himself' and to announce only the end result aloud.

The general method outlined above was employed by Gal'perin in his efforts to accelerate the formation of elementary geometrical concepts. The subjects of his study were 48 pupils between 13 and 16 years of age. Sixteen of them were described by their teachers as 'hopeless' and failed the problems set in a geometry pre-test. The remainder had made no previous study of geometry and were of low attainment in other school subjects. The criterion of formation of a concept adopted was a change by the subject from searching for its separate components to applying it directly as a whole to the particular task in hand. This was shown by the child glancing quickly over the problem set and then giving the answer immediately. When asked the reason for his opinion, the child would usually turn once more to the problem and indicate the necessary and sufficient components of the concept in the conditions of the problem.

The results obtained with this approach not only indicate that all of the subjects attained the criterion levels of performance but that the formation of the concepts proceeds almost faultlessly from the very beginning.

In Gal'perin's opinion his findings are consistent with the view that there are two ways of forming a concept. These are distinguished chiefly by the extent to which the process underlying the formation of new concepts is organized, controlled or facilitated. When a subject's mental processes are not controlled and organized to apply a definition of the concept to the problem in hand, he finds himself in the position of an investigator searching for and establishing for himself the essential and sufficient features of the new concept.

This takes place by means of trial and error, and the essential nature of the new concept becomes established only after it has evolved through a number of intermediate stages. In contrast when, as in Gal'perin's approach, the subject is provided from the outset with a precise and objective account of the essential features of the concept and is shown how to apply them in the clearest possible way, the process of concept formation takes place without any intermediate 'hybrid' forms and the path taken becomes very much shorter.

In reaching an over-all assessment of the achievements of research aimed at accelerating conceptual development care had to be taken not to be led into making an over-estimate on the basis of the high degree of success reported in the Russian studies. It proved salutary to remember that in spite of the efforts which Smedslund had expended in the cause of acceleration the percentage of successful subjects had been less than fifty in all of his experiments. The importance of making a realistic estimate of achievement in the period up to 1965 lay in its effect on policy decisions. A high degree of success supported the view that as the conditions *sufficient* for the purpose had been discovered the main focus of the work should be the determination of those which are *necessary* for acceleration to take place. If Gal'perin's findings were discounted, however, the results of the other studies did not appear to justify the adoption of this policy; on the contrary, they indicated that the principal research goal should remain the search for experimental treatments sufficient to produce acceleration in the process of concept formation. This assessment of the import of the existing experimental evidence and the resulting prescription for action formed the basis for the approach to the problem of acceleration adopted in the present study.

This description of the outcome of the review of experimental studies of acceleration completes the account of the preliminary appraisal of work relevant to the four selected problem areas. The next chapter will deal with the task of applying the guidance gained from it to the difficulties encountered in planning an empirical attack on the chosen issues.

CHAPTER TWO

The Experimental Study : The Initial Phase

IT WAS DECIDED as a first step in the design of the present investigation that it would focus on four important problems to the exclusion of the myriad others which are raised by the topic of concept formation. The first chapter has reviewed work relevant to two methodological issues: the relative merits of the verbal and non-verbal approaches, and the need for an objective method of analysing qualitative data; and to the theoretical questions of the existence of stages and the possibility of acceleration. The next task which had to be undertaken was that of drastically narrowing the field of concern to permit a conceptual area and experimental design to be selected which would enable a potentially useful empirical attack to be made simultaneously on all four problem areas. The questions of stages and analysis of qualitative data are compatible with the study of any type of conceptualization and, accordingly, guidance in selecting the particular conceptual area to be investigated had to be exclusively sought in the literature concerned with acceleration and the relative merits of the verbal and non-verbal approaches.

A consideration of the existing studies of acceleration suggested that number conservation provided a suitable focus for the purpose in view. It had been the most popular subject within the area in the period up to 1965 and thus had the advantages over other possible themes of having the main controversial issues more clearly delineated and of affording more sets of results for comparison purposes. It has also more fundamental assets as the subject of an acceleration attempt. The conservations are relatively easily detected landmarks in conceptual development. Their key importance has been emphasized by Piaget (1952) with particular reference to conservation of number. 'Conservation is a necessary condition of all rational activity. . . . This being so, arithmetical thought is no exception to this rule. A set or collection is only conceivable if it remains unchanged irrespective of change occurring in the relationship between the elements. For instance, the permutations of elements in a given set do not change its value. A number is only intelligible if it remains identical with itself, whatever the distribution of the units of which it is composed. . . . In a word, whether it be a matter of continuous or discontinuous quantities, or quantitative relations perceived in a sensible universe, or of sets and numbers conceived by thought, whether it be a matter of the child's earliest contacts with number or the most refined axiomatisations . . . in each and every case the conservation of something is postulated as a necessary condition for any mathematical understanding. From the psychological point of view the need for conservation appears then to be a kind of functional *a priori* of thought'.

Among the various forms of conservation which Piaget has highlighted, conservation of number appears to be a particularly suitable subject for an acceleration study in which the main aim is the discovery of sufficient conditions. The use of discontinuous material clearly facilitates the task of verification of conservation by the subjects when this is necessary. The task of combating reliance on a perceptual mode of operation should, also, be easier when discrete elements are used. Smedslund (1961) has expanded on the latter point. In his view, the sequence of development may be a function of the amount of perceptual disturbance involved and the disturbing influence of perception is clearly less when discontinuous rather than continuous materials are in use. It is also plausible that the presence of perceptually separate and invariant parts in the discontinuous material may facilitate an additive composition of these parts, and thereby conservation. By an 'additive composition' Smedslund means that the whole object is seen as a sum of its parts, and as long as all the parts are retained the whole is conserved. The choice of number conservation as a focus, also, fitted well with the state of play in studies of the relative merits of the verbal and non-verbal approaches, since this was the only one of the conservations for which both a verbal and a non-verbal test were readily available.

In the case of experimental design, unlike that of conceptual area, the intention to tackle the problem of stages imposed constraints. The shortcomings of cross-sectional studies as an approach to this problem were highlighted in Chapter One and the need for longitudinal studies was emphasized. As long-term longitudinal studies are fraught with difficulties the adoption of the short-term longitudinal study as a compromise solution was urged. The development of number conservation is a theme which is well-suited to this approach since the available data indicates that it takes place in a relatively short period of time in the five to seven years region.

The material obtained by repeated testing of subjects on verbal and non-verbal tests of number conservation should be eminently suitable for investigation of the problems encountered in analysing qualitative data. The general features of the short-term longitudinal approach are, also, in accordance with some of the requirements of the acceleration issue. For example, the desirability of determining the stability and permanence of any changes produced by the experimental treatments adopted decrees that at least two post-tests separated by a reasonable interval of time should be a feature of the design. In addition to these shared features, the problem of acceleration made demands of its own on experimental design. A study involving a single experimental group and a control group poses the intractable problem of devising a treatment for the control group which will compensate for the action of the Hawthorne effect on the performance of the experimental group. In view of this pitfall it seemed desirable as a method of obtaining a clearer indication of the efficacy of an experimental treatment to adopt a design in which two experimental groups were involved and, thus, the results of each treatment could be compared with those of another as well as with the results of a control group.

The above considerations led to the adoption of the following general design in the present study.

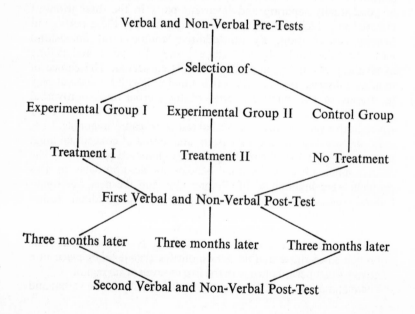

As indicated in the outline the main aim in the initial phase of the study was to obtain data on the basis of which the two experimental and control groups could be selected. The subjects accordingly underwent verbal and non-verbal tests of number conservation. The sample comprised 227 children drawn from Bristol schools with nursery classes and widely differing socio-economic backgrounds. The children were divided into three age groups. Thirty-seven (25 girls, 12 boys) were between 4.0 and 4.6 years, ninety-seven (50 girls, 47 boys) between 5.0 and 5.6 years, and ninety-three (47 girls, 46 boys) between 6.0 and 6.6 years. Half of the children were tested on the non-verbal test first and the other half underwent the verbal test first.

The non-verbal pre-test

The non-verbal test of number conservation used was based on that of Wohlwill (1960). This was preferred to Wohlwill's (1962) later version on the grounds that the latter involved the making of a match between a given collection of elements and the corresponding symbolically indicated number, while the former paralleled the verbal test to be used (Dodwell, 1960) in that it entailed appreciation of the equivalence of the numerosity of two collections of elements.

(a) *Apparatus*

This consisted of an aluminium sheet (18 × 12 in.) mounted vertically on a base of the same material (see Figure I). Three rectangular apertures (4 × 2½ in.) separated by intervals of 2½ in. were cut in the centre of the sheet in a horizontal row. These apertures were approximately at eye level for a subject seated in front of the apparatus and were covered with doors which opened upwards towards the child. Behind each door there was a ledge on which the experimenter could place the small, coloured, wooden blocks with which correct responses were reinforced. Each door was, also, equipped with two projections on which cards were hung.

(b) *Administration*

Initial practice trial. Three choice cards were hung on the doors in the presentation apparatus. These comprised, from left to right, two blue dots arranged horizontally, three blue dots forming an isosceles triangle, and two purple concentric circles. The sample card, which was placed on the table in front of the apparatus, also showed two purple concentric circles, though somewhat larger than those of the third choice card.

FIGURE I: *Non-verbal pre-test apparatus*

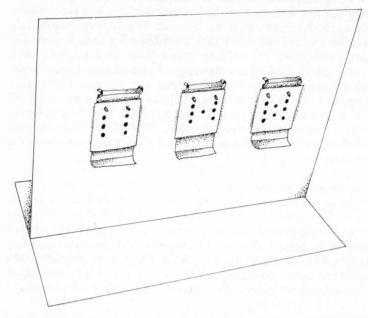

The experimenter told the child that he wanted to play a game with him. He would hide a block behind one of the doors and the subject was to try to find it and string it with the other blocks on a wire with which he had been provided. He would be able to find the block every time if he looked carefully at the (sample) card and then at the (choice) cards on the doors, for they would tell him which was the correct door. The child was now allowed to choose and open one of the doors. If this initial choice was incorrect, he was permitted to correct it until he found the block. He was, also, urged to look very closely at the cards, since there was something on them which would tell him which door had the block behind it. This correction procedure applied only to this single practice trial.

Training series. After the practice trial, the choice card with the concentric circles was replaced with one showing four blue dots in a diamond arrangement. The three choice cards, thus, represented the numbers two, three and four, respectively, from left to right on the doors. These choice cards remained in place throughout the training series.

The training series involved the use of a set of eighteen sample cards, carrying two, three and four dots in varying configurations, none of which was identical to any of the choice cards on the doors. As in the practice trial, the sample cards were placed, one at a time in random order, on the table directly in front of the apparatus. The subject was not, however, permitted to correct wrong choices. The criterion of learning was six consecutive correct responses: if this criterion was not met in forty-eight trials, the child did not undergo the test series.

Test series. 1. Extension Series. In this test the range of numbers being used was extended Six, seven and eight dots were shown on the choice cards as well as, in varying configurations, on the sample cards. Procedurally, this test constituted an extension of the training series.

2. Conservation of Number (Unprovoked Correspondence). For this test the choice cards from the previous test, representing the numbers six, seven and eight, were retained. A number of plastic counters, however, were employed instead of the sample cards. At the start of each trial, the counters were arranged in a pattern exactly duplicating the configuration of the dots on the corresponding choice card. The subject was instructed to look at the counters, because there was one card which looked just like them. He then made his choice. Since the purpose of this preliminary choice was only to inform him of the choice card whose dots were in numerical correspondence with the set of counters, the experimenter prevented him from carrying out an incorrect choice by stopping him short if he moved to open the wrong door. He was asked to try again and urged to look carefully at the card. These preliminary choices were not scored. After the information portion of the trial, the experimenter scrambled the counters by hand in full view of the subject, and calling his attention to this rearrangement of them. The child then responded anew to one of the doors.

The last part of this procedure was a departure from Wohlwill's (1960) practice. He believed that it was necessary to cover the counters after the act of scrambling to prevent the subject recounting them and, thus, succeeding on the scored trial without truly conserving. Covering the rearranged counters was rejected in the present study because it seemed to limit the variety of modes of approach which the children could adopt to the problem and, thus, would result in a loss of potentially valuable developmental data. In addition, it was considered that success by recounting could be detected by careful observation of the subjects' verbalization, lip and hand movements, and of the difference in the time taken to make the scored responses. Covering the counters, also, places a burden on the subjects' short term memory and, thus, makes the task of interpreting fail responses all the more difficult since they may be due to memory lapses rather than to inadequate conceptual development.

3. Addition and Subtraction (Unprovoked Correspondence). This test consisted of a set of trials similar to those of the previous test, with which they were interspersed in the following order: c (=conservation); a (=addition); s (=subtraction); a; c; s; s; c; a; c; c. The only difference between Tests 3 and 2 was that in Test 3 one counter was either added to or subtracted from the collection in front of the subject, immediately after his initial configurational match and just before the experimenter disarranged the counters. In either case, the experimenter alerted the child to the action which he was taking.

4. Provoked Correspondence. This test was identical in administration to Test 2 and 3 and, like them, comprised twelve addition, subtraction and conservation trials. The choice cards, however, depicted six, seven and eight egg-cups and the counters were replaced with toy eggs.

All the tests consisted of six reinforced trials with the exception of Test 1 (Extension Series) which was presented for twelve trials in order to provide adequate familiarization with the choice cards for the following conservation and addition-subtraction tests. To facilitate comparison the arbitrary criterion used by Wohlwill (1960) for determining the number of passes on the individual tests was adopted. This was five correct responses out of six trials and ten out of twelve on Test 1.

The verbal pre-test

The verbal test used was that of Dodwell (1960). This was selected as being the nearest approach to a standardized version of Piaget's number conservation test situations available. There were seven conservation items. Two of these entailed the relation of perceived size to number (beakers and beads), three dealt with provoked correspondence (eggs and egg cups) and two with unprovoked correspondence (red and blue counters). Complete details of the procedure item by item will be found in Appendix A.

The results of the pre-tests

The results of the pre-tests support the view that the attainment of conservation of number constitutes a definite developmental land-

FIGURE II: *Distribution of conservation scores on the verbal pre-test*

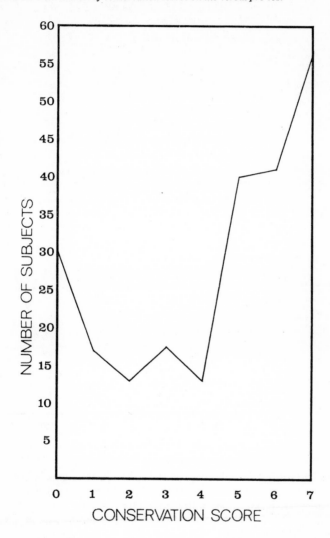

FIGURE III: *Distribution of conservation scores on the non-verbal pre-test*

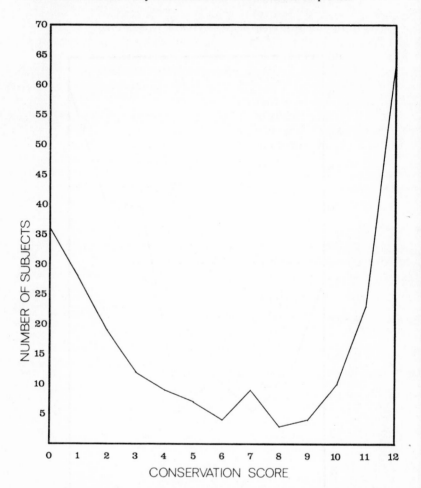

mark. The subjects' total scores on the conservation items in both the verbal and non-verbal tests yielded U-shaped frequency distributions consistent with an all-or-none character for the concept being tapped. In the verbal test (see Figure V) the mode was at seven. Fifty-six subjects attained this level, while thirteen scored four and thirty had a zero score. As Figure VI indicated, the mode was at twelve in the non-verbal test. Sixty-three subjects achieved this score.

Four subjects had a score of six and thirty-six had a zero score. Both the unprovoked and provoked conservation sub-tests (Tests 2 and 4), also, yielded U-shaped frequency distributions with a mode at six.

Thirty-one of the original 227 subjects failed to reach the criterion of six consecutive correct responses in the Training Series of the non-verbal test. Of this group sixteen (9 girls, 7 boys) belonged to the 4.0–4.6 year groups, twelve (3 girls, 9 boys) to the 5.0–5.6 years and three (1 girl, 2 boys) to the 6.0–6.6 years group.

The order of difficulty of the non-verbal sub-tests as judged by the total number of subjects who attained the pass level is indicated in Table 1. As any variations in the order of difficulty of the sub-tests from age group to age group are of considerable importance for developmental issues, Table 1 comprises a breakdown of the pass frequency figures into age group totals. To preserve the parallel with Wohlwill's work, Loevinger's (1947) co-efficient (H_{it}) was accepted as an index of the homogeneity of each test with the total scale. It reveals the extent to which a test scales with the set as a whole, in terms of power to discriminate subjects with a relatively higher total score from subjects with a relatively lower total score.

TABLE 1: *Frequency of passes on tests and homogeneity (H_{it}) of tests with total scale*

	ADDITION SUBTRACTION (PROVOKED CORRESPONDENCE)	ADDITION SUBTRACTION (UNPROVOKED CORRESPONDENCE)	CONSERVATION (PROVOKED CORRESPONDENCE)	CONSERVATION (UNPROVOKED CORRESPONDENCE)	EXTENSION SERIES
H_{it}	0·88	0·86	0·97	0·95	0·97
4·0–4·6 years group	4	4	0	1	1
5·0–5·6 years group	37	37	31	27	26
6·0–6·6 years group	70	67	74	65	64
Total number of passes	111	108	105	93	91

In addition to the total and sub-test scores outlined above a detailed account of performance, including observations on verbalization and other lip movements, hand movements, and delays in responding, was available for one hundred and seventy-nine subjects.

This data revealed that, in both the verbal and non-verbal tests, a number of subjects overtly counted the counters, eggs or other elements after they had been rearranged and before making their scored conservation test responses. The frequency of the adoption of this mode of approach in relation to the children's age group and total conservation score on the non-verbal test is given in Table 2. The same verbal test data reveal a similar increase in overt counting activity with total conservation score.

TABLE 2: *Frequency of overt counting before scored conservation test responses*

	CONSERVATION SCORE												
	0	1	2	3	4	5	6	7	8	9	10	11	12
4·0–4·6 years Group	0	0	0	0	0	0	0	0	0	0	0	0	0
5·0–5·6 years Group	0	0	1	2	2	2	0	1	1	3	2	4	4
6·0–6·6 years Group	0	1	0	0	0	0	0	2	0	1	2	8	11

Shortcomings of the Non-Verbal Pre-Test

In considering the results of the non-verbal pre-test, attention will be mainly devoted to Tests 2 and 3, the conservation and addition-subtraction sub-tests in which the correspondence between the counters and choice cards was unprovoked or spontaneous. This will be done since, except at points which will be indicated, the results of Test 4 in which the materials were qualitatively complementary and correspondence was provoked, are entirely in accordance with those of the earlier tests. That the provoked correspondence totals are higher than the unprovoked totals is in line with expectations based on the order of administration of the tests and the difference in the materials employed. The superiority is most marked in the results of the six-year-old group and this may be attributed to a greater ability to benefit from practice or to an interaction between the subjects' level of numerical competence and the difference in the test materials.

More remarkable are the relative positions in order of difficulty of the extension series, conservation and addition-subtraction tests. The critical ratio associated with the difference between the proportion of subjects passing the unprovoked addition-subtraction test (Test 3) and the extension series is 2.67 ($p < 0.01$). The greater ease with which the subjects dealt with the addition-subtraction test is surprising since, theoretically, it demands all of the symbolic operations involved in the extension series and, also, an understanding of the relationship between adjacent numbers involved in operations of the type $x + 1 = y$.

A consideration of the relative performance of the three age groups suggests a possible explanation. In the six-year-old group the number of subjects who passed the unprovoked addition-subtraction test is not significantly superior to the number of passes on the extension series. In addition, seven of the ten children who failed the extension series and passed the addition-subtraction test would have passed the former if the high arbitrary criterion of ten correct responses had been lowered to eight correct responses. These subjects were clearly working on a numerical basis but found accurate counting more difficult in the extension series, where there was no perceptual correspondence between the choice and sample cards, than in the addition-subtraction test in which there was exact perceptual correspondence between the counters and choice cards on the initial match.

In the five-year-old and four-year-old groups, fourteen and four subjects respectively failed the extension series and passed the unprovoked addition-subtraction test. Only two five-year-olds and none of the four-year-olds would have passed the extension series on the suggested revised criterion. The scores of the remainder were sufficiently low to suggest that it was highly probable that they had not been working on a numerical basis at all. Although Wohlwill (1960) admitted that a successful response on the training series might only indicate a discriminative capacity of a fairly primitive order, he proceeded with the rest of the tests on the assumption that success could only be achieved if the subjects adopted a number matching set. This is highly problematical since a subject who attains the training criterion by matching the sample and choice cards on the basis of purely perceptual cues (such as, for example, total stimulus area or extent of figure-ground segregation) is easily able to find the correct door on the initial trials of the addition-subtraction test as there is an exact configurational correspondence between the counters and the choice cards. A high measure of success on the scored responses can then be achieved, entirely without numerical working, by making choices guided by a simple, empirical rule such as 'the correct door is always a different one from the one which is correct the first time'. This would give a 1/2 chance of responding to the correct door on each trial.

Eight of Wohlwill's subjects, also, failed the extension series and passed the unprovoked addition-subtraction test. The explanation which he offers of this finding cannot be regarded as the most parsimonious. He comments that 'on the lowest level, success on this test was based less on a precise realization of the arithmetical relationships involved than on a possibly still rather intuitive perception of the order among the choice cards, and of the effects of addition and subtraction'.

Although equally open to this type of approach there is less evidence of success achieved in the unprovoked conservation test by an empirical rather than a numerical attack. Its high homogeneity with the total scale provides a general indication of a largely numerical approach by the subjects. Only nine six-year-olds, seven five-year-olds and a single four-year-old failed the extension series and passed the unprovoked conservation test. Eight of the six-year-olds and one of the five-year-olds would have passed the extension series if a less stringent criterion of eight correct responses had been adopted. The remaining six-year-old and a further five-year-old were among the group who overtly counted the counters before making their scored conservation test responses. This leaves six of the younger subjects who gave no apparent evidence of numerical working and may have succeeded on the unprovoked conservation test by employing an empirical rule such as 'the correct door is the same on both choices'.

The Developmental Relationship of Addition-Subtraction and Conservation

An interesting developmental issue is raised by the greater total of passes on the addition-subtraction than on the conservation tests. The result is contrary to expectations based on an analysis of the numerical operations involved since addition-subtraction trials appear to entail a grasp at a symbolic level of the relationships among numbers which does not seem to be demanded by the conservation trials. On the basis of a similar, statistically significant critical ratio Wohlwill (1960) asserted that success on the addition-subtraction trials appeared to be virtually a prerequisite for the manifestation of conservation, and that, interspersed with the conservation trials, they had the effect of suggesting to the subject the conservation of the number aggregate in the conservation trials, where no element was either added or subtracted but only the perceptual configurations were changed.

Although this assertion about the course of the development of conservation of number derives a certain amount of support from the results of studies by Williams (1958) and Churchill (1958), and the modest success reported by Wohlwill (1962) in establishing the notion of conservation by repeated exposure to the effects of addition and subtraction, it is extremely doubtful if Wohlwill's (1960) results and those of the present study can be reconciled with it. Twelve of Wohlwill's subjects passed the addition-subtraction test and failed the conservation test. Six of these subjects, however, although failing to achieve the pass criterion of five concept responses, gave definite evidence of conservation in that, after responding incorrectly on the first two or three trials, they made correct responses on the last four or three trials. As Wohlwill does not provide details of individual performance on the extension series, it is not possible to assess how many of the six remaining subjects were clearly functioning on a numerical rather than an empirical basis.

In the present study, seven six-year-olds, twelve five-year-olds and three four-year-olds passed the unprovoked addition-subtraction test and failed the unprovoked conservation test. Only one of the six-year-olds and two of the five-year-olds gave definite evidence of conservation although failing to achieve the pass criterion. The comparatively large numbers of subjects remaining might seem to support Wohlwill's views on the sequence of development but a consideration of their scores on the extension series deprives this evidence of its validity. All three of the four-year-olds, seven of the five-year-olds and one of the six-year-olds scored six or less correct responses on the extension series. It is thus highly uncertain that these subjects were employing a numerical set in tackling the tests. The performance of the five six-year-olds and three five-year-olds who were clearly working on a numerical basis and who passed the addition-subtraction test and failed the conservation test still seems to support Wohlwill's viewpoint. This evidence is counter-balanced by the performance of the five six-year-olds and two five-year-olds who failed the addition-subtraction test and passed the conservation test. With the exception of a single five-year-old, all of these subjects were clearly working on a numerical basis since one scored twelve correct responses on the extension series, two scored eleven, one scored ten and two scored nine and eight respectively.

Other features of the results are inconsistent with Wohlwill's assertion. At the six-year-old level where most of the subjects were clearly working with a numerical set the total number of subjects who passed the unprovoked addition-subtraction test was only slightly, and not significantly, greater than the total of those who passed the unprovoked conservation test. In addition, although the results obtained in the addition-subtraction and conservation tests with the provoked correspondence materials were, in general, very similar to those obtained with the unprovoked correspondence materials, at the six-year-old level the number of passes on the provoked conservation test was slightly, but not significantly, superior to the number of passes on the provoked addition-subtraction test.

In short, although an appreciation of the effects of addition and subtraction is evidently closely linked to the appearance of conservation of number, neither Wohlwill's (1960) results nor those of the present study give clear grounds for regarding the former as a pre-requisite for the development of the latter. Indeed, the results of the present study suggest that the concept of conservation would be more likely to be established in children by presenting them with both addition-subtraction and conservation trials in a mixed sequence than by repeated exposure to the effects of addition-subtraction alone. Support for this viewpoint is provided by the work of Smedslund (1961) on accelerating the development of conservation of weight in children aged from five to seven years, which was discussed in Chapter One.

The Relationship Between Counting and Conservation

The marked increase, revealed in both the verbal and non-verbal pre-test results, in the frequency of adoption of the overt counting approach with the rise in the subjects' age and total conservation score has some interesting developmental implications. In general, it suggests the existence of a close connexion between the use of counting by the children and their attainment of conservation. We can be more specific. Two variations of the counting approach were observed. Some of the subjects counted the counters or eggs before making the initial choice and then, after they had been rearranged, proceeded to recount them before making their scored responses. Others gave no evidence of counting on the initial match but after the elements had been rearranged, counted before making their scored responses. The behaviour of the former group is consistent with the interpretation that they have discarded the perceptually dominated approach which produces non-conservation and clearly realize the relevance of enumeration to the situation. The concept of conservation is not yet sufficiently established, however, for them to accept it as logically necessary that, in the absence of addition or subtraction of an element, the number of objects in the collection must be unchanged. They are, therefore, obliged to recount the elements in the group to make sure of this fact. The latter group, also, appreciate the relevance of enumeration; that they do not apply it in making the initial match appears to be due to the realization that the correct response can easily be determined by relying on the obvious one-one correspondence between the counters or eggs and the arrangement of the elements on the appropriate choice card. They do find it necessary, however, to resort to counting to discover the correct response on the conservation trial.

These findings are not consistent with the features stressed by Piaget (1952) in his account of the genesis of conservation. His account is based on the results obtained in a series of highly verbal test situations in which, as in the present study, the establishment of an initial one-one correspondence between the elements of two equal collections was followed by a disruption of the perceptual configuration of one of them. In it he asserts that the reasoning which leads to the affirmation of conservation essentially consists of co-ordination of relations with its twofold aspect of logical multiplication of relations and mathematical composition of parts and proportions. The child is able to co-ordinate the displacements made in the elements of the disturbed collection and realizes, for example, that although they may have been pressed together and occupy a smaller area they have not become fewer since the change has been offset by a corresponding increase in their density. He realizes that the spatial modification in the distribution of the elements can be corrected by an inverse operation which would restore the original correspondence. Thus, it is the development of the ability to employ logical multiplication of relations and reversible operations in his thought processes that enables the child to establish the quantifying operational correspondence which guarantees the necessary and lasting numerical equivalence of corresponding sets in spite of changes in their appearance.

Piaget accords little importance to counting in the evolution of conservation. He asserts that there is no connection between the acquired ability to count and the actual operations of which the child is capable. At the point at which correspondence becomes quantifying, thereby giving rise to the beginnings of equivalence, counting aloud may hasten the process of evolution but the process is not begun by numerals as such. The results of the present study not only suggest that Piaget may have underestimated the part played by counting in the development of conservation but, also, that he may have over-emphasized the role played by appreciation of the multiplication of relations. If his claims for the importance of multiplication of relations are justified it is particularly difficult to explain the behaviour of the subjects who made their initial choice on the basis of one-one correspondence and yet found it necessary to resort to counting before making their scored responses. This suggests that one-one correspondence may have to be linked with counting before necessary equivalence is accepted. Renwick (1963) quotes examples of children's responses which indicate that the establishing of one-one correspondence is not at first regarded as giving valid information about the relative number of objects in two collections. It is only when the act of pairing becomes connected with the familiar operation of counting and the use of the well-known verbal sequence that its numerical significance is appreciated and it is accepted as a valid alternative to counting as a source of numerical information.

Two further points support the suggestion that counting may have a fundamental rather than an ancillary role to play in the development of conservation. Piaget's account is based on a series of test situations in which the subject is called upon to deal simultaneously with two collections of elements. This is not structurally the simplest situation in which children's appreciation of conservation can be tested. The simplest approach would involve confronting the subject with a single collection of elements and testing his grasp of the invariance of the number in the group despite changes in the position of the elements. The fundamental part played by counting in the development of conservation is very evident in this situation since the child must employ counting to establish a correspondence between the elements in the collection and the units of the familiar verbal sequence before the initial situation necessary for the investigation of conservation can be established.

The importance of counting is also emphasized if we accept the suggestion made by Churchill (1958) that it is through repeated counting acts, particularly if accompanied by finger pointing as they often are, that the child becomes aware of the units comprising a group, one of the basic factors necessary to the number concept. The realization is vital for the appearance of conservation. The child must be aware of the units comprising a group before he can discard the global or perceptual method of reaching numerical decisions and become capable of employing the critical test for conservation—that at least one element must be added to or subtracted from a collection before the number changes.

Shortcomings of the Verbal Pre-Test

As in the case of the non-verbal test, the performance of a number of subjects on the verbal pre-test indicated that it was possible to achieve success on the conservation items by functioning at an empirical rather than a conceptual level. The empirical rule involved was simply to follow the suggestion in the experimenter's questions. A considerable degree of success could be attained by means of this approach since in six of the seven conservation items the crucial question was worded in a form which was suggestive of the correct response. Although the subjects were required to give explanations of their answers on five of these six items this additional information was of very limited usefulness in detecting working on an empirical basis since 'Don't know' replies were frequent particularly among the younger children. Had all seven conservation items been alike the existence of functioning at the empirical level would have remained a suspicion rather than a certainty and there would, of course, have been no means of determining its frequency of occurrence. Fortunately Item 13 was unique in being worded in a manner which suggested the wrong answer. This permitted the compilation of Table 3 which presents a frequency distribution of the subjects who followed this suggestion and produced the wrong response and a 'Don't know' explanation on Item 13 and, also, one or more correct answers and 'Don't know' explanations on the other conservation items.

TABLE 3: *Frequency of pass–'Don't know' response in verbal test made by subjects giving a fail–'Don't know' response on Item 13*

AGE GROUP	N	1	2	3	4	5	Total
4·0–4·6 years	37	3	2	2	4	5	16
5·0–5·6 years	97	6	6	8	10	3	33
6·0–6·6 years	93	0	0	0	3	0	3
Total	227	9	8	10	17	8	52

(No. OF PASS–'DON'T KNOW' RESPONSES IN VERBAL TEST)

It is evident from the data on the incidence of empirical rule working in the verbal pre-test provided in Table 3 and the above discussion of the shortcomings of the non-verbal pre-test that neither would be satisfactory for assessing the effectiveness of attempts to accelerate the attainment of conservation. The nature of their faults and failings is such, however, that it is still possible for the pre-tests to fulfil their principal function of making possible the selection of the subjects for the acceleration study. It seems reasonable to conclude that children have not yet attained conservation of number if they do not achieve a substantial degree of success on tests in which success can be attained either by working on a conceptual or an empirical rule basis. The decision as to what constitutes a substantial degree of success is facilitated by the U-shaped nature of the frequency distribution of scores on both tests. These suggest a score of four on the verbal test and of six on the non-verbal test as suitable dividing points and these will be employed as the criterion levels in the description of the sampling procedure with which the account of the acceleration study in the next chapter begins.

CHAPTER THREE

The Experimental Study:
Training Procedures and the Post-Tests

The sample for the acceleration study

TWO CONSIDERATIONS determined the choice of the 90 subjects who constituted the sample for the acceleration study. It was decided that there should be equal numbers from the three age groups and that subjects representing three types of non-conservation performance detected by the pre-tests should be included. The first type was entirely confined to fourteen of the thirty-seven four-year-olds and involved not only failure to achieve a single success in the conservation items on either pre-test but inability to appreciate the numerical equivalence of two rows of six counters arranged in one to one correspondence. Twenty of the four-year-olds, forty-seven of the ninety-seven five-year-olds, and sixteen of the ninety-three six-year-olds exhibited the second type. They were able to appreciate numerical equivalence but failed to attain criterion levels of more than four correct conservation responses on the verbal test and more than six on the non-verbal test. These scores were selected as criterion levels because, as indicated above, their positions in their respective frequency distributions indicated that they represented something of a watershed in the subject's performance. The third type of performance was fully described in the discussion of the pre-tests in Chapter Two. Subjects adopting this approach established the initial numerical equivalence between two collections with or without overt counting and, then, after the elements in one of the collections had been rearranged by the experimenter, proceeded to overtly count them before making the correct conservation response. The adoption of this method of approach can be interpreted as evidence that these children had discarded the perceptually dominated attitude which produces non-conservation and clearly realized the relevance of enumeration to the situation. The concept of conservation was not yet sufficiently established, however, for them to accept it as logically necessary that, in the absence of addition or subtraction of an element, the number of objects in the collection must be unchanged. They were, therefore, obliged to count the elements in the group to make sure of this fact. An account of performance in sufficient detail to permit the detection of this approach was available for 179 of the subjects. None of the four-year-olds, twenty-two of the five-year-olds and twenty-five of the six-year-olds adopted it. All but seven of the five-year-olds and one six-year-old surpassed the criterion levels on the pre-tests. The combination of age and type of pre-test performance outlined in Table 4 was adopted as a basis for the selection of the ninety children to take part in the acceleration study. The members of each sub-group were randomly selected from the subjects satisfying the various age and pre-test performance requirements.

TABLE 4: *Composition of acceleration study sample (90 subjects) sub-groups*

	4 YEAR I	4 YEAR II	5 YEAR	6 YEAR I	6 YEAR II
Age of subjects	4·0–4·6	4·0–4·6	5·0–6·6	6·0–6·6	6·0–6·6
Number of subjects	12	18	30	15	15
Type of pre-test performance	Type 1	Type 2	Type 2	Type 2	Type 3

Each of the sub-groups was randomly divided into three sections and these were combined to form three groups of thirty subjects, each of which retained the same divisions by age and pre-test performance as the original sample of ninety subjects. The three groups were randomly designated as Experimental Group I, Experimental Group II and a Control Group. The Control Group was not seen by the experimenter while Experimental Group I and Experimental Group II were respectively undergoing the so-called non-verbal and verbal training procedures outlined below. The training procedures were administered by the writer and a second experimenter. Half of the children in each of the sub-groups of Experimental Groups I and II were randomly assigned for treatment to each experimenter. This avoided any possible identification of an experimenter with one of the acceleration techniques.

The non-verbal training procedure

The training procedure adopted with Experimental Group I was based on a number of hypotheses derived from the discussion in Chapter One of theoretical and empirical work on the topic of acceleration.

1. An attempt to foster conceptual conflict should be a feature of any acceleration technique. In the case of number conservation an appropriate method of achieving conceptual conflict is the employment of trials in which the effects of perceptual change are juxtaposed with those of addition and subtraction. External reinforcement should be a feature of such trials. If it takes a suitably motivating form it should increase conceptual conflict by raising the absolute strengths of the responses involved. At the same time by providing feedback on the accuracy of responses external reinforcement should help to emphasize the consistency of the addition-subtraction schema and the ambiguity and contradiction of the perceptual mode of operation.

2. Since attention must be given to the acquisition of 'content' as well as 'structure', a treatment aimed at acceleration should include trials involving direct, externally reinforced practice on the principle to be inculcated in addition to trials aimed at initiating appropriate conceptual conflict. In conjunction with the first hypothesis this supports the adoption of a mixed sequence of conservation and addition-subtraction trials of the type comprising the addition and subtraction treatment in the Wohlwill and Lowe (1962) study. The pre-test results in the present study, also, suggest that the concept of number conservation is more likely to be established by presenting both addition-subtraction and conservation trials in a mixed sequence than by repeated exposure to the effects of addition-subtraction alone.

3. True conservation, as distinct from the acquisition of a narrow, empirical rule, is more likely to be produced by confronting children with an extended series of relevant learning experiences involving the use of a wide variety of materials. This hypothesis was prompted by Wohlwill's (1962) suggestion that the restricted nature of the learning produced by his own training conditions might be due to the use of a single set of materials throughout, and by Smedslund's (1963) view that it should be worthwhile to use more practice sessions, extending, for example, over two weeks, in order to obtain more definite results in acceleration studies. It is also in line with Harlow's (1959) account of learning set (LS) formation and his emphasis on generalized experience as a prerequisite for the learning of broad concepts and principles in primates as well as in man.

Apparatus

In the non-verbal training procedure this was constructed of wood and consisted of two platforms (each 9 × 11 inches) side by side but

c

separated by a depression. Beneath the platforms and facing the subject were three apertures covered by doors which opened upwards towards the subject. Reinforcement was delivered to these openings from the rear of the apparatus by means of a sliding drawer. The rear of the apparatus was low to allow the experimenter to place objects on the platforms but it was flanked by high sides and equipped with a roller blind (see Figure IVa) which effectively cut off both the doors and platforms from the subject's view between trials.

Administration

The members of Experimental Group I were seen individually by the experimenter for thirty minutes on eight successive school days. The child was seated in front of the apparatus and the situation was introduced as a game of hide and seek. He was given a board with a partly completed mini-mosaic on it and instructed that he would be able to find more mini-tiles behind the doors. He would find the correct door every time if he looked carefully at the objects which would be placed on the platforms. The decision to employ a form of positive reinforcement which involved manipulatory activity by the subjects was prompted by the work of Terrell (1959) on motivation and by the practical consideration that it provided time for the setting up of the next trial. Negative reinforcement, in the shape of two wooden blocks placed behind the incorrect doors, was also employed on every trial.

A complete, detailed account of the sequence of trials used in the non-verbal acceleration method is available (Wallace, 1967). Considerations of bulk, however, dictate that it cannot be included in the present volume. The description of the procedure which follows will, accordingly, consist of an outline of its general features.

Training series. This had the twofold aim of ascertaining the numerical level at which each child could work successfully and of allowing him to discover for himself the rule governing the location of the reinforcement. The relative number of objects on the platforms was the determining factor. When there were more objects on the left platform than on the right the positive reinforcement was discovered behind the left door. When the right platform held more objects, the right door was positively reinforced. When equal numbers of objects were on the platforms the centre door was correct.

Small, red blocks were the materials used throughout the training series. They were arranged in an irregular fashion and there was no configurational correspondence between those on the two platforms

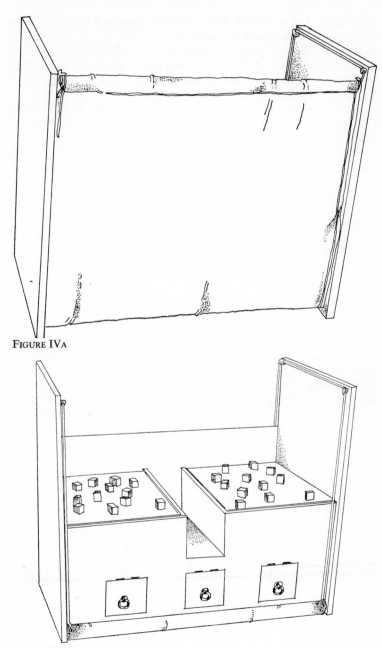

FIGURE IVa

FIGURE IVb

(see Figure IVb). The series began with a sequence of twenty trials using one or two objects on each platform. The child was allowed to correct his choices on the first three trials, thereafter no further correction was permitted at any point in the series. This sequence, like those used throughout the period of training, was designed, as far as possible, to ensure that subjects did not begin to rely on empirical rules based on position preferences due to one door being positively reinforced more frequently than the others. It was repeated until a criterion of six successive correct responses was attained.

Similar sequences employing three or four and seven or eight objects on each platform followed. These were, also, continued until the criterion was attained. The training series concluded with six trials using twelve or thirteen objects. They were not repeated and three successive correct responses terminated this section. Subjects underwent the entire series or followed it to a point at which their attainment of the criterion at one or more of the lower numerical levels indicated that they had learned the rule governing the location of the positive reinforcement but their unsuccessful performance with a greater number of objects suggested that they had gone beyond the numerical level at which they could count accurately. Attainment of the criterion at the three-four level was set as the condition for entry to the Conservation Series.

Conservation series. This was based on a repeated sequence of twenty trials comprising ten conservation and ten addition-subtraction trials in a random order. At the commencement of each trial the roller blind was lowered to reveal the objects in position on the platform (see Figure Va). Unlike the Training Series three types of initial arrangement were used—objects on both platforms in rows; objects on one platform in a similar irregular arrangement to those on the other; objects on one platform in a different irregular arrangement from those on the other. The three types of arrangement occurred a similar number of times in random order in the course of the conservation and addition or subtraction trials. These variations were introduced to provide the children with experience of dealing with situations in which their initial choice could be based entirely on visual correspondence and, also, others in which the intervention of symbolic activity (i.e. counting) was essential. As the initial choice constituted the information portion of the trial the subject was prevented from making an incorrect response and urged to look again carefully at the objects on the platform.

In a conservation trial, after the initial choice, the experimenter called the subject's attention to the fact that the group of objects on

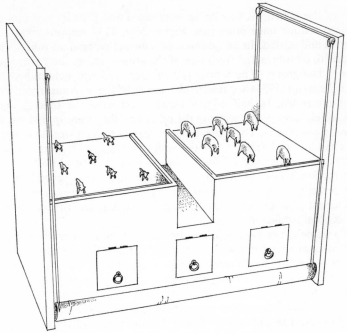

FIGURE VA

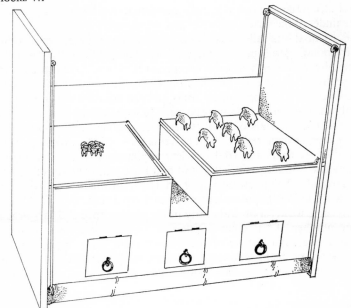

FIGURE VB

one of the platforms was being rearranged and then invited him to choose a door once more (see Figure Vb). This response was recorded and scored. In an addition or subtraction trial an object was added to or subtracted from one of the groups before the rearrangement. The group to be rearranged in each trial was determined by a Gellermann (1933) sequence. The nature of the rearrangement was also controlled. In half of the conservation trials the objects were pushed closer together while in the other half they were spread out to cover a wider area. These two types of rearrangement were employed in a random order. In all of the addition trials the rearrangements increased the density of the group of objects while in all of the subtraction trials the density was diminished. This procedure set the perceptual cues consistently at variance with the nature of the numerical change and was intended to maximize the degree of conceptual conflict involved.

To allow the maximum use to be made of the comparatively brief period available for training, parallel forms of the Conservation Series were produced corresponding to the three–four, seven–eight and twelve–thirteen numerical levels in the Training Series. In accordance with the degree of competence which they had displayed all the subjects began their training either at the three–four or seven–eight level. Flexibility was retained, however, and if the subject appeared to be coping easily with the trials at a particular numerical level below the maximum he was transferred to a higher level for the remainder of the series.

Each of the parallel forms was divided into four major sections corresponding to four main types of materials employed in the trials. The third and fourth sections comprised three and four sub-sections respectively. The first problem in each section and sub-section consisted of ten conservation trials and ten addition or subtraction trials arranged in a random sequence. The sequence was continued for the full twenty trials or until the subject attained a criterion of six successive correct responses. The remainder of the problems consisted of six trials and trial two learning applied (i.e. if the subject responded correctly on the second and third trials the problem was terminated). This distribution of trials per problem was based on Harlow's (1959) hypothesis that a small fixed number of trials per problem is wasteful of trials early in LS performance and too large a fixed number of trials per problem is wasteful of trials late in LS performance. An outline of the Conservation Series indicating the number of problems and the type of materials employed in the four main sections and their sub-sections follows:

1. Provoked Correspondence. Six problems. The materials on the platforms were qualitatively complementary (e.g. cups on one and saucers on the other) and correspondence was, thus, provoked.

2. Unprovoked Correspondence. Six problems similar to those in the previous section but non-complementary, identical materials (e.g. blue cubes) were used.

3. Varying Materials. (a) Two problems. Dissimilar everyday objects on both platforms (see Figure VIa). (b) Two problems. Dissimilar objects on both platforms. These were randomly selected from a collection of twenty-eight geometrical shapes (see Figure VIb). (c) Two Problems. A mixture of objects on both platforms randomly selected from the collections used in (a) and (b).

4. Varying Containers. Throughout this section identical materials (beads) were used. (a) Three problems. Beads on both platforms at beginning of each trial. Those on the platform on which the addition, subtraction or conservation change was performed were placed in a glass container (e.g. a cylinder). (b) Three problems. Beads on both platforms at beginning of each trial. Both those on which the addition, subtraction or conservation change was carried out and those on the other platform were placed in glass containers (e.g. a beaker and a cylinder respectively). (c) Two problems. Beads were initially presented on the platforms in identical glass containers. Those on which the addition, subtraction or conservation change was carried out were transferred to another container (e.g. two beakers at outset and contents of one transferred to a cylinder). (d) One problem. Beads were initially presented on the platforms in identical glass containers. Both the group on which the addition, subtraction or conservation change was performed and the other group were transferred to different containers (e.g. two beakers at outset, bead added to one and contents transferred to a wide, low container; contents of the other transferred to a cylinder).

The verbal training procedure

The treatment accorded to Experimental Group II was based on the work of Gal'perin (1961). This decision was in accordance with the conclusion in Chapter One that the impressive results achieved with his methods justify attempts to determine their efficacy in other conceptual areas and with subjects of varying age levels. The hypotheses on which the procedure were founded was derived from Gal'perin's explicit statements and from features implicit in hi technique.

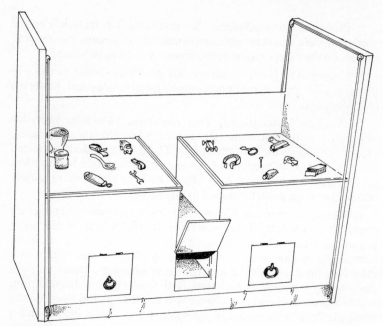

FIGURE VIA

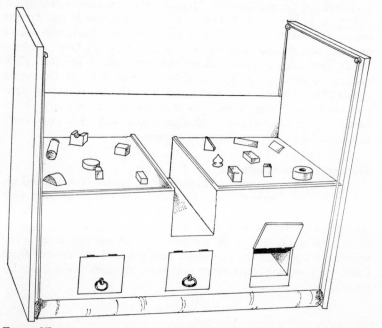

FIGURE VIb

1. When a subject is provided from the outset with a precise and objective account of the essential features of a concept and is shown how to apply them in the clearest possible way, the process of concept formation is greatly shortened since a number of intermediate stages which occur when the subject's mental processes are not controlled and organized in this way are avoided.

2. Conceptualization consists of a process of progressive internalization of a structure which should be presented in its entirety at the outset in an externally observable form. The first step is the development of a correct set of reference points on the basis of which the material or overt, concrete form of concept may be developed. In the second stage the concept becomes independent of material, concrete formulations and, in contrast, is reflected in audible speech. Finally this audible speech form of the concept is transmuted into an internal mental arrangement and takes the form of the individual talking to himself. The concept becomes an act of verbal thinking and, as a result of abbreviations and complete assimilation, attains a final form which is hard to follow by introspection.

3. By presenting a variety of problems involving variations in the material such that the conditions stipulated in the conceptual definition may be completely or incompletely fulfilled, the subject is led not only to internalize but, also, to generalize the complete structure with which he has been provided.

Administration

The first task in adapting Gal'perin's method for an attempt at accelerating the appearance of number conservation in four- to six-year-old children was the production of the initial, material form of the concept. As a written, verbal definition was clearly unsuitable for use in this age range a largely pictorial method of presenting the basic features of the concept was adopted. Figure VII illustrates the layout of the captions and the three series of pictures on the card which constituted the concrete form of the concept. Two examples of the type of pictures used (1D and 2A respectively) are provided in Figure VIII. The choice of monkeys as the characters through which the definition was presented was prompted by the existence in Bristol of an excellent zoo with which all of the children were familiar and, also, by the ready availability of suitable pictures.

The general procedure adopted will be outlined first and then a detailed account of the method of introducing and presenting the problems will be provided. As in the case of Experimental Group I, the members of Experimental Group II were seen individually by the

FIGURE VII: *Materials for verbal training procedure*

1.   NO CHANGE

4 monkeys on swing	4 monkeys around box	4 monkeys on see-saw	4 monkeys being fed through bars of cage
A	B	C	D

2.   CHANGE

monkey leaving box

3 monkeys on see-saw	1 monkey peeping out of box	3 monkeys on see-saw and fourth monkey approaching from box	4 monkeys playing on see-saw
A	B	C	D

3.   CHANGE

monkey approaching box

4 monkeys on see-saw	3 monkeys on see-saw and 1 going towards box	1 monkey peeping out of box	3 monkeys on see-saw
A	B	C	D

FIGURE VIII: *Materials for verbal training procedure*

experimenter for thirty minutes on eight successive school days. At the outset the child was shown the pictorial definition of number conservation. The basic features of the concept were explained and he was informed that he would be able to solve a number of problems, which were about to be presented to him, by a systematic application of the components to the features of each problem.

The problems used were a sub-set of the sequence devised for the non-verbal acceleration technique. This decision was prompted by the fact that they satisfied the requirement, stated in the third hypothesis above, for variations in material and in the degree of fulfilment of the defining conditions. A detailed description of the specific problems and trials used cannot be presented within the confines of this account but it is available elsewhere (Wallace, 1967). Only the procedural changes necessitated by their adaptation for use in the verbal acceleration technique will be described below. As in the non-verbal trials use was made of parallel series of problems corresponding to the three–four, seven–eight and twelve–thirteen numerical levels. The subject's degree of numerical competence was determined at the outset in the trials which comprised Problem 1 and this enabled a sequence of problems at the appropriate level to be presented. Once again flexibility was retained and if the subject appeared to be coping easily with the trials at a particular level below the maximum he was transferred to a higher numerical level for the remainder of the training.

Initially, the subject was guided to the solution of the problems by applying all of the aspects of the concept as delineated on the card. When he had thoroughly assimilated the contents of the card and appeared to be able to do without it, it was, first, turned over on the table and later removed completely. The subject was asked to continue tackling the problems by reciting the components of the concept aloud from memory and, also, by describing aloud how they applied to the features of each problem. When this procedure, too, began to be accomplished quickly without any mistakes and usually in an abbreviated form, the subject was instructed to carry out the same process in the same order but to speak 'to himself' and only announce the answer aloud. If a subject gave an incorrect reply he was directed to return to the preceding level of the process. In the cases where mistakes occurred when the subject was at the final stage and the process was internal and he was operating under his own control, it was suggested that he should repeat the components of the concept to himself and then look, once more, at the problem. If this procedure did not help, the experimenter suggested that the subject recite the features of the concept aloud (i.e. return to the preceding level) and then see how they applied to the conditions of the problem.

The above description of the general procedure gives an overall view of the technique. To add detail to the picture an account follows of the introduction and method of presentation of problems used.

Introduction. The experimenter told the subject "We are going to look at some puzzles, but first of all, I am going to show you three stories. If you look carefully at the stories they will help you to find the answers to the puzzles'.

The subject was shown the first cartoon strip. 'Have you been to the zoo? Did you see the monkeys?'

The experimenter pointed to the first picture in the strip. 'What are the monkeys doing here?' 'How many monkeys are there?'

The experimenter now pointed to the second picture. 'Are the monkeys still in the same part of their cage?' 'They have moved. What are they doing now?' 'How many monkeys are there now?' 'How many were there here (pointing to first picture)?' 'The monkeys have moved but the number of monkeys has not changed. There is *no change* (repeated and accompanied with pointing to the caption over the strip) in the number of monkeys.'

The same sequence of questions was gone through with respect to the third and fourth pictures.

The subject was shown the second cartoon strip. The experimenter pointed to the first picture. 'What are the monkeys doing here?' 'How many monkeys are there?' The subject's attention was switched to the second picture. 'What is happening in this picture?' 'Another monkey is coming out of the box.' The third picture was indicated. 'What is he doing now?' 'He is going to play with the other three monkeys.'

The experimenter pointed to the fourth picture. 'How many monkeys are there now?'

The subject was once again directed to the first picture. 'How many monkeys were there here?' 'The number of monkeys has changed. 'Why has the number of monkeys changed?'

'The number of monkeys changed because another monkey came out of the box.'

The experimenter pointed to the caption over the strip (the word CHANGE and a picture of the monkey leaving the box).

The subject was shown the third cartoon strip. The experimenter pointed to the first picture. 'What are the monkeys doing here?' 'How many monkeys are there?' The second picture was indicated.

'What is happening in this picture?' 'One of the monkeys is going away from the other monkeys.'

The subject's attention was switched to the third picture. 'What is he doing now?' 'He is going into the box.'

The experimenter pointed to the fourth picture. 'How many monkeys are there now?'

The subject was again directed to the first picture. 'How many monkeys were there here?' 'The number of monkeys has changed. Why has the number of monkeys changed?'

'The number of monkeys changed because one of the monkeys went into the box. The experimenter pointed to the caption over the strip (the word CHANGE and a picture of the monkey approaching the box).

The introduction concluded at this point with the experimenter telling the subject, 'We are going to look at the puzzles now and remember that these three stories (card laid beside the subject) will help you to find the answers'.

Method of presentation. As in the case of the non-verbal acceleration technique, the problems were presented in terms of two groups of objects. In the verbal training procedure, however, no presentation apparatus was employed and the two sets of objects were simply arranged on a table top, one group in front of the experimenter and the other in front of the subject. The same general procedure was followed in each of the problems.

The experimenter initially arranged his objects in rows or in an irregular configuration as demanded by the particular trial. The subject was then presented with his group of objects and, as appropriate, instructed to put them in rows like the experimenter's or to arrange them like the experimenter's (i.e. in the same irregular configuration) or just to lay his objects out as he saw fit (i.e. in a different, irregular configuration from the experimenter's group). If it proved necessary, the experimenter subsequently altered the subject's arrangement to make it correspond more closely with his own or in order that the perceptual change to greater or less density which was to follow in the later portion of the trial might be more definite.

After the objects had been satisfactorily arranged in the two initial groups, the experimenter asked the subjects:

'Have we got the same number of things?'

'Have you got more than me?'

'Have you got less than me?'

In each case if the subject was wrong the experimenter asked: 'How many have you got?' 'How many have I got?' and then repeated the original question.

This series of questions was followed by the perceptual change required by a +, — or conservation trial.

The experimenter then asked the subject:

'Have you got the same number as*⎫
            more than ⎬ me now?'
            less than ⎭

*whichever was correct in the initial situation.

Regardless of whether the subject replied correctly, incorrectly or not at all, the experimenter proceeded.

'The monkeys will help you to find the right answer. When did the number of monkeys change?' The experimenter directed the subject to the first cartoon strip. 'The number of monkeys changed because another monkey came out of the box and joined them. Has another thing come out to join my/your (the group which had been perceptually altered) ones?'

The experimenter directed the subject to the second cartoon strip. 'When did the number of monkeys change?' 'The number of monkeys changed because one of the monkeys went away into the box. Has one of my/your things gone away?'

In a + or — trial the experimenter proceeded: 'The number of my/your things has changed? How many have I/you got now?' 'How many have I/you got?' The experimenter then returned to the original question:

'Have you got the same number as⎫
            more than ⎬ me now?'
            less than ⎭

and followed it with the other two possible variations of this question.

In a conservation trial the experimenter proceeded to direct the subject to the third cartoon strip. 'The monkeys have moved but the number of monkeys has not changed. Have my/your things moved?' 'Has the number of my/your things changed?' 'My/your things have moved but the number has not changed.'

The experimenter then returned to the original question:

'Have you got the same number as⎫
            more than ⎬ me now?'
            less than ⎭

If the subject still could not answer, the experimenter asked, 'How many have I/you got?' 'How many have I/you got?'

The original question was then repeated and followed by the other two possible variations of this question.

As indicated above, during the sequence of problems when the subject appeared to have thoroughly assimilated the contents of the card and to be able to do without it, it was first turned over on the table and, after some more problems had been dealt with, removed completely. The subject was asked to continue tackling the problems by applying the three stories to the problem situations *aloud from memory*.

When, after the solution of further problems, the subject appeared to be able to go through this procedure quickly and without error, the experimenter instructed him to continue to use the three stories in the same way but to 'speak to himself' and only to say the answer to the questions 'out loud'.

At the conclusion of the eight day training sequence, Experimental Group I, Experimental Group II and the Control Group underwent the first post-tests. Three months after the training sequence they were retested on the verbal and non-verbal tests employed as the first post-tests.

Performance in the non-verbal training procedure

The average number of trials at each numerical level attempted by the members of the five sub-groups of Experimental Group I during the Conservation Series in the non-verbal training sequence is presented in Table 5.

TABLE 5: *Average number of trials attempted at each numerical level in conservation series*

NUMERICAL LEVEL	SUB-GROUPS				
	4 Year I	*4 Year II*	*5 Year*	*6 Year II*	*6 Year II*
3–4	30·5	23·25	11·6	7·5	1·2
7–8	8·5	47·5	39·7	24·75	9·0
12–13	0	0	9·8	24·5	29·4

The Developmental Relationship of Addition-Subtraction and Conservation

Two aspects of the children's performance during the non-verbal training procedure are directly relevant to the unresolved issue of the course of the development of conservation. The first of these is the relative degree of success achieved by the subjects on the addition-subtraction and conservation items. The average number of successes obtained by the members of the sub-groups and of the Experimental Group as a whole were compared. Neither the within sub-groups differences nor the total difference between the scores on the two types of item were statistically significant. (Wilcoxon Matched-Pairs Signed-Ranks Test). These results are in accord with the conclusion reached on the basis of the non-verbal pre-test findings that there are no clear grounds for regarding success on addition-subtraction items as a prerequisite for success on conservation items.

A detailed account of performance, as distinct from a record of correct and incorrect responses, is, unfortunately, only available for fourteen of the subjects in Experimental Group I (0 from 4 Year I; 2 from 4 Year II; 8 from 5 Year, 1 from 6 Year I and 3 from 6 Year II). This represents a very tenuous basis for comment but the developmental picture suggested is, nevertheless, interesting. With the exception of two subjects in the 5 Year Group, all of the records were consistent with the following developmental sequence: (a) before making the scored response on both conservation and addition-subtraction trials the subject finds it necessary to recount the objects on the platforms; (b) the subject responds immediately on conservation trials but still finds it necessary to recount on addition-subtraction trials; (e) the subject responds immediately without recounting on both types of trial.

Performance in the verbal training procedure

As anticipated, despite the identical nature of the materials and the basic similarity of the procedure, the administration of the trials which comprised the verbal training sessions proved to be more time consuming than that of their counterparts in the non-verbal training sequence. The extent of the differential can be gauged from a comparison of Table 5 above and Table 6 which indicates the average

TABLE 6: *Average number of trials attempted at each numerical level in verbal training series*

NUMERICAL LEVEL	SUB-GROUPS				
	4 Year I	*4 Year II*	*5 Year*	*6 Year I*	*6 Year II*
3–4	15·0	3·0	3·0	3·0	3·0
7–8	22·5	23·5	15·9	3·0	3·0
12–13	0	9·0	17·4	25·2	27·0

number of trials at each numerical level undergone by the members of the five sub-groups of Experimental Group II.

As will be seen from the above table, additional trials at the 3–4 level beyond the minimum number of three presented in the course of Problem 1, were only necessary in the case of the 4 Year I sub-group. At the numerical level dictated by their individual variations in counting competence all of the subjects in Experimental Group II before the end of the training sequence produced the type of performance regarded by Gal'perin (1961) as the criterion of concept formation. They gave immediate accurate responses to the problems and were able to support their answers with appropriate explanations derived from the conceptual definition which was, of course, absent at this juncture. The relative pace at which the subjects in the sub-groups passed through the various stages in the process of internalizing the definition is indicated in Table 7 which provides details of the number of children for whom the definition was turned over or removed from view in each of the training sessions.

TABLE 7: *Details of training sessions in which the definition was turned over (DTO) and removed (DR)*

SUB-GROUPS		1	2	3	4	5	6	7	8
4 Year I	DTO	0	0	0	0	0	2	0	0
(N = 2)	DR	0	0	0	0	0	2	0	0
4 Year II	DTO	0	0	2	0	4	0	0	0
(N = 6)	DR	0	0	0	2	0	4	0	0
5 Year	DTO	0	0	0	5	5	0	0	0
(N = 10)	DR	0	0	0	0	5	5	0	0
6 Year I	DTO	0	0	4	1	0	0	0	0
(N = 5)	DR	0	0	3	1	1	0	0	0
6 Year II	DTO	0	2	3	0	0	0	0	0
(N = 5)	DR	0	1	2	2	0	0	0	0

The results paralleled those of Gal'perin not only in that all of the subjects attained the criterion level of performance but in the fact that, after their level of numerical competence had been determined at the outset, the formation of the concept proceeded almost faultlessly. A return to a preceding level of operating was only found necessary in the case of a single member of the 5 Year sub-group whose level of performance slumped when the definition was turned over during the course of the third session. This step was repeated in the following session without affecting his functioning. Three subjects, one member of the 4 Year I sub-group and two of the 5 Year sub-group, had difficulty at the outset of training in coping with questions involving the use of the word 'more'. The technique of informing the child that he was wrong, instructing him to count both collections of objects and then repeating the original 'more' question was found to be effective in surmounting this difficulty.

Modifications incorporated in the post-tests

As indicated in Chapter Two, the shortcomings of the non-verbal and verbal pre-tests, and in particular the possibility of achieving a substantial degree of success by dint of empirical rule working, rendered them unsuitable for assessing the effectiveness of the two training procedures. The non-verbal and verbal post-tests were, accordingly, based on the corresponding pre-tests but included modifications aimed at removing their shortcomings.

The Non-Verbal Post-Test

In the case of the non-verbal test the number of conservation and addition-subtraction trials was increased to eighteen respectively. With a view to preventing subjects who were functioning on the basis of purely perceptual rather than numerical cues from attaining the criterion in the training series six, seven or eight dots were placed on the sample and choice cards instead of two, three or four. As an additional precaution to detect purely perceptual working twelve trials in the test proper began with only a numerical, not a perceptual, correspondence between the counters and the dots on the choice cards. In the remainder of the trials an initial perceptual correspondence was retained.

The third major modification was aimed at excluding the possibility of arriving at the correct response by adopting empirical rules of a positional type. In the conservation trials, for example, this might take the form of the conclusion that 'The correct door is the same on both choices' and in the addition-subtraction trials that 'The correct door is always a different one from the one which is correct the first time'. To combat such sequential hypotheses the mode of administration was altered to permit the relative positions of the choice cards over the doors in the presentation apparatus to be changed after the subject's initial match and before his scored response. As indicated in Figure IX, this was accomplished by mounting rings on the top edge of the apparatus from which a deck of cardboard strips was suspended. Each of the strips presented the three choice cards in a row above their corresponding doors. These relative positions were altered by simply bringing over the next strip in the deck from the rear to the front of the apparatus.

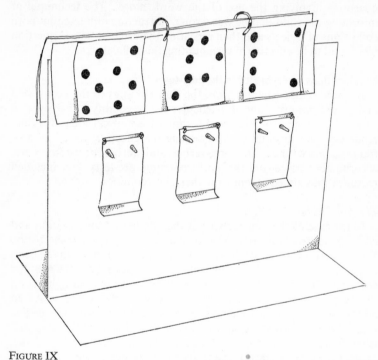

FIGURE IX

A further change in the procedure stemmed from a desire to explore a specific aspect of the development of conservation of number rather than to check a further form of 'pseudoconservation'. The records of children's performance on the non-verbal pre-test suggested the existence of a close connexion between the use of counting and the attainment of conservation. With a view to elucidating the nature of this relationship the non-verbal post-test was divided into equal numbers of 'covered' and 'uncovered' items. In the former the counters were covered over after they had been disarranged to prevent the subjects from counting while in the latter, as throughout the pre-test, no attempt was made to prevent the adoption of this approach. A detailed account of the modified, non-verbal post-test and of the modified verbal post-test is presented in Appendix A.

The Verbal Post-Test

The main procedural modification made in the verbal pre-test to fit it for use as a post-test was designed to remove the possibility of achieving success by simply following the suggestion in the experimenter's questions. The single conservation question in each item was replaced with two questions. The first of these was designed to guide suggestible subjects to the wrong answer. In a typical unprovoked correspondence item, for example, the subject was first asked 'Have you got more pieces than me?' and 'Have we got the same number of pieces?' A correct answer to both questions was required to pass the item.

The number of items in the verbal post-test was also increased. There were twelve conservation items and, to enable a comparison to be made with the non-verbal test, four items were included in which an object was added to or subtracted from one of the collections before it was rearranged. For the reason already outlined above, in four of the conservation items the group rearranged was covered over immediately after the rearrangement while in the remainder this step was omitted. A further innovation introduced as a result of the speculations instigated by the subjects' performance in the pre-tests was the use of only a single collection of objects in five of the conservation items and three of the addition-subtraction items. These items began with the child being asked how many objects there were in the single collection. This procedure replaced the establishment of numerical equivalence between two collections of objects which remained the initial step in the other trials. It was hoped that a comparison of the results obtained with these two procedures would provide a test of the hypothesis that confronting the subject with a single collection of objects constitutes a structurally simpler situation for investigating appreciation of conservation than an approach in which he is called upon to deal simultaneously with two collections of elements.

Wastage from the Sample

Twenty-seven of the thirty subjects in Experimental Group I completed the training sequence and underwent the first post-tests. Unfortunately all of the missing subjects belonged to one age group since it was one member of the 4 Year I Group and two members of the 4 Year II Group who dropped out. Experimental Group I was further reduced to twenty-six by the loss of a member of the 5 Year Group between the first and second post-tests. Experimental Group II, also, suffered casualties in the lowest age range since two members of the 4 Year I Group dropped out of the study before the first post-tests. The total of twenty-eight subjects who completed the first post-tests was reduced to twenty-seven before the second series of post-tests by the loss of a member of the 5 Year Group. Twenty-eight of the Control Group underwent the first post-tests. The two missing subjects belonged respectively to the 5 Year and 6 Year II Groups. The total membership of the Control Group was reduced to twenty-six between the first and second post-tests by the loss of two members of the 4 Year II Group.

Results of the verbal and non-verbal post-tests

The first and second post-tests were administered by the two experimenters who had conducted the training sessions. On both occasions half of the children in each sub-group of the two Experimental and Control Groups were randomly assigned for testing to each experimenter. As in the pre-tests, alternate subjects underwent the verbal and non-verbal tests first.

In presenting the results of the post-tests the total scores relevant to the issue of the effectiveness of the training sequences in accelerating the development of conservation of number will be dealt with first. A consideration of the more detailed aspects of the subjects' performance will follow.

Table 8 presents the mean conservation scores of the Experimental and Control Groups on the verbal and non-verbal tests in the two post-tests. The Mann-Whitney U Test was used in investigating the significance of the differences between the groups' scores. Figures X and XI provide a graphical representation of the distributions of conservation scores.

These overall figures, however, include the scores of children who cannot be regarded as having achieved a sufficient number of correct responses to indicate attainment of conservation. Accordingly Table 9 comprises the numbers of individual subjects who attained levels of performance arbitrarily selected as indicating conservation on the verbal, non-verbal and both tests. The criteria were 11/12 correct responses on the verbal and 15/18 correct responses on the non-verbal test. In view of the safeguards incorporated in the post-tests, these scores appeared to be sufficiently high to exclude the possibility

TABLE 8: *Mean conservation scores and standard deviations of the experimental and control groups on the verbal and non-verbal tests in the two post-tests*

First post-test

Verbal test

Sub-Groups	Exp. Group I	s	Exp. Group II	s	Control Group	s
4 Year I	5·00	(4·97)	8·00	(4·00)	1·80	(1·23)
4 Year II	8·75	(4·49)	11·25	(0·83)	3·00	(1·79)
5 Year	9·20	(2·09)	11·10	(1·22)	7·00	(2·83)
6 Year I	10·25	(2·05)	11·60	(0·80)	11·20	(0·75)
6 Year II	11·00	(1·82)	11·80	(0·40)	9·75	(3·44)
Total	9·22	(3.40)	11·13	(1·63)	6·50	(3·91)

p = ·0132   p = ·00006

p = ·0032

Non-verbal test

Sub-Groups	Exp. Group I	s	Exp. Group II	s	Control Group	s
4 Year I	4·33	(4·43)	0	(0)	1·20	(2·15)
4 Year II	5·00	(3·41)	6·00	(5·12)	2·20	(2·59)
5 Year	6·70	(3·48)	7·40	(3·69)	4·78	(4·84)
6 Year I	12·75	(4·15)	8·00	(2·29)	6·00	(5·83)
6 Year II	16·00	(2·31)	13·20	(4·75)	9·25	(5·22)
Total	9·15	(4·40)	7·60	(4·43)	4·54	(5·19)

p = ·1788   p = ·0672

p = ·002

Second post-test

Verbal test

Sub-Groups	Exp. Group I	s	Exp. Group II	s	Control Group	s
4 Year I	5·67	(4·50)	8·00	(4·00)	1·00	(0·45)
4 Year II	11·50	(0·87)	11·75	(0·43)	8·00	(4·32)
5 Year	12·00	(0)	11·78	(0·42)	9·22	(3·05)
6 Year I	12·00	(0)	11·40	(1·20)	12·00	(0)
6 Year II	12·00	(0)	11·60	(0·80)	10·25	(2·48)
Total	11·19	(2·002)	11·41	(1·35)	8·19	(4·22)

$p = ·4902$ $p = ·0014$

$p = ·00054$

Non-verbal test

Sub-Groups	Exp. Group I	s	Exp. Group II	s	Control Group	s
4 Year I	0	(0)	0	(0)	0	(0)
4 Year II	12·25	(3·70)	7·13	(5·65)	0	(0)
5 Year	13·89	(3·23)	5·33	(3·28)	2·33	(4·19)
6 Year I	15·75	(1·48)	6·80	(3·91)	8·80	(4·68)
6 Year II	16·17	(1·95)	15·00	(4·56)	10·25	(4·57)
Total	12·85	(3·28)	7·38	(4·73)	4·08	(5·11)

$p = ·0058$ $p = ·0478$

$p = ·00006$

FIGURE X: *Distribution of conservation scores on:* (a) *First verbal post-test;* (b) *Second verbal post-test*

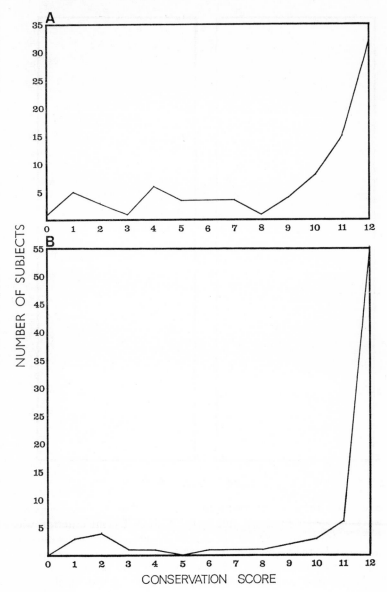

FIGURE XI: *Distribution of conservation scores on: (a) First non-verbal post-test;*
(b) Second non-verbal post-test

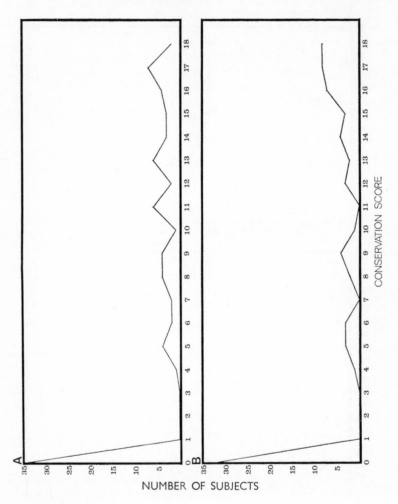

of children being credited with conservation when they were actually
working on an empirical rule basis. A more lenient criterion was
adopted for the non-verbal test as it clearly presented a more difficult
task. Unlike the verbal test, it demanded that the subjects remember
the exact number of units involved on any item before they could
make a correct response. Lapses in short term memory could, thus,

result in errors by subjects who had attained conservation. The significance of the difference between the proportions of the Experimental and Control Groups who attained the criteria was, also, investigated (chi-square test, d.f.$=1$, Yates' correction applied) and the results are included in Table 9.

The greater difficulty of the non-verbal test is evident in Table 9. When the Experimental and Control Groups were considered singly and as a combined group the differences between the proportion of subjects who passed the verbal test and those who passed the non-verbal test were, with one exception, found to be significant at least at the five per cent level (by the chi-square test) in both post-tests. The only non-significant difference was provided by the Control Group on the first post-test in which few of them passed either the verbal or the non-verbal test.

The proportion of subjects in Experimental Group I who attained the pass criterion in the second post-test was significantly higher than in the first post-test on both the verbal test ($\chi^2=8\cdot1$, d.f.$=1$, $p<0\cdot01$) and the non-verbal test ($\chi^2=5\cdot79$, d.f.$=1$, $p<0\cdot025$). There was no significant difference between the proportion of subjects in Experimental Group II who attained the pass criterion on the first and second verbal and non-verbal post-tests. In the case of the Control Group the proportion was significantly higher on the verbal test ($\chi^2=5\cdot14$, d.f.$=1$, $p<0\cdot025$) but there was not a significant difference on the non-verbal test.

Relationship Between Post-Test Performance, Age and Pre-Test Performance

The nature of the relationship between the subjects' post-test performance and their age and level of functioning on the pre-test was investigated on the basis of the data presented in Table 9. In the case of age the 4 Year I and 4 Year II Groups were combined and, also, the 6 Year I and 6 Year II Groups, while for level of pre-test performance the 4 Year II, 5 Year and 6 Year I Groups were combined. Appropriate values of chi-square were calculated separately for the Experimental and Control Groups on the first and second post-tests. The overall values of chi-square obtained for both age and pre-test performance were then partitioned by means of the method outlined by Maxwell (1961, pp. 65–69) into a portion attributable to linear regression and another representing departure from the regression line. Only three significant departures from linear regression were detected and, in view of the comparatively small number of subjects in the sub-groups comprising the Experimental and Control Groups,

TABLE 9: *Number of subjects attaining pass criteria on verbal (11/12), non-verbal (15/18) and both conservation tests in the two post-tests*

First post-test

Sub-Groups	VERBAL TEST			NON-VERBAL TEST			BOTH TESTS		
	Exp. Group I	*Exp. Group II*	*Control Group*	*Exp. Group I*	*Exp. Group II*	*Control Group*	*Exp. Group I*	*Exp. Group II*	*Control Group*
4 Year I	1	1	0	0	0	0	0	0	0
4 Year II	3	6	0	0	2	0	0	2	0
5 Year	4	8	1	0	0	1	0	0	1
6 Year I	2	4	2	3	0	1	1	0	1
6 Year II	5	5	3	4	3	2	4	3	2
Total	15	24	8	7	5	4	5	5	4
p <	0·05	0·001	NS	NS	NS	NS	NS	NS	NS

Second post-test

Sub-Groups	VERBAL TEST			NON-VERBAL TEST			BOTH TESTS		
	Exp. Group I	*Exp. Group II*	*Control Group*	*Exp. Group I*	*Exp. Group II*	*Control Group*	*Exp. Group I*	*Exp. Group II*	*Control Group*
4 Year I	1	1	0	0	0	0	0	0	0
4 Year II	3	6	1	3	3	0	3	3	0
5 Year	9	9	5	6	0	0	6	0	0
6 Year I	5	4	5	4	0	1	4	0	1
6 Year II	5	4	3	3	4	2	3	3	2
Total	23	24	14	16	7	3	16	6	3
p <	NS	0·025	0·025	0·025	NS	0·001	0·01	NS	0·001

these must not be overstressed as indicators of important interaction effects. In the case of Experimental Group I, for example, a significant departure from linear regression was found in the association between pre-test performance and attainment of the conservation criterion in the second non-verbal post-test (chi-square=4·11, d.f.=1, $p < 0.05$). This finding can be directly traced to the performance of a single subject in the 6 Year II Group who attained the criterion level with a score of 17 on the first non-verbal post-test and failed to do so on the second non-verbal post-test with a score of 13. The other two significant interaction effects were found in the performance of Experimental Group II on the second post-test. The first was between pre-test performance and attainment of the conservation criterion on the verbal test (chi-square=4·16, d.f.=1, $p < 0.05$) and the second between age and criterion attainment on the non-verbal test (chi-square=4·69, d.f.=1, $p < 0.05$). It is clear from Table 10 which presents the frequencies of conservers and non-conservers on which these findings are based that only the complete lack of success in the five-year-old group underlying the second significant departure from linear regression comes anywhere near to representing a sufficiently marked trend in terms of numbers to warrant speculation on the existence of a psychologically interesting interaction effect. Accordingly, no speculative explanations will be offered.

Effect of Subjects' Failure in Training Series of Non-Verbal Post-Test
  Before turning to a consideration of the more detailed aspects of the subjects' performance a further feature of the total conservation

TABLE 10: *Frequencies of conservers and non-conservers in experimental group II on second verbal and non-verbal post-tests giving rise to significant departures from linear regression*

	VERBAL TEST Pre-test performance					NON-VERBAL TEST Age		
	4 Year I	4 Year II	5 Year	6 Year I	6 Year II	4 Years	5 Years	6 Years
Conservers	1		19		4	3	0	4
Non-Conservers	1		1		1	5	9	6
Total	2		20		5	8	9	10

FIGURE XII: *Distribution of conservation scores on non-verbal post-tests with subjects who failed to train omitted*

First post-test

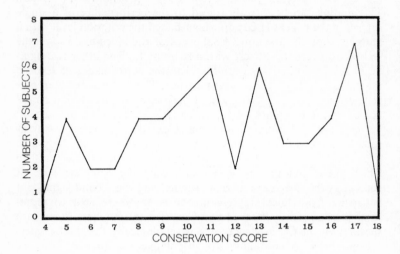

Second post-test

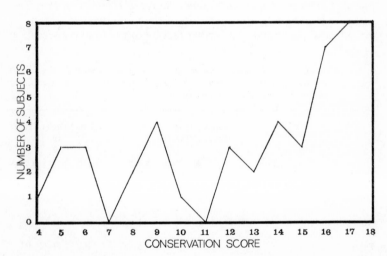

scores on the non-verbal post-test which, with the corresponding scores on the verbal post-tests, formed the basis for the tabulated results presented above, must be considered. This is the fact that a conservation score for all of the subjects was included in the statistical calculations. Children who failed to attain the criterion level in the initial training series in the non-verbal post-tests and, thus, did not undergo any of the conservation or addition-subtraction trials were allocated a zero conservation score. To provide a full picture of the relative effectiveness of the training sequence Table 11 presents details of the number of subjects in each group who did not pass beyond the training series. The significance of the differences in the group totals were investigated by means of the chi-square test (degrees of freedom$=1$) and the results are included in Table 11.

TABLE 11: *Number of subjects in each group who failed to attain the criterion level in the training series in the non-verbal post-tests*

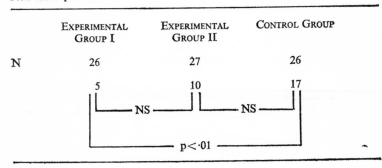

Non-verbal post-test I

	EXPERIMENTAL GROUP I	EXPERIMENTAL GROUP II	CONTROL GROUP
N	27	28	28
	7	10	17

NS — $p < \cdot025$ — NS

Non-verbal post-test II

	EXPERIMENTAL GROUP I	EXPERIMENTAL GROUP II	CONTROL GROUP
N	26	27	26
	5	10	17

NS — $p < \cdot01$ — NS

In view of the large number of subjects, particularly in the Control Group, who failed to attain the criterion level in the non-verbal training series the significance of the difference between the groups' mean conservation scores, already explored in Table 8 above, was re-examined with the zero scores of those who failed to train being omitted. The revised means and probabilities obtained in this fashion comprise Table 12. Figure XII provides a graphical representation of the revised distributions of non-verbal conservation scores.

TABLE 12: *Mean conservation scores and standard deviations of the experimental and control groups on the non-verbal test omitting scores of subjects who failed the training series*

First post-test

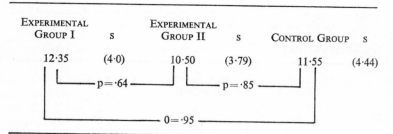

EXPERIMENTAL GROUP I	S	EXPERIMENTAL GROUP II	S	CONTROL GROUP	S
12·35	(4·0)	10·50	(3·79)	11·55	(4·44)

p = ·64, p = ·85, 0 = ·95

Second post-test

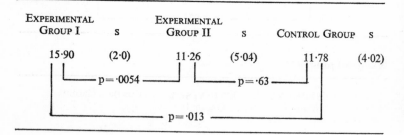

EXPERIMENTAL GROUP I	S	EXPERIMENTAL GROUP II	S	CONTROL GROUP	S
15·90	(2·0)	11·26	(5·04)	11·78	(4·02)

p = ·0054, p = ·63, p = ·013

Although the number of subjects, indicated in Table 9 above, who attained the pass criterion of 15/18 correct responses on the conservation items was unaffected, the number of non-conservers was, of course, diminished by the exclusion of those who failed the training series. Accordingly the significance of the difference between the number of conservers and non-conservers in the Experimental and Control Groups was also recalculated. The revised results are presented in Table 13.

TABLE 13: *Number of subjects attaining pass criterion (15/18) on non-verbal conservation test. Significance of group differences calculated omitting subjects who failed the training series*

FIRST POST-TEST			SECOND POST-TEST		
Exp. Group I	Exp. Group II	Control Group	Exp. Group I	Exp. Group II	Control Group
7	5	4	16	7	3
NS	NS	NS	0·05	NS	NS

Subjects' Scores in subsections of Post-Tests

In making comparisons between the subjects' scores in the subsections of the tests, the Wilcoxon Matched-Pairs Signed-Ranks Test was used whenever, as in the case of the conservation and addition-subtraction items in the non-verbal post-tests, the possible total scores were the same. When the possible totals were unequal but comparable arbitrary pass criteria could be selected (for example, in the non-verbal test 5/6 for the conservation items with initial numerical correspondence and 10/12 for those with initial perceptual correspondence) chi-square was used in determining the significance of the difference between the corresponding proportions, Yates's correction being applied where appropriate. In cases where the nature of the possible total scores prevented the selection of suitable comparable pass criteria (for example, totals of 8 and 10 or 5 and 7 respectively) recourse was had to the expedient of expressing each individual score as a proportion of the corresponding possible total score and then deriving a value for chi-square by applying the Sign Test to the two sets of proportions obtained in this fashion. This procedure was necessary in making three comparisons—conservation scores on items with a single and with two collections of objects in the verbal post-test, and in the non-verbal post-test scores on addition-subtraction items with and without 'covering' and on conservation items with and without 'covering'.

D

Conservation and Addition-Subtraction Items

The comparison of the subjects' scores on the conservation and addition-subtraction items in the verbal test yielded a single significant difference in favour of addition-subtraction in the case of the Control Group in the second post-test (chi-square $= 5 \cdot 0$, d.f. $= 1$, $p < \cdot 05$). This finding was not exactly paralleled in the non-verbal test since it was Experimental Group I which provided the only significant differences in the first (Wilcoxon, $T = 30 \cdot 5$, $p < \cdot 05$) and second (Wilcoxon, $T = 31 \cdot 5$, $p < \cdot 05$) post-tests. As in the verbal test both results indicated a superior performance in the addition-subtraction items.

'Covered' and 'Uncovered' Items

A greater divergence between the subjects' performance on the verbal and non-verbal tests was revealed by the comparison of scores on 'covered' and 'uncovered' items. The verbal test yielded a single significant difference in favour of the 'covered' conservation items in the performance of the Control Group in the first post-test (chi-square $= 5 \cdot 0$, d.f. $= 1$, $p < \cdot 05$). In contrast the scores of Experimental Group I and Experimental Group II in the non-verbal post-tests indicated a consistently significantly superior performance on the 'uncovered' items. The details for the total scores are as follows: Experimental Group I, first post-test (Wilcoxon, $T = 1 \cdot 5$, $p < \cdot 01$), second post-test ($T = 0$, $p < \cdot 01$); Experimental Group II, first post-test ($T = 5 \cdot 5$, $p < \cdot 01$), second post-test ($T = 4 \cdot 5$, $p < \cdot 01$). These findings were mirrored when the total scores were divided up into 'covered' and 'uncovered' addition-subtraction items and 'covered' and 'uncovered' conservation items. Once again the only significant differences were found in the performance of Experimental Groups I and II and all were in favour of the 'uncovered' items. The details of these comparisons are provided in Table 14.

Incidence of Overt Counting Activity

The 'covered' and 'uncovered' items were included in both post-tests primarily with a view to determining the role of counting in the development of number conservation. As in the pre-tests a record was also kept of the number of subjects who overtly counted in the post-tests after the perceptual rearrangement had taken place and before they made their scored conservation responses. These frequencies are presented in Table 15.

As the relationship between the adoption of this mode of approach and the subjects' scores on the 'covered' and 'uncovered' items has

TABLE 14: *Details of performance of experimental groups I and II on 'covered' and 'uncovered' addition-subtraction and conservation items on non-verbal post-tests*

First post-test

	EXPERIMENTAL GROUP I			EXPERIMENTAL GROUP II		
	chi-square	*d.f.*	*p*	*chi-square*	*d.f.*	*p*
+ −	10·32	1	<·01	8·44	1	<·01
conservation	10·32	1	<·01	7·56	1	<·01

Second post-test

	chi-square	*d.f.*	*p*	*chi-square*	*d.f.*	*p*
+ −	17·56	1	<·001	12·5	1	<·001
conservation	14·42	1	<·001	6·72	1	<·01

considerable developmental implications, Table 16 comprises a complete account of the scores obtained on these items in the verbal and non-verbal post-tests by all of the children who engaged in overt counting activity.

Items Confined to the Verbal or Non-Verbal Post-Tests

The results presented in Table 15A have stemmed from aspects common to both the verbal and non-verbal post-tests. It remains to consider the data obtained from the sections peculiar to each of the tests. The comparison of items commencing with a single collection of objects and those in which two sets of objects were initially arranged in one to one correspondence was entirely confined to the verbal post-test. No significant difference was found between the subjects' total conservation scores on these two types of item in either first or second post-test. The non-verbal post-test had a monopoly of the items aimed at investigating the relative difficulty of an initial perceptual and an initial numerical correspondence between two collections. The only significant difference detected was provided by Experimental Group II's scores in the first post-test (chi-square=4·0, d.f.=1, p<0·5) and indicated that the items with initial perceptual

TABLE 15A: *Total scores on covered and uncovered items obtained by subjects who adopted overt counting approach in post-tests*

First post-test

	EXPERIMENTAL GROUP I				EXPERIMENTAL GROUP II				CONTROL GROUP			
	Verbal test		Non-verbal test		Verbal test		Non-verbal test		Verbal test		Non-verbal test	
Sub-Groups	Cov. (4)	Uncov. (8)	Cov. (8)	Uncov. (10)	Cov. (4)	Uncov. (8)	Cov. (8)	Uncov. (10)	Cov. (4)	Uncov. (8)	Cov. (8)	Uncov. (10)
4 Year I	—	—	3	10	—	—	0	8	2	2	—	—
4 Year II	—	—	2 / 1	10 / 7	4	7	7	10	3 / 0	3 / 4	—	—
5 Year	4 / 3 / 1	8 / 3 / 5	5	8	1 / 3	7 / 7	2 / 3 / 3	6 / 8 / 10	4	8	—	—
6 Year I	4	6	1 / 3 / 5	5 / 10 / 10	—	—	—	—	4	6	—	—
6 Year II	4	8	7 / 3	10 / 8	—	—	—	—	4	8	6 / 8	10 / 8

Second post-test

Group	Scores
4 Year I	— — — — — — — — — — 6
4 Year II	— — 8 2 10 6 — — 10 — — / 6 5 2 7 7 4 7 7 6 4 / 10 10 8 10 10 10 9 10 10
5 Year	6 3 5 2 3 5 — —
6 Year I	9 3 — — 9 3 — — 9 / 7 8 / 4 7
6 Year II	9 8 8 10 3 — 5 — — 10 10 7 8 — — 10

TABLE 15B: *Frequency of overt counting before scored conservation responses in the post-tests*

		FIRST POST-TEST				SECOND POST-TEST		
	N	Verbal	Non-verbal	Both	N	Verbal	Non-verbal	Both
Experimental Group I								
4 Year I	3	0	1	0	3	0	0	0
4 Year II	4	0	2	0	4	0	2	0
5 Year	10	3	1	0	9	0	7	0
6 Year I	5	1	3	1	5	0	1	0
6 Year II	5	1	2	1	5	0	2	0
Total	27	5	9	2	26	0	12	0
Experimental Group II								
4 Year I	2	0	0	0	2	0	0	0
4 Year II	6	1	3	0	6	0	2	0
5 Year	10	2	2	1	9	0	1	0
6 Year I	5	0	0	0	5	0	1	0
6 Year II	5	0	0	0	5	0	2	0
Total	28	3	5	1	27	0	6	0
Control Group								
4 Year 1	4	1	0	0	4	0	0	0
4 Year II	6	2	0	0	4	1	0	0
5 Year	9	1	0	0	9	1	1	1
6 Year I	5	1	0	0	5	0	2	0
6 Year II	4	1	2	1	4	0	2	0
Total	28	6	2	1	26	2	5	1
Overall Totals	83	14	16	4	79	2	23	1

correspondence had presented less difficulty. This brief treatment of the aspects confined to one or other of the post-tests concludes the account of the experimental results. Their import for the focal issues of the study will be considered in the next three chapters. Chapters Four and Five will deal respectively with the problem of acceleration and the question of the issues of the existence of developmental stages, and the analysis of qualitative data, which will necessitate a substantial amount of reworking of the data presented above, will be dealt with in Chapter Six.

CHAPTER FOUR

The Acceleration Issue Revisited

IN ORGANIZING THE RESULTS relevant to the issue of acceleration for comment the division between the outcome of the verbal and non-verbal post-tests appears to constitute a natural line of cleavage. Accordingly, the former will be dealt with first and then any tentative conclusions reached will be reconsidered in the light of the much more complex set of data derived from the non-verbal post-tests.

'Delayed action' effect of non-verbal training sequence on verbal post-tests

The emphasis in the present study has been placed on the discovery of conditions sufficient to produce acceleration in the process of concept formation. The results of the second verbal post-test, presented in Tables 8 and 9 (Chapter Three) indicate that the training sequences undergone by both of the Experimental Groups constitute sufficient treatments for this purpose in the case of number conservation. The fact that the superiority of the Experimental Groups over the Control Group is to be attributed, in the main, to the performance of the 4 Year II and 5 Year sub-groups is particularly impressive evidence of their efficacy. Such blanket comments on the two experimental treatments cease to be appropriate, however, when the focus is widened to include not only the subjects' terminal performance but also their results on the first verbal post-test. A comparison of the outcomes of the first and second verbal post-tests highlights the comparative tardiness of the acceleration produced by the non-verbal training sequence undergone by Experimental Group I. In contrast to the position on the second post-test, the number of subjects trained by the non-verbal method who attained the conservation criterion in the first post-test was not significantly greater than the corresponding figure for the Control Group and was significantly less than that for Experimental Group II. This finding appears to be in accord with Gal'perin's (1961) assertion that providing a subject with a precise and objective account of the essential features of a concept at the outset and showing him how to apply them in the

clearest possible way greatly shortens the process of concept formation by cutting out a number of intermediate stages which occur when
the subject's mental processes are not controlled and organized in this
fashion.

Any attempt at providing an answer to the intriguing question of
the causation of the 'delayed action' effect exhibited in the performance of the non-verbally trained group in the two post-tests
must, in view of the design of the study, be of a purely speculative
and tentative nature.

The attempt to provide an answer appears worthwhile, however,
since a similar result has been reported by Lunzer (1970) in a large-
scale acceleration study dealing with conservation in four content
areas; number, length, area and substance. The most successful of
the four treatments used, a free-teaching method, yielded both
further improvement and transfer between content areas in the
second post-test which was administered six weeks after the first
post-test.

A reply to the causation question consistent with Gal'perin's
approach would be to attribute the delay to the unguided subjects'
need for additional time to allow them to complete the process,
begun during the training sessions, of establishing the essential and
sufficient features of the new concept by means of trial and error.
Another, similar explanation, in line with Harlow's (1959) emphasis
on generalized experience as a prerequisite for the learning of broad
concepts, would be that the training procedure had brought some of
the members of Experimental Group I to a point in development
at which the additional varied experience, provided by the first
post-test and by everyday events during the three month period
between the post-tests, was sufficient to produce number conservation.

A third, more detailed and, thus, even more speculative reply
hinges on the distinction made by Piaget (1959) between the acquisition of content and structure in intellectual development. The
former as indicated above, is the province of learning on the basis of
external reinforcement and involves the type of appreciation of
the physical facts of the situation imparted by the conservation trials
of the non-verbal training sequence. The latter consists of the active
formation and reorganization by the subject of the logical structures
necessary to cope with the content derived from experience and is
identified by Piaget with equilibration. This was precisely the goal at
which the addition-subtraction trials in the training series were
directed. It was hypothesized that by encouraging conceptual

conflict they would be likely to lead the subjects to engage in structural reorganization and, thus, be conducive to the operation of
the process of equilibration. In the case of 'spontaneous' development, learning and equilibration together lead to the acquisition of
physical content and logical structure concurrently. It seems reasonable to assume, however, that when efforts are made to encourage the
operation of both, the comparatively passive process of registering
the physical facts of the situation will be of shorter duration than the
active process of structural formation and reorganization. On the
basis of this assumption the most probable outcome of the acceleration sequence undergone by Experimental Group I would be that the
acquisition of content would outstrip that of structure. In Piaget's
view, imposition of knowledge of content before a corresponding
development of logical structure necessitates retrospective structural
reorganization. The comparative tardiness of the acceleration produced by the non-verbal training sequence could be attributed to the
need for time for such retrospective structural reorganization to take
place.

The Genevan group themselves have been struck by the general
importance of the time element in the learning process. Inhelder and
Sinclair (1969) in the course of conducting acceleration studies
concerned with quantity and length conservation and class inclusion
report that they were astonished to notice that several of their
subjects who learned quickly and surely, without regressions or
hesitations from one session to the next, showed no sign of transfer of
what they had acquired to a different field, whereas other subjects,
who during two or three sessions seemed to have great difficulties in
progressing from one item to another and who frequently regressed
from one session to another, finally showed a true mastery of the
learned concept as well as transfer to another field.

Necessary conditions for acceleration of number conservation

Having embarked on speculation with the above consideration of
the reasons underlying the differences between the performance of the
two Experimental Groups there is a strong temptation to indulge in
escalation and to speculate on the nature of the conditions necessary
to produce acceleration in the development of number conservation.
What basis is there for yielding to such temptation? The design of the
study was, of course, aimed at the detection of sufficient rather than
necessary conditions. In view of the success of both experimental
treatments as measured by the verbal post-tests, however, any
features common to both of the training sequences would appear to

merit attention in a search for the conditions necessary for acceleration to take place. Due to the widely differing orientations represented by the two techniques no commonality can be expected at the theoretical level and, accordingly, any efforts at detecting common features must be confined to the practical procedures adopted. Three obvious common features exist at the procedural level. Both techniques involved exposing the subjects to a mixed sequence of conservation and addition-subtraction problems. It should be mentioned, parenthetically, at this point that a mixed sequence of this type was also, an integral part of the treatment adopted by Wallach and Sprott (1964) in a highly successful attempt to accelerate the appearance of number conservation in a group of 15 children with a mean age of 6:11 years which has been reported since the commencement of the present study. Its presence in the training series was, however, purely coincidental since the keystone of Wallach and Sprott's procedure, in their own view, was the provision of experience with reversibility aimed at inculcating the appreciation that whenever changes in form or arrangement occur, the initial situation can be brought about again by an inverse change. In order to establish whether conservation could be induced by training in reversibility alone, Wallach *et al.* (1967) conducted a second experiment which involved the comparison of a reversibility training sequence with a series of trials indicating the effects of addition and subtraction. The fact that the latter procedure proved to be ineffective in producing number conservation is not at variance with the outcome of the present study since the addition and subtraction trials did not involve any perceptual deformation of the collections of objects, nor were they intermingled with conservation trials. The reversibility training sequence proved to be successful, but a detailed consideration of the results has led Wallach to conclude that this success cannot be regarded as providing evidence for the rôle of the recognition of reversibility in conservation. Its effectiveness appeared, at least in large part, to be attributable to its success in inducing the subjects to stop using misleading perceptual cues.

The explanations which can be offered for the efficacy of a mixed sequence of conservation and addition-subtraction problems are as numerous as the training methods. In the case of the non-verbal training series, it could be attributed to catering for the acquisition of both content and structure as outlined above. From Gal'perin's standpoint its contribution would be explained in terms of the provision of problems in which the conditions stipulated in the conceptual definition may be completely or incompletely fulfilled.

The use of a wide variety of materials in the presentation of the problems was, also, a common feature of the training procedures. The rationales offered from the two standpoints are, in contrast, in this case, essentially similar. The invocation of Harlow's dictum on the importance of generalized experience and the emphasis on avoiding narrow empirical rule learning on which this aspect of the non-verbal method is predicated differ little from the stress in the verbal technique on varying the materials used to ensure that the subjects generalize the complete structure with which they have been provided at the outset.

The third common element of the procedures is equally obvious but, unlike the two aspects already dealt with, is an incidental feature lacking a direct link with one of the fundamental hypotheses on which the techniques were based. It is, however, possible to advance theoretical and experimental evidence from other sources in support of the likely importance of its contribution in producing acceleration. Both Experimental Groups were encouraged by the nature of the treatments which they underwent to engage in a considerable amount of counting activity. In the case of Experimental Group I, the subjects were confronted with situations involving comparisons between collections which were unlikely to be successfully accomplished on a perceptual basis and were provided with feedback on the accuracy of their judgements. That this treatment resulted in the adoption of an approach based on repeated counting is attested to by the available detailed accounts of subjects' performance during training. For Experimental Group II the encouragement could scarcely have been more direct since they were explicitly asked questions which demanded counting activity during both the presentation of the definition and the subsequent guided solution of the problems. Further consideration of the possible rôle of counting appears justified not only by the results of the present study but also by the findings in two Japanese investigations of the development of number concepts. Ito and Hatano (1963) found that a training sequence consisting of repeated confirmation of the numerical invariance of sets by counting was the most successful of three techniques employed with a view to accelerating the appearance of number conservation in 27 five-year-old children. It resulted in an increase in the frequency of conservers in the experimental group which was significant at the five per cent level. More recently, Azuma (1965) reported that a treatment involving counting was found to be most efficacious in a similar acceleration study of four-year-old, disadvantaged children. He also discovered a perfect tetrachoric correlation between the ability to accurately count collections of six stones and the possession of number conservation in a larger group of 100 three-to eight-year-olds.

The results of an American acceleration study which, unlike the Japanese investigations, did not have counting as the focal feature of a training procedure, are, none the less, consistent with it being accorded considerable importance. Gruen (1965) found that verbal pre-training alone was about as effective as either direct training or cognitive conflict in the inducement of number conservation. The prime objective of the verbal pre-training was to ensure that, when questions were posed, subjects interpreted the key words 'more' and 'same' to mean more or same in number and did not associate them with length, a variable which typically shows substantial correlation with number. Of greater interest in the present context, is the fact that the verbal pre-training involved the subjects in counting, and if necessary recounting, aloud the number of blocks in rows of varying lengths. The parallel with the outcome of the present study can be carried further since the most intriguing characteristic of the verbal pre-training was the facilitative effect it had in inducing conservation when it was combined with the cognitive-conflict training. The latter resembled the non-verbal training procedure in that it was aimed at producing conflict between the perceptual deformation and addition-subtraction schemata, but differed in the method which was adopted to accomplish this. It, for example, did not include the provision of feedback to the subjects on the accuracy of their responses.

The effectiveness of a combination of conceptual conflict and counting activity in producing conservation is not confined to the area of number. Inhelder and Sinclair (1969) employed it successfully in training conservation of length. In the acceleration treatment the six-year-old children were asked to use matches to construct a straight line equal in length to a zig-zag or straight line constructed by the experimenter. The subjects, in typical non-conserving fashion, were at first satisfied if the ends of the two lines coincided. When encouraged to apply the numerical operations which they had already acquired to the situation, however, the children readily recognized that equivalence of length entailed having the same number of matches in both lines and began to count to ensure that this criterion was satisfied. This led to conceptual conflict since it was not possible to construct a straight line with the same number of matches as the experimenter's zig-zag line without violating the constraint that the ends of the two lines should coincide. Before the non-conserving, end matching approach was abandoned and the conflict permanently resolved some amusing compromise solutions were tried out by the children. Some of the subjects, for example, broke one of the matches in their row in two, thus creating a line with the same number of elements as the experimenter's without destroying the correspondence of the ends.

Counting activity and number conservation

Although the evidence presented above can scarcely be regarded as of crushing weight, agreement between independently conducted acceleration studies on the merits of a particular mode of treatment is such a novelty that a more detailed analysis of possible links between counting activity and the appearance of number conservation appears to be necessary. Some tentative remarks on this theme were offered in the discussion of the results of the pre-tests in Chapter Two but these will now be substantially amplified.

A consideration of number conservation as exemplified in the type of situation employed in the verbal and non-verbal tests in the present study suggests three ways in which counting may facilitate its appearance. These are best appreciated if they are described with reference to three successive points in the administration of a standard conservation trial. At the outset the adoption of a numerical as opposed to a perceptual approach by the subject towards the collections about which he is asked to make judgements is at a high premium. Zimiles (1963) has highlighted the importance of this division in children who have reached a point in development at which they employ a rudimentary command of numbers together with various perceptual criteria in their evaluation of quantity. It is conceivable that an extended period of training in which counting is the dominant activity may lead the subject to adopt this mode of approach to the test collections. Once the decision to count the elements in the collections has been taken the likelihood that the subject will make a perceptually based judgement, even in the initial test situation in which the elements are arranged in one-to-one correspondence, is greatly diminished. The act of counting leads him to the awareness of the units comprising the collections and, thus, banishes global, perceptually based judgements in favour of a numerical approach. This is precisely the appreciation of the 'additive composition' of the parts of an object from which Smedslund (1961) asserted that conservation stems.

The second way in which the activity of counting may make a contribution concerns another important point in the conservation process which has been stressed by Smedslund (1964). He maintains that his findings have revealed one partial explanation of the persistent and 'illogical' absence of conservation in young children, namely that the 'equality' of the two collections is not accepted at the beginning of the test. If this suggestion, which Smedslund supports not only with evidence from his own study but with supportive material from Birch and Lefford's (1963) work on intersensory judgements, is accepted it seems to afford potential scope for counting to play a part. If the subject counts both of the collections of objects, the act of reaching the same point in the familiar verbal sequence provides him with an identical symbol for the numerical property of the two sets which will, presumably, greatly increase the likelihood of reaching a judgement that they are 'equal'. The suggestion that one-one correspondence may, in some cases, have to be linked with counting before necessary equivalence is accepted has already been advanced in Chapter Two and supported by Renwick's (1963) observations.

The focal point in the conservation test situation is, of course, the effect of the transformation in the perceptual dimension on the subject's judgement of the quantitative aspect. At this juncture the effectiveness of the adoption of an initial numerical set and the subsequent acceptance of the numerical equivalence of the two collections is entirely dissipated if the child fails to recognize that the perceptual rearrangement of the aggregates is both irrelevant and misleading. Counting appears, once again, to be a suitable instrument for ensuring that the seductive properties of the perceptual cues are resisted. As in the initial situation, recourse to it leads the subject to awareness of the units comprising the collections. The resulting fragmentation of the global features of the situation may well substantially decrease their impact and, consequently, diminish the likelihood of recourse to an erroneous perceptually based judgement. The attribution of this significant rôle to counting can be reconciled with the apparent importance of exposure to a mixed sequence of conservation and addition-subtraction problems. Children who achieve success on addition-subtraction and conservation trials by counting the elements after the addition-subtraction and/or deformation has taken place appear to have discarded the perceptually dominated approach which produces non-conservation and clearly realize the relevance of enumeration to the situation but the concept of conservation is not yet sufficiently well established for them to accept it as logically necessary that, in the absence of addition or subtraction of an element, the number of objects in a collection must be unchanged. It is at this point in development that exposure to a mixed sequence

of addition-subtraction and conservation trials is of crucial importance. To conserve, the child must realize that by focusing on the
presence or absence of the key acts of addition or subtraction he
obviates the need to count. The addition-subtraction and conservation trials making up the training sequences differ in only one respect,
the adding or subtracting of an element before the deformation of the
collection in the former. The fact that it is the only procedural
variation highlights the act of addition or subtraction for the subject
and leads him gradually to infer that it is the critical feature determining the numerical properties of the final test situation. When he
realizes this the child no longer requires to count and conservation
is attained. The above hypothetical account of the development of
conservation is consistent with the available detailed records of the
children's performance during the non-verbal training series but this
constitutes a very tenuous basis of supportive evidence. It is not
suggested that this is the path traversed to conservation by all
children, but at most that it may have been followed by some of the
subjects who underwent the training accorded to Experimental
Group I. An attempt to obtain further data which might help in
assessing the accuracy of the account would provide a suitable
theme for further research.

The relationship between perception and conceptualization

Before leaving the topic of counting it is proposed to adduce some
studies bearing on the relationship between perception and conceptualization. They are relevant to the present discussion since they
illustrate the power of the perceptual dimension and the possible
efficacy in facilitating concept formation of techniques which, like the
use of counting, combat this influence. As we have seen above, the
outcome of her most recent experiment has led Wallach (1967) to
stress the importance in inducing conservation of employing techniques likely to lead subjects to abandon the use of misleading
perceptual cues. Another and particularly fine example of the power
of the perceptual aspect of a situation is provided by the work of
Frank (1964). Having first submitted her four-, five-, six- and
seven-year-old subjects to the classic tests of conservation of quantity with beakers and water, she then went on to other procedures,
among which was the following. Two standard beakers were partly
filled so that the child judged them to contain equal amounts of
water. A wider beaker of the same height was introduced and the
three beakers were now, except for their tops, hidden by a screen.
The experimenter poured the water from one of the standard beakers

into the wider beaker and then removed the empty standard beaker from view. The child, without seeing the water, was asked whether the remaining standard beaker or the wider beaker had more to drink, or did they have the same amount. The results revealed a striking increase in correct equality judgements in comparison with the unscreened pre-test. Correct conservation responses leaped from none to 50 per cent among the four-year-olds, from 20 to 90 per cent among the five-year-olds, and from 50 to 100 per cent among the six-year-olds. The significantly superior performance of the Control Group on the 'covered', as opposed to the 'uncovered', items in the first verbal post-test in the present study is consistent with these results.

Frank's findings in an extension of her procedure confirm the seductive nature of the perceptual dimension but, also, emphasize the possibility of accelerating conceptual development by means of a method which, even temporarily, frees the child from the influence of the irrelevant perceptual cues. After the relative quantities question had been posed and answered, the screen was removed. All of the four-year-olds promptly changed their minds. The perceptual display overwhelmed them and they decided that the wider beaker contained less water. But virtually all of the five-year-olds and all of the six- and seven-year-olds stuck to their previous judgement. The brief respite afforded by the intervention of the screen appears to be sufficient to emancipate them from the irrelevant perceptual dimension. This improvement in performance was maintained in the vast majority of cases in a post-test, involving a tall thin beaker with the standard ones and no screen, which was administered a few minutes later.

In Frank's study the technique adopted for combating perceptual influence required no action whatsoever of the subject but was entirely dependent on the experimenter. Other, apparently equally efficacious, methods cast the child in a more active, as opposed to reactive, rôle. In the standard, conservation of quantity test the subject is first led to agree that two identical receptacles contain an equal quantity of material and then confronted with a transformation which places the perceptual and quantitative dimensions of the situation in opposition. Dienes (1965) has experimented with a situation dealing with discontinuous quantity in which this opposition is gradually built up as the result of a series of steps rather than a single action. Five-year-old children who had not yet achieved conservation of discontinuous quantity were instructed to place beads alternately one by one in two separate receptacles one of which was low and wide and the other high and thin. From time to time they were asked if the number of objects in the receptacles was the same. With this procedure it was discovered that, even after the number of beads had reached a point at which the effect of the misleading perceptual aspect was very marked, the subjects continued to insist that in spite of appearances there were the same number of objects in each receptacle. They gave as their reason that since they put one in each, it must be the same. This appreciation of the continuing numerical equality between the sets is clearly founded on the operation of one-to-one correspondence. There is, also, a similarity between this technique and counting, however, in that both procedures combat irrelevant perceptual cues by making the subject aware of the units comprising the collections and, thus, reducing the likelihood of a global judgement.

A method, which resembled Dienes' approach in that it demanded action of the subject, emerged as the most successful of a number of techniques of accelerating the development of conservation of substance examined by Sonstroem (1965). A remarkably high degree of learning was produced among a group of six- and seven-year-old children, who had initially failed the classic test of conservation of substance involving quantitative comparisons between two balls of clay, by training which involved manipulation and labelling. In each trial the subject was asked to take one of two balls of clay, which he had just declared to be equal, and to convert it into a sausage or other shape. The experimenter now posed questions designed to highlight the compensating attributes of the two shapes, for example, 'Which is the longest?' and 'Which is the fattest?', and then asked the child to make a judgement on the relative amounts of clay in each piece. To complete the trial the child was instructed to 'make the fat ball as long as the sausage'. or (in half the instances) 'make the long sausage as fat as the ball'.

The explanation of the effectiveness of this technique offered by Sonstroem is founded on Bruner's account of the successive development of the enactive (motoric), ikonic (perceptual) and linguistic modes of representation. The young child, relying on his usual ikonic mode of representing events, makes the erroneous judgements which he does in the conservation situation because perceptual cues are dominant. The teaching problem is to lead him to represent the events before him in other ways which will conflict with his perceptual rendering to the extent that he will reject it in favour of the more compelling alternatives. The successful training sequence induced precisely such conflict in the child by the use of manipulation and labelling. Enactive representation was encouraged by offering him manipulation, and symbolic representation was fostered by offering him verbal labels for compensating attributes. Their combined influence was strong enough to counteract the considerable influence of perceptual cues since two messages—the enactive and the symbolic ones—were saying 'same', whereas only one—the ikonic—was saying 'different'. The one was forced to yield to the combined effect of the two. This account is compatible with the suggested rôle allotted to counting in the present discussion. Counting as a process resembles Sonstroem's technique in that it involves the use of enactive (finger pointing) and linguistic (recitation of the number sequence) representation in combating perceptual cues. It should be mentioned, parenthetically, at this point that the authenticity of conservation produced by acceleration treatments based on Bruner's theory, and by Frank's screening technique in particular, has been questioned by Piaget (1967). The grounds on which this criticism is advanced will be discussed below.

It seems appropriate to end this wide ranging, speculative discussion by presenting two pieces of evidence from the results of the present study which are in accord with the line of argument developed above. The marked decline between the first and second verbal post-tests in the number of subjects who overtly counted the elements in the collections before making their scored conservation responses (see Table 15) suggests that, at any rate in some cases, the employment of counting is a stepping-stone to the attainment of conservation. The comparative failure of both the verbal and non-verbal training sequences to produce improvement in the performance of the 4 Year I sub-groups is, also, suggestive. Tables 5 and 6 indicate that the vast majority of the training trials which they underwent involved collections of only three or four objects. At this numerical level, accurate perceptual judgements of relative quantity can easily be made. Also, the effect of the misleading perceptual cues produced by the transformation after the initial judgement is minimal. As a result, even when counting is employed there is no conflict between it and the irrelevant perceptual dimension since the effect of the latter is so weak. The employment of counting as an approach when the misleading perceptual cues are strong, is, thus, hardly to be expected. Azuma's (1965) discovery of a close connection between the possession of number conservation and the ability to count collections of six objects is consistent with the hypothesis since six appears to be the numerical level at which accurate perceptual judgements become difficult and the seductive power of the perceptual dimension becomes marked.

In summary, it is contended that three procedural features common to both the verbal and non-verbal experimental treatments merit serious consideration in a search for the conditions necessary to produce acceleration in the development of number conservation. These comprise exposure to a mixed sequence of conservation and addition-subtraction problems, the use of a wide variety of materials in the presentation of the problems and the encouragement of counting activity. Varying amounts of experimental evidence have been cited in support of the importance of these components as individual features. Before widening the scope of the discussion to include the results of the non-verbal post-tests, some evidence which is consistent with their effectiveness as a combination will be presented. As this is derived from a recent study concerned with teaching children length and weight conservation its relevance to the present discussion is of an indirect rather than direct nature.

The investigation conducted by Kingsley and Hall (1967) differs from the present study not only in its choice of specific theme but in the rationale underlying the acceleration treatments employed. They maintain that the failures, reported in the literature, to train young children to master different types of conservation are to be attributed to experiential variables rather than to internal considerations such as the effect of cognitive conflict on cognitive structure. Most of these earlier attempts at training have ignored the large amount of background knowledge necessary and, consequently, the extended period of time required to train children for conservation mastery. Kingsley and Hall have tried to avoid these pitfalls by founding their experimental treatment on Gagné's learning set procedure. This approach involves the analysis of the material to be taught into a hierarchy of subtasks. Attainment of these subtasks provides a successful route to the mastery of the criterion task. In the case of conservation of weight, for example, the application of this technique produced the following sequence of six subtasks arranged in order of increasing difficulty:

1. know the meaning of appropriate relational terms, e.g. heavier, lighter, equal, more, less, same;

2. know the meaning of weight independent of amount of substance;

3. know what a scale is and how to determine heavier, lighter and equal on it;

4. know the scale is more accurate than kinaesthetic cues;

5. know the effect of adding and subtracting clay on weight;

6. know the effect of changing shape on weight regardless of other extraneous cues, e.g. labels and appearance.

A similar sequence of five sub-tasks formed the basis for the training aimed at producing conservation of length. The experimental groups underwent both treatments which were administered on an individual basis during a maximum of nine 20-minute sessions. A comparison of their performance, with that of the control groups, on post-tests of conservation of weight and length, revealed highly significant training effects which were still in evidence when the post-tests were repeated four months later.

In spite of the obvious differences in theoretical background and practical objectives, the procedures adopted by Kingsley and Hall exhibit the three components which were common to both the verbal and non-verbal experimental treatments in the present study. The function discharged by counting activity of leading the subjects to abandon reliance on perceptual judgements is paralleled by the training geared to the fourth sub-task listed above. The children were urged to estimate the relative weight of clay pieces varying in size and shape. They then weighed the objects, stated the relations, and evaluated their prediction as 'right' or 'wrong'. The experimenter encouraged the children, praised correct predictions and evaluations, and emphasized the accuracy of decisions made after reference to the balance rather than on a perceptual basis.

To train conservation one of two balls of equal weight was removed from the scale and its shape was deformed. The standard question asked was, 'Do you think this one weighs more, or the same amount as, or less than the ball?' After every answer, the child was told to check his prediction by comparing both objects on the scale. More deformations were made, verbal labels were given to some of the objects and clay of different colours was used. After each shape change, the same standard question was asked and the child checked his prediction. As the children began to predict quality of weight, the experimenter began breaking the ball into many pieces, making several long 'snakes' with the clay and using labels like 'a small ball of dust' and 'a big, fat rock'. At the same time the children were allowed to transform the other piece of clay into whatever they desired. The same sequence of prediction, validation, and evaluation was demanded of the children. Finally, pieces of clay that were initially unequal in weight were introduced and the sequence of deformation was repeated. Although this training sequence did not involve as varied a collection of materials as the experimental treatments in the present study, the permutations of shape, colour and verbal labels certainly confronted the subjects with a very considerable degree of variation in the situations presenting the conservation principle. There is, also, a similarity between the treatments in the two studies in that both involved conservation trials in which the two balls or collection of objects were in some trials initially equal in weight or number while in others there was initial inequality.

Kingsley and Hall did not follow the present study in confronting the subjects with a mixed sequence of conservation and addition-subtraction problems. As the sequence of sub-tasks indicates, the conservation training was preceded by a series of trials aimed at leading the children to understand the effects on relative weight of 'putting some on' and 'taking some off'. Despite this apparent procedural divergence it seems likely that the effect of the treatment on the subjects would be very similar to that achieved by a juxta-position of conservation and addition-subtraction trials. This assertion is based on the fact that during the conservation training an attempt was made by the experimenter to relate the shape changes to the children's recently acquired knowledge of addition and subtrac-tion. Many of them, for example, thought that any change at all changed weight. After they admitted that their prediction had been wrong, they were asked, 'You said it was heavier (or lighter) but what do you have to do to make things heavier (or lighter)?' 'Did you do that?' 'Then, could it get heavier (or lighter)?' Such questions are calculated to produce as close a liaison between conservation and addition-subtraction as their physical proximity in a mixed sequence of trials. It should be mentioned before concluding this brief treat-ment of Kingsley and Hall's study that, in spite of their avowed emphasis on experimental as opposed to internal variables, the existence of this parallel with the present study in the use made of addition-subtraction and conservation trials throws the success of their training technique wide open to explanations based on the very structural concepts, such as cognitive conflict, which they are so anxious to avoid.

Comparison of the results of the verbal and non-verbal post-tests

The above comments on the acceleration issue founded on the outcome of the verbal post-tests must now be submitted to the acid test. To what extent are they in accord with the results of the non-verbal post-tests? In general the differences between the verbal and non-verbal results are much more marked than the similarities. One of the few resemblances is the emergence of the same 'delayed action' effect in the performance of the non-verbally trained group in the non-verbal tests as they exhibited in the verbal tests. The number of subjects in Experimental Group I who attained the conservation criterion in the first non-verbal post-test was not statistically significantly greater than the corresponding figures for Experimental Group II and the Control Group. In the second non-verbal post-test, however, the performance of Experimental Group I was significantly superior to that of both of the other groups. No further speculation will be offered on the causation of this delayed acceleration since it has already been considered at some length in the discussion of the verbal test results and the tentative explanations advanced appear to be equally appropriate to the non-verbal case.

The most striking contrast between the verbal and non-verbal test results is provided by the much poorer performance of the verbally trained group in the non-verbal post-tests. In neither of them was the number of subjects in Experimental Group II who achieved the conservation criterion statistically significantly superior to the corresponding figure for the Control Group. It appears justifiable on the basis of this finding to assert that the non-verbal acceleration technique may be superior to its verbal counterpart in the degree of generalization of the concept of number conservation which it produces. There is another important aspect of the non-verbal test data which must be adumbrated before the merits of this assertion can be assessed. This concerns the effect on the inter-group comparisons of the number of subjects who failed to pass the training series in the non-verbal post-tests. When these subjects are excluded from consideration the significant superiority of Experimental Group I over Experimental Group II in the number of subjects attaining the conservation criterion on the second non-verbal post-test is maintained but the superiority of Experimental Group I over the Control Group ceases to be statistically significant. The latter result constitutes less of a departure from the earlier picture than it might appear. The superiority of Experimental Group I over the Control Group falls just short of significance at the 5 per cent level ($\chi^2 = 3\cdot31$; $3\cdot841$ required for $\cdot05$ level) and this is to be attributed to the fact that only nine members of the Control Group passed the training series. If the mean conservation scores, rather than the number of subjects achieving the conservation criterion, are compared the performance of Experimental Group I is significantly superior ($p < \cdot01$) to that of the Control Group. The grounds for the assertion that the non-verbal training sequence may be conducive to a greater degree of generalization than the verbal acceleration technique appear, therefore, to be little, if at all, weakened by this revision of the non-verbal test results.

Before speculating on the possible reasons underlying this divergence in the relative effectiveness of the training methods, further consideration will be given to the question of what is involved in passing or failing the training series in the non-verbal test. This decision is founded on the conviction that such an inquiry will throw light on another dimension of the subject of generalization and, thus, provide an additional yardstick against which to compare the acceleration techniques. What experimental results are relevant to this theme? The most striking finding is, undoubtedly, that thirteen subjects in the first post-test and seventeen in the second post-test made ten or more correct conservation responses in the verbal test and yet failed to pass the training series in the non-verbal test. Table 16 provides details of the distribution of these totals among the Experimental and Control Groups. The incidence of this pattern of

TABLE 16: *Number of subjects having a conservation score of 10+ in the verbal post-tests who failed the training series in the corresponding non-verbal post-tests*

	FIRST POST-TEST			SECOND POST-TEST		
Verbal Conservation Score	*10*	*11*	*12*	*10*	*11*	*12*
Experimental Group I						
4 Year I	0	0	0	0	0	1
4 Year II	0	1	0	1	0	0
5 Year	0	0	1	0	0	1
6 Year I	0	0	0	0	0	0
6 Year II	0	0	0	0	0	0
Experimental Group II						
4 Year I	0	0	1	0	0	1
4 Year II	0	0	2	0	1	1
5 Year	1	1	1	0	0	3
6 Year I	0	0	1	0	0	1
6 Year II	0	0	0	0	0	0
Control Group						
4 Year I	0	0	0	0	0	0
4 Year II	0	0	0	1	0	1
5 Year	1	0	0	0	2	2
6 Year I	0	1	2	0	0	1
6 Year II	0	0	0	0	0	0
Total	2	3	8	2	3	12

performance raises the fundamental question of what is meant when a child is said to have attained conservation of number. The steps which must be mastered en route to the criterion of conservation have already been described above in terms of the classic verbal test situation. In the order of their occurrence they comprise the ability to establish numerical equivalence between two collections, to retain the fact of their equivalence, and connect their previous equivalence with the rearrangement of the collections so that the manipulation of the conflicting perceptual cue is recognized as both irrelevant and misleading. This catalogue, however, deals with one, admittedly basic, aspect of the learning process and omits a number of other important characteristics. For example, two children may reach the same level of acquisition of a concept but one may be able to use it to create new ideas and the other may not; one may be able to employ it under stress and the other may not; and, most relevant to the present discussion, one may be able to apply it in a new and novel setting and the other may not. In the case of number conservation the two points in the process at which the presence or absence of the ability to generalize to a new situation becomes manifest are right at the outset when the subject must decide whether to adopt a numerical, perceptual or other approach and after the perceptual transformation has been effected when this decision must be retaken. The non-verbal test situation provides a suitable means of comparing the relative success of the training sequences in producing generalization at both of these junctures since, unlike its verbal counterpart, it does not comprise a series of questions which signal the relevance of number as the appropriate dimension of operation. It is entirely left to the subject to determine the angle of approach to be adopted.

The superiority of the non-verbal, acceleration technique in producing the adoption of a suitable numerical approach to the making of the conservation judgement after the perceptual transformation has already been mentioned. A comparison of the number of subjects in each group who failed the training series in the non-verbal tests should indicate the relative effectiveness of the training sequences in imparting when it is appropriate to adopt a numerical initial approach to a new situation. The results of both post-tests present an identical picture. The number of failures in Experimental Group I was significantly less than the corresponding figure for the Control Group. The Experimental Group II total fell between the Control Group and Experimental Group I totals but did not differ significantly from either of them. Although the superiority of Experimental Group I is less clear-cut, the trend of these findings favours the view that the non-verbal training sequence is more conducive to the adoption of a numerical initial approach when this is appropriate.

Indirect confirmation of the relative failure of the verbal acceleration technique to produce generalization of the conservation principle is provided in the results obtained by Beilin (1965) in a complex study involving number, length and area conservation tasks and the assessment of the effectiveness of three training procedures. None of the procedures bore a detailed resemblance to the acceleration techniques used in the present study but Beilin's verbal rule instruction (VRI) method, which proved to be most effective in facilitating conservation performance paralleled the verbal technique in involving repeated verbal explanations of the conservation rule. In the case of number, for example, the explanation took the following form: 'Now I am moving them. See, they are standing in a different place, but there are just as many dots as before. They only look different. See, I can put them back just the way they were, so you see, there are still the same number as before because I did not add any dots or take away any dots, I only moved them'. The post-test results indicated that the VRI treatment had significantly improved the subjects' performance in the areas in which they were trained (i.e. number and length conservation) but of greater import for the present discussion is the finding that there was no improvement on a conservation test, namely conservation of area, in which they had not been trained.

Reasons for variations in generalization produced by treatments

What are the reasons behind the disparate ability exhibited by the children who underwent the acceleration sequences in the present study to successfully tackle a new situation in which the relevance of their training experiences was not signalled? Any attempt to suggest an answer to this question must be prefaced with the same warning on its speculative nature which preceded the discussion of the conditions necessary for the acceleration of the development of number conservation. The distinction made by Schroder *et al.* (1967) between unilateral and interdependent training environments provides what appears to be a promising approach to this problem. They maintain that whatever the content or goal of training, the training agent (parent, teacher, and so on) can create one of two basic types of environment to which the subject has to adapt while learning the required responses. The agent can provide the subject with ready-made rules and control his behaviour until he learns the required response. Such training, referred to as unilateral, creates an environment in which the trainee learns to adapt by looking for externally provided schemata. By structuring the learning situation and inhibiting the emergence of alternate schemata delineated by the trainee himself this approach unrealistically over simplifies the environment to which he is adapting and endangers the potential development of abstract structural properties. Its authoritarian nature, also, maximizes the development of an adaptive orientation anchored in external and absolute control. The more the trainee is rewarded for adapting in this way, the more the development of his conceptual structure becomes arrested or stabilized at a low level or inflexible type of integration.

In the interdependent method of training the learner is provided with an environment which affords information as feedback or as a consequence of his own questions or exploratory behaviour. The feedback, of course, is designed to enhance efficient learning of the required response. The agent does not provide ready-made schemata or rules of integration and the trainee is required to generate these himself. As no schemata are imposed, the environment possesses certain characteristics aimed at ensuring that responses and attitudes are learned. For example, it contains all the components of the required goal. Further, it encourages the subject to explore the environment, ask questions, and at the same time, it permits him to experience the consequences of these exploratory actions. In this sense, the environment encourages the evolvement of complex integrative rules without relying upon external control. These conditions permit the development of conceptual properties which generate a more complex perception of the environment as well as increased potential for differentiation and flexible integration. In the unilateral condition, the subject learns a response pattern through an adaptive orientation characterized by applying fixed rules; in the interdependent condition, the subject learns a response pattern through an adaptive orientation characterized by applying self-generated rules.

The two acceleration techniques being compared in the present study constitute fine examples of the two basic types of training environment distinguished by Schroder. The verbal and non-verbal training sequences can clearly be identified as a unilateral and an interdependent method respectively. It would, accordingly, be predicted that the latter technique would result in the formation of conceptual structures exhibiting a greater degree of flexibility and adaptability. The performance of the subjects on the two non-verbal post-tests was consistent with this prediction. In view of the conformity of these results with Schroder's viewpoint it appears worthwhile to enter on a more detailed consideration of the specific features of the two training sequences which may, to some extent, account for the disparity in the degree of generalization of the learning which they produce.

One of the dimensions of variation between the two techniques which may be relevant in this connection is their treatment of the question of mediation. In the verbal acceleration method the subjects were from the outset provided with the entire structure to be internalized expressed in terms of verbal and imaginal mediators which the experimenter deemed appropriate. The non-verbal method, in contrast, left it to the children to derive the principle for themselves and to devise suitable mediators for its operation. It can be hypothesized that structures founded on externally provided mediation do not become integrated into the child's conceptual structure as a whole since they are not expressed in his characteristic mediational mode. They are, consequently, only brought into action when the child encounters a problem posed in terms of these same external mediators and generalization to situations lacking these cues does not take place. There is, on the other hand, no obstacle to the complete integration of new structures formulated by the child himself since they are based on the same mediators as the totality of his existing conceptual structure. This integration renders the new structures more flexible and adaptable and, thus, facilitates their generalization.

An alternative, or possibly complementary, explanation can be advanced which offers an almost identical picture of the conceptual structures involved but focuses on conceptual conflict rather than mediation. One of the fundamental features of the non-verbal acceleration technique was an attempt to foster conceptual conflict by confronting the subject with trials in which the effects of perceptual change were juxtaposed with those of addition and subtraction. It was hoped that this experience, coupled with feedback on the accuracy of responses, would emphasize the consistency of the addition-subtraction schema and the ambiguity and contradiction of the perceptual mode of operation and, thus, lead to a basic reorganization of the subjects' conceptual structure. This restructuring would have the result of placing the addition-subtraction schema in a dominant position in any situation in which the perceptual mode of operation had, hitherto, been paramount. The production of conceptual conflict was not numbered among the objectives of the verbal acceleration method and it seems to be a reasonable assumption that little or no such conflict was inadvertently instigated by it. As the essence of the technique was the guided application of the definition to the features of the problem situations, the child was never placed in a situation in which rival schemata were activated and, consequently, indecision and conceptual conflict ensued. It can, therefore, be argued that, in contrast to the non-verbal sequence, it was highly unlikely that any fundamental reorganization of the subject's conceptual structures would be initiated and that, at best, the internalized definition would become a specialized structure of narrow applicability, divorced from the totality of his conceptual structures and, thus, from the possibility of generalization.

The relative importance of mediation and structural change in development

Having offered alternative explanations of the differential effectiveness of the acceleration techniques which, respectively, stress the rôle of mediation and structural modification due to conceptual conflict, it seems a logical development to consider the import of the results of the present study for the confrontation between the Geneva and Harvard schools on the relative importance of mediation and structural change in intellectual growth. In '*Studies of Cognitive Growth*', Bruner (1966) has presented the most extended account, to date, of the position of the Harvard group. The point of view adopted represents a development of the position outlined in his seminal paper on '*The Course of Cognitive Growth*' in the *American Psychologist* (1964). The label which Bruner has suggested for this view of growth is 'instrumental conceptualism' and its point of departure is the observation that man seems to have evolved with a unique capacity for helplessness that can be relieved by outside shaping and external devices. As a result cognitive growth occurs as much from the outside in as from the inside out. Much of it consists in a human being's becoming linked with culturally transmitted 'amplifiers' of his motive, sensory and reflective capacities. The earliest of these cognitive 'technologies' for representing the world to be acquired, is based on action. Knowledge is represented by knowing how to do something. This is then supplemented by a system of ikonic representation in which serially ordered events and actions are now rendered in simultaneous form in imagery. Finally, a third component is added—symbolic representation, in which experience is now encoded in the more powerful notation of language, with its rules not only for representing but also for transforming experience.

There is some need for the preparation of experience and mental operations before language can be used in this way. Although the syntactic aspect of language reaches maturity very swiftly, the child, in order to use it as an instrument of thought, must first bring the world of experience under the control of principles of organization that are in some degree isomorphic with the structural principles of syntax. Once language is applied, then it is possible, by using language as an instrument, to scale to higher levels. In essence, once he has coded experience in language, the child can (but does not necessarily) read surplus meaning into the experience by pursuing the built-in implications of the rules of language.

Bruner and his colleagues make no claim to have constructed a 'finished' theory of cognitive growth nor to have devised an entirely new approach to ontogenetic problems. They fully acknowledge their debt to Piaget and have adopted a basically similar cybernetic feedback model of cognitive development. Their major innovation is a matter of adjustment of emphasis rather than of fundamental reconstruction. The Cambridge school disagree with Geneva on the how of intellectual growth. They maintain that by viewing the problem of development in terms of the formation of logical structures in the child's organized experience Piaget and his colleagues have failed to recognize the supreme importance of the psychological processes which sustain logical behaviour and have, thus, tended to ignore or play down the rôle of imagery and the other internalized, culturally transmitted cognitive technologies. Although the Genevan investigations of imagery (Inhelder, 1965; Piaget and Inhelder, 1966) cast some doubt on the accuracy of this charge, the series of experiments reported in '*Studies*' was aimed at repairing the alleged omission.

Two of these experiments, those conducted by Sonstroem and Frank, have already been described as illustrations of the power of the perceptual dimension and the possible efficacy in facilitating concept formation of techniques which combat this influence. These studies had their genesis in the Harvard view that non-conservation reflects the dominance of ikonic reckoning by appearance and, consequently, preventing the subject from reckoning on this basis, by, for example, compelling him to do his reasoning with the relevant objects behind a screen, will produce conservation. Piaget (1967) has argued that, although Harvard subjects gave conservation—like responses after treatment of this type, it was really convariation that the children had achieved and not conservation. They recognized, for example, that width narrowed when height increased but recognized it empirically and not in terms of quantitative necessity.

This contrast between performance founded on an empirical basis and on a reversible system of operations is paralleled in the distinction which Piaget (1964) makes within the cognitive function between the figurative and the operative aspects. The former deals with static configurations and comprises such activities as perception, imitation and mental imagery. The latter includes operations and the transformations which lead from one static configuration to another. There is constant interaction between these two facets but the operative component constitutes the basic aspect of intelligent knowing and, as development proceeds, it increasingly dominates and determines the figurative aspect. In children who have attained the stage of concrete operations and in adults, the figurative aspects are subordinated to the operative aspects. Any given state is understood to be the result of some transformation and the point of departure for another transformation. But the pre-operational child does not understand transformations. He does not have the operations necessary to understand them and, as a result, puts all the emphasis on the static quality of the states. It is because of this, for example, that in the conservation experiments he simply compares the initial state and the final state without being concerned with the transformation. Piaget maintains that a training technique which concentrates on the perceptual aspect will reinforce the figurative component without touching the operative component and is, thus, unlikely to accelerate the development of cognitive structures. To achieve the latter objective the focus should be on the operative aspect, on the understanding of transformations not the analysis of states.

Piaget does not regard language as being in any way an exception to the principle of the dominance in intellectual development of the operative, structural aspect over the symbolic, mediational function. He made this abundantly clear in a discussion of the relation between language and thinking: 'If it is legitimate to consider language as playing a central rôle in the formation of thought, it is insofar as it constitutes one of the manifestations of the symbolic function while the development of this symbolic function is itself dominated by the intelligence in all its aspects' (Piaget, 1963, p.57).[1]

A consideration of the part played by language in the striking changes in cognitive functioning which characterize the five- to seven-year period provides a suitable illustration of how this viewpoint clashes with that of the Harvard group. Bruner maintains that a child living in an advanced society becomes 'operational', in the Piagetian

[1]Hans G. Furth's translation.

sense, at this stage in development because his structural experience is brought under the control of principles of organization isomorphic with the structural principles of syntax and this allows him to use the rules of language to transform his experience. The importance of language as an instrument of thought is ineluctable but there is a fair amount of experimental evidence which appears to conflict with Bruner's account of its function at this specific juncture. Piaget (1960), in arguing the case for the importance of the factor of equilibration in the development of conservation, stresses the fact that the various types of conservation appear in a temporal sequence. The child arrives at conservation of substance, weight and volume by exactly the same reasoning using the same words yet they appear on the average at about 7–8, 9–10 and 11–12 years respectively. Piaget maintains that if conservation is explained on the basis of a linguistic, syntactic structure there is no obvious reason why it should not be immediately applied to all content areas. More recently, the Genevan group (Inhelder *et al.*, 1966; Sinclair, 1967; Inhelder and Sinclair, 1969), on the basis of a series of experiments aimed at assessing the rôle of language in the attainment of conservation, have reached the general conclusion that, although language training, among other types of training, operates to direct the child's interactions with the environment and thus to 'focus' on relevant dimensions of task situations, and although changes observed in the justifications given for answers in the conservation task after training suggests that language does aid in the storage and retrieval of relevant information, the evidence offered little, if any, support for the contention that language learning *per se* contributes to the *integration and co-ordination* of 'informational units' necessary for the achievement of the conservation concepts. This line of argument is also supported by Oléron (1961) and Furth's (1966) studies of deaf-mutes which show that they develop operational structures quite normally in spite of being cut off from social transmission by language. It is, also, consistent with the results of studies of transposition learning reviewed by White (1963) since they include both examples of operational behaviour antedating the appearance of the type of verbal explanations regarded by Bruner as evidence of the existence of the critical isomorphism between syntactic structure and organized experience, and others in which the reverse temporal relationship applied.

What light, if any, do the results of the present study throw on the issue of the nature of the relationship between mediation and structural change in intellectual development? Any attempt at answering this question must be of a highly tentative nature since it lies well beyond the declared objectives of the experimental work. For what they are worth in this foreign context, the results do seem to favour the Genevan position. The relative failure of the verbal acceleration technique to produce generalization of the conservation principle is consistent with the prediction based on Piaget's viewpoint that a treatment, which depends for its effectiveness on inducing the child to abandon his dependence on misleading ikonic forms of representation by providing him with alternative verbal and enactive mediators, will result in a purely empirical recognition of conservation based on experience and confined in its application to the situations in which this experience was gained. It will not produce the structural changes which, in Piaget's view, are the basis of conservation proper with its quality of logical necessity. The Geneva-Harvard debate continues, however, and seems likely to attract even more widespread attention since Piaget and Bruner have agreed on the production of a joint book which will present the common ground between the two theoretical viewpoints and, also, point up the issues on which they 'agree and disagree'. The publication of this volume should present something of a landmark in the history of research on cognitive development.

'Covered' and 'uncovered' items and overt counting
Before concluding this consideration of the import of the results of the non-verbal post-tests for the acceleration issue and turning to the methodological question of the relative merits of the verbal and non-verbal approaches, there are two further findings which cannot be passed over without a brief comment. In the discussion of the outcome of the verbal post-tests the significantly superior performance of the Control Group on the 'covered', as opposed to the 'uncovered', items in the first post-test was cited as an illustration of the power of the perceptual dimension and as being consistent with the apparent efficacy in facilitating concept formation of techniques which combat this influence. In addition, the marked decline in the incidence of overt counting between the first and second verbal post-tests was quoted in support of the view that, in some cases, the employment of counting is a stepping-stone to the attainment of conservation. The results of the non-verbal post-tests, presented in Chapter Three, seem to subvert both of these lines of argument since the scores of Experimental Group I and Experimental Group II, indicated a consistently significantly superior performance on the 'uncovered' items and there was a marked rise in the frequency of overt counting between the first and second post-tests.

A case can be made for the assertion that these disparities between the results of the two sets of post-tests are to be attributed to specific features of the non-verbal test procedure and, in particular, to the prominent rôle which it accords to short-term memory. In contrast to the verbal test, a correct response on an item in the non-verbal test demands not only a correct conservation judgement but also that the subject knows the exact number of elements in the perceptually altered collection. It is, thus, hardly surprising that the 'covered' items proved to be more difficult than the 'uncovered' items since in the case of the latter the subjects were able to check the accuracy of their recollections by counting before making their scored responses. The emphasis placed on short-term memory in this suggested explanation is consistent with the contrast between the irregular distributions of conservation scores yielded by the two non-verbal post-tests (see Figure XII) and the U-shaped frequency distribution obtained in the non-verbal pre-test in which there was no attempt to cover the collections of elements.

The same procedural features of the non-verbal post-test can be adduced to account for the increase in the incidence of counting between the first and second post-tests. The contrasting decrease in the case of the verbal post-tests can be attributed to the fact that as the subjects attained conservation they no longer found it necessary to count after the perceptual rearrangement. In the non-verbal post-tests the appearance of conservation was not accompanied by the disappearance of counting. The subjects continued to employ it, whenever possible, to ensure that they had remembered the correct number and to ease the burden on their short-term memory. This hypothesis is supported by the performance of the three subjects on the first non-verbal post-test and ten on the second non-verbal post-test who attained a high level of success (6+/8) on the 'covered' trials yet still employed counting in obtaining a perfect score (10/10) on the 'uncovered' trials.

Since a consideration of the implications of the results of the present study for future research on the acceleration question will be deferred to the concluding chapter, the detailed discussion of this issue will be terminated at the point now reached. As indicated in Chapter One, the next chapter will be devoted to a reconsideration of the important methodological issue of the relative merits of the verbal and non-verbal approaches.

CHAPTER FIVE

The Verbal and Non-Verbal Approaches to the Investigation of Concept Formation—II

IT IS EVIDENT that the present study has provided ample testimony of the difficulties involved in adopting the non-verbal approach to the study of the process of conceptualization. Smedslund (1963) stressed the double danger involved in any assessment of cognitive functioning. The presence of a selected symptom-response may be falsely interpreted as indicating the presence of a particular level of functioning and the absence of the symptom response may be falsely interpreted as indicating the absence of the level of functioning in question. As we have seen in Chapter Two, the non-verbal pre-test provided a fine illustration of the first of these pitfalls since it was possible for the subjects to produce correct conservation responses by working on a perceptual and empirical rule basis. There are grounds for the assertion, on the other hand, that the non-verbal post-tests perpetrated the error of underestimating the children's conceptual status. As indicated in Chapter Four, success on the 'covered' trials demanded not only that the children conserve but that they remember the exact number of elements in the hidden collection. The likelihood of this burden on short-term memory being successfully sustained is diminished by the necessity for the subjects to cope with the rearranged positions of the choice cards before making their scored responses. In short, the procedural features of the post-tests which are conducive to underestimation are among the modifications introduced to counteract the possibility of overestimation inherent in the pre-test. This insoluble dilemma appears to be an unavoidable feature of the non-verbal approach. Efforts to exclude empirical rule working and other sources of spurious success inevitably increase the likelihood of an underestimate of the subject's conceptual status. A possible method of circumventing this difficulty is to concentrate on devising trials aimed at detecting the adoption of specific empirical rules rather then seeking to refine the test procedure to a point at which success can only be achieved by means of the conceptual ability being assessed.

This was the point of departure for a pilot study of transitivity of length conducted by the writer with a view to resolving the dilemma presented by the stage reached in the Smedslund-Braine controversy in 1965, as described in Chapter One. At that juncture it appeared that any acceptable experimental approach to the problem would have to satisfy two procedural constraints. To prevent attention to the measured object being an additional basis for responses it must involve the application of the measuring rod to both uprights on each trial. Secondly, it must facilitate the detection of children who are employing non-transitive hypotheses. In the pilot study an attempt is made to satisfy these conditions by using two types of pseudo-measurement trial which resemble transitivity trials in that both sticks are measured but which do not permit the making of a valid transitivity judgement ($A > B$. $C > B$ and $A < B$. $C < B$). It is hypothe-sized that if these pseudomeasurement trials are incorporated in a series of straightforward transitivity trials children with genuine transitivity will be puzzled by both types of inconclusive trial. They may react by reverting to guessing or a non-transitive hypothesis as the basis for their responses but it is probable that if the pseudo-measurement trials are separated by numerous genuine trials their puzzlement will reveal itself in verbalization and a substantially increased response time. Two of the main non-transitive hypotheses should, also, be detectable and discriminable. Subjects employing the $A > B : \supset A > C$ hypothesis should deal happily with the $A > B$ and $C > B$ pseudomeasurement trials and be puzzled by the $A < B$ and $C < B$ variety while exactly the reverse should be true of those depending on the $A < B : \supset A < C$ non-transitive hypothesis.

In a further effort to illuminate the currently confused situation results will be presented which were obtained by testing a group of five-year-old subjects with both Braine's non-verbal procedure and Smedslund's verbal procedure.

While the present study was underway Smedslund (1966a), in a further contribution to the mainstream of the controversy, reported an experiment in which he, too, attempted to demonstrate the existence of non-transitive hypotheses by using pseudomeasurement situations in which both comparison sticks were measured but valid transitive inferences were excluded. His results, however, do not per-mit conclusions to be reached on the crucial questions of which individual children employed non-transitive hypotheses and of what type since his findings are based on a contingency analysis of the incidence of passes and failures on the genuine measurement (G) and pseudomeasurement (P) tests in the group of subjects as a whole. Since the coefficients of constraint (Attneave, 1959) between the two

G-tests and between the two *P*-tests show no tendency to be higher than the coefficients of constraint between the *G*-tests and the *P*-tests, he maintains that there is no evidence for the existence of separate factors in the *G*-tests and *P*-tests, but, on the contrary, some support for the hypothesis that a single factor may be generating the successful performance in both types of tests. Since successful performance in the *P*-tests appears to be generated entirely by non-transitive hypotheses, it follows that these hypotheses must also constitute the factor common to both types of tests. Smedslund concludes that the genuine measurement tasks were solved by the subjects quite probably on the basis of non-transitive hypotheses. This also means that Braine's non-verbal method is not a valid instrument for diagnosing transitivity of length, and that his five-year-old subjects most likely did not have a grasp of transitivity.

The subjects for the pilot study conducted by the writer were 30 children, 16 boys and 14 girls, aged from 4:10 to 6:4 years with a median age of 5:3 years. They were selected from the children in the given age range in four Bristol infant schools on the basis of their performance in the training series described below.

Apparatus

This consisted of a wooden base 32 inches in length, $2\frac{3}{4}$ inches in height and 3 inches in width. Two inches from either end of the base was a half-inch-deep slot into which the comparison sticks used in the experiment could be placed in an upright position. On the front of the base facing the subject and situated directly under the stick slots were two rectangular apertures ($3\frac{1}{2} \times 2\frac{3}{4}$ in.) each covered with a door which opened upwards towards the child. Behind each door was a compartment in which the experimenter could place the small, coloured, wooden blocks with which correct responses were reinforced. The child was prevented from seeing the operation by a flap $9\frac{1}{2}$ inches high and 32 inches in length which was hinged to the rear of the base and was in a vertical position throughout the test.

Four comparison sticks ($1 \times 3/16$ in. in cross section) were used in the training series. Their respective lengths, from the top to the point where they entered the base, were 18 inches (A), 9 inches (B), 7 inches (C) and $6\frac{1}{2}$ inches (D). Only two comparison sticks were employed in the test series. They were both 12 inches in length and will be referred to as E1 and E2. All of the comparison sticks were painted turquoise. The measuring stick used in the test series was a round, hollow, metal rod $11\frac{3}{4}$ inches in length. A wooden dowel fitted inside it projected

$\frac{1}{2}$ inch beyond its base and increased its overall length to $12\frac{1}{4}$ inches. This projection was spring loaded and when light pressure was exerted on its base it disappeared from view into the interior of the rod. The overall length of the rod was thus, reduced to $11\frac{3}{4}$ inches. A metal spigot, $1\frac{3}{4}$ inches in length and $\frac{1}{2}$ inch wide, was fixed at right-angles to the top of the rod. The entire measuring stick was painted black and the spigot was orange.

Procedure

The experimenter told the children, who were seen individually, that he wanted to play a game with them. He would hide a block behind one of the doors and the subject was to try and find it and string it with the other blocks on a wire with which he had been provided. He would be able to find the block every time if he looked very carefully at the sticks.

The training series began with twenty trials using sticks A (18 in.) and B (9 in.). The relative positions of the sticks to the left and right of the child were alternated in accordance with a random Gellermann (1933) sequence to prevent responses on a positional basis. If the child selected the wrong door on a trial he was shown that the compartment behind that door was empty and that the block was behind the other door. This correction procedure was followed throughout the training series. The criterion of learning was eight consecutive correct responses; if this criterion was not met after the sequence had been gone through twice (i.e. in 40 trials), the child did not undergo the test series. The second stage of the training series involved the presentation of sticks C (7 in.) and B (9 in.), C and D ($6\frac{1}{2}$ in.) and B and D in successive trials in a random sequence. As in the first stage the relative positions of the long and short sticks were randomly alternated from trial to trial. The criterion was again eight consecutive correct responses and any child who did not attain this level in 40 trials took no further part in the experiment.

The test series, which immediately followed the training series, comprised four types of trial-genuine measurement trials, two varieties of pseudomeasurement trials and retention trials. The two sticks (E1 and E2) of identical length (12 in.) were used throughout the genuine measurement trials. This avoided any possibility of correct responses being made on a perceptual basis. They were removed from the slots in the wooden base at the end of each trial, taken out of the subject's sight and then replaced as if they were a new pair of sticks. Apparent variations in their relative lengths from trial to trial were produced by varying the length of the measuring stick by means of the spring device described above. In each trial, the experimenter informed the subject that he was going to help him to find the block and then juxtaposed the measuring stick with the comparison stick on the subject's left and then with the comparison stick on his right. The measuring stick always appeared to be shorter than one of them and longer than the other. It was placed vertically alongside each comparison stick and then rotated so that the spigot passed over the top of the one which appeared shorter or rested against the side of the one which appeared longer. While making the comparisons, the experimenter kept his hand around the base of the measuring stick as an additional precaution against the detection of the subterfuge. If the child did not seem to be watching during this procedure, the measuring stick was knocked against the top of the comparison stick to attract his attention and he was told, 'Look at the tops of them'. The subject was not allowed to choose a door until the measuring operations had been completed. If he failed to select a door immediately after their completion, the measuring procedure was repeated and he was then instructed to find the block.

Both types of pseudomeasurement trial used the same pair of sticks (E1 and E2) and the same general procedure employed in the genuine measurement trials. In one type the measuring stick was made longer than both of the comparison sticks and in the other the measuring stick was shorter than both of the comparison sticks. The former was aimed at detecting the use of the $A > B: \supset A > C$ non-transitive hypothesis and the latter the $A < B: \supset A < C$ hypothesis. None of the subjects' choices on the pseudomeasurement trials was reinforced.

The time which elapsed between the completion of the measurement procedure by the experimenter and the subject's choice of a door was recorded in both the genuine and pseudomeasurement trials, as were all relevant verbalizations by the subjects.

The retention trials were similar to those which comprised the training series and the same pairs of comparison sticks were used in them. They were administered at intervals in the sequence of genuine and pseudomeasurement trials and were intended as a check that the children were still responding on a basis of relative length. A repetition of the training series was to follow any error on these items. In fact, no errors occurred and no such repetition was required.

In the full description of the sequence which follows and in the remainder of this account of the pilot study, genuine, pseudomeasurement and retention trials will be indicated by the letters G, P and R respectively. *E1* will be used to indicate the comparison rod which appeared to be longer than the measuring stick and *E2* that which appeared to be shorter; thus, *P-E1 E1* will represent a pseudo-measurement trial in which both comparison sticks appeared to be longer than the measuring stick, and *G-E2 E1* will represent a genuine measurement trial in which the apparently shorter comparison stick was on the subject's left and the longer stick on his right. The test series consisted of forty trials, comprising twenty eight *G*-trials, three *P-E1 E1* trials, three *P-E2 E2* trials, and six *R*-trials, in the following order:

G-E1 E2, G-E1 E2, G-E2 E1, G-E2 E1, R, G-E2 E1, G-E2 E1, P-E2 E2, G-E1 E2, G-E1 E2, G-E1 E2, R, G-E2 E1, G-E1 E2, P-E2 E2, G-E1 E2, G-E2 E1, R, G-E1 E2, G-E2 E1, P-E1 E1, G-E1 E2, G-E2 E1, R, G-E1 E2, P-E2 E2, G-E2 E1, G-E2 E1, G-E1 E2, R, G-E1 E2, P-E1 E1, G-E2 E1, G-E1 E2, G-E2 E1, R, G-E2 E1, G-E1 E2, P-E1 E1, G-E2 E1.

For purposes of comparison with the results obtained by the non-verbal procedure three additional *G*-trials were administered at the conclusion of the test series. The base, the two comparison sticks and the measuring stick were the same as in the test series but the transitivity problems were posed verbally. The three *G*-trials were preceded by an *R*-trial in which the subject was asked, 'Which one is longer of these two sticks?' If the child chose the correct one, the experimenter said 'That's right'. To preserve continuity with what had gone before he was, also, rewarded with a block. Each of the comparisons in the *G*-trials was accompanied by the following words: 'Before you tell me which one is longer, I will place this black stick (the measuring rod) like this. Can you see the difference? Which one of the sticks is longer?' If the subject gave the wrong answer he was corrected and asked to look more closely. If he was correct, the experimenter said, 'Yes, that's right, this one is longer than that one'. After the second comparison the measuring stick was rapidly removed and the child was asked, 'Which one of these two (comparison) sticks is the longer one?' If he delayed his answer too long, the procedure was repeated. If he answered correctly, the measuring stick was laid on the table (without emphasis) and he was asked, 'How do you know that this stick is longer than that one?' or 'From what do you know that this one is longer than that one?' Every explanation was greeted with signs of approval by the experimenter.

Results

The objectives of the pilot study dictate that attention should be focussed on the subjects who passed on the non-verbal test series and would, thus, be regarded by Braine as having transitivity of length. The pass criterion adopted was nineteen correct responses out of twenty-seven trials. The first of the twenty-eight *G*-trials in the test series was regarded as a practice trial and was not scored. This represents a slightly more stringent criterion than that adopted by Braine (1959) since $p = \cdot 026$ of obtaining nineteen or more correct responses by chance in twenty-seven trials while for his criterion (13/18) $p = \cdot 048$. On this basis, nineteen subjects attained the pass level and eleven failed. At 63 per cent the proportion of passes exceeded the corresponding figure of 50 per cent obtained by Braine with children of this age level.

The Incidence of Non-Transitive Hypotheses

Did any of the children who passed achieve success by employing non-transitive hypotheses as opposed to transitive inferences? An answer to this question is sought by considering the extent to which

TABLE 17: *Subjects' mean response times in seconds on G-trials and two types of P-trials. Also P-trial means expressed in terms of standard deviation units from G-trial mean*

SUB-JECTS	AGE	G-TRIALS		P-E1 E1 TRIALS		P-E2 E2 TRIALS	
		Mean	S	Mean	Z	Mean	Z
1	4–10	0·74	0·35	5·66*	14·06	2.33*	4·54
2	5–2	1·59	2·77	1·50	0·03	3·16	0·57
3	5–2	1·20	0·45	1·16	0·09	1·33	0·29
4	5–3	0·57	0·20	1·33	3·80	1·66*	5·45
5	5–3	1·06	0·95	1·16	0·12	2·00*	0·99
6	5–3	1·90	1·20	15·66*	11·47	8·33*	5·36
7	5–3	1·18	0·41	2·66	3·61	2·33	2·80
8	5–3	1·20	0·44	3·16	4·45	8·66	16·95
9	5–4	0·61	0·48	5·83	10·88	0·66	0·10
10	5–5	0·69	0·32	0·50	0·59	2·00*	4·09
11	5–5	2·70	1·72	4·33*	0·95	5·66*	1·72
12	5–5	0·79	0·60	1·91	1·87	1·91	1·87
13	5–6	1·40	0·78	3·00	2·05	1·33	0·09
14	5–7	1·48	0·69	2·00	0·75	2·50	1·48
15	5–8	0·85	0·58	3·00	3·71	2·66	3·12
16	5–11	1·00	0	2·33	0	1·00	0
17	6–1	1·05	0·85	0·50	0·65	1·00	0·06
18	6–4	0·81	0·64	1·66	1·33	2·33	2·38
19	6–4	2·16	4·26	10·00*	1·84	17·33*	3·56

* Indicates relevant verbalization of P-E1 E1 and/or P-E2 E2 trials

the subjects revealed by appropriate verbalization and increases in response time that they realized the two types of *P*-trial did not permit the making of a valid transitivity judgement. In the case of the verbal evidence establishing a criterion of such a realization is relatively simple. A subject who indicates on the *P-E1 E1* trials that both comparison sticks are longer than the measuring rod and on the *P-E2 E2* trials that both are shorter and, consequently, that he cannot make a meaningful choice can reasonably be regarded as likely to be employing transitive inferences on the *G*-trials.

The seven subjects who made relevant verbal comments when confronted with the *P*-trials are indicated in the above table. The quality of the verbalizations of the four children who commented on both types of *P*-trial is exemplified by subject 16. On the *P-E1 E1* trials he responded 'Both (comparison sticks) big (when compared to the measuring rod)' and on the *P-E2 E2* trials 'Both the littlest'. The response 'Both are short' made by subject 15 is typical of the three children who commented on only the *P-E2 E2* trials.

When the nineteen subjects are considered as a group the evidence from response time is clearcut. Both in the case of the *P-E1 E1* trials ($t = 2 \cdot 93$, d.f.$= 18$, p (one-tailed test) $< \cdot 005$) and the *P-E2 E2* trials ($t = 2 \cdot 80$, d.f.$= 18$, p (one-tailed test) $< \cdot 01$) their mean response times significantly exceeded their mean response times on the *G*-trials. These figures, however, provide no information on the crucial details of the performance of individual subjects. Table 1 accordingly contains the mean and standard deviation of their response times on the twenty-seven *G*-trials and their mean response times on the three *P-E1 E1* and three *P-E2 E2* trials.

The selection of a criterion in the case of response times is more difficult. Clearly any increase in a subject's response time when confronted with a *P*-trial must be interpreted in the light of the variations in his response time on the *G*-trials. The method of achieving this adopted is to regard each child's mean response times on each type of *P*-trial as scores in the distribution of his response times on the *G*-trials and then to express their deviation from the *G*-trial mean as a *z* score. The decision as to what will be viewed as a significant deviation must be taken on an arbitrary basis and for the purpose of the present discussion a *z* score of $1 \cdot 64$ ($p < \cdot 05$) is viewed as indicating a significantly greater response time on a group of *P*-trials than on the *G*-trials. Children attaining a *z* score of $1 \cdot 64$ or more on both types of *P*-trials are accordingly considered as likely to be employing transitive inferences on the *G*-trials.

Applying the criteria outlined above nine of the nineteen subjects who passed on the non-verbal series appear to have done so on a transitivity basis. Three satisfied both the verbal and response time criteria, one only the former and five the latter. The verbalization and response time of five of the ten remaining subjects were consistent with the patterns attributed to the two types of non-transitive hypotheses on which the *P*-trials were based. Three of these subjects appeared to be using the $A > B: \supset A > C$ hypothesis since they gave no indication of appreciating that a valid transitivity judgement was impossible on the *P-E1 E1* trials yet gave verbal (one subject), response time (one subject) or both types (one subject) of indication of such a realization on the *P-E2 E2* trials. The other two children satisfied the response time criterion on the *P-E1 E1* trials but attained neither criterion level on the *P-E2 E2* trials, and thus, seemed to be employing the $A < B: \supset A < C$ non-transitive hypothesis. No conclusion can be reached on the basis underlying the performance of the other five subjects since they failed to attain the criteria on either type of *P*-trial.

The number of correct transitivity judgements on the three additional verbal trials made by the nineteen children who passed on the non-verbal series are presented in Table 2. In judging the quality of their verbal explanations of the basis for their decisions the criterion advocated by Smedslund (1963) was adopted. An acceptable explanation is one which explicitly mentions both premises, i.e. $A > B$ (or $B < A$) and $B > C$ (or $C < B$). Only subject 15 satisfied this criterion.

TABLE 18: *Number of correct transitivity judgements on three verbal trials by 19 subjects who passed on the non-verbal series*

SUB-JECTS	SCORE	SUB-JECTS	SCORE	SUB-JECTS	SCORE	SUB-JECTS	SCORE	SUB-JECTS	SCORE
1	3	5	2	9	2	13	2	17	2
2	2	6	3	10	3	14	3	18	0
3	2	7	3	11	3	15	3	19	3
4	3	8	2	12	3	16	3		

The Detection of Non-Transitive Hypotheses

The main aim of the pilot study was to determine the feasibility of detecting individual children who employ non-transitive hypotheses on non-verbal transitivity items by means of a method which avoids the major shortcomings of the earlier attempts by Smedslund and

Braine. The results obtained indicate that the *P*-trial procedure goes some way towards achieving this objective. There appears to be little room for doubt that children who attain the verbal criterion on both types of *P*-trial are working on a transitive inference basis. There may seem to be less justification for reaching the same conclusion about subjects who attain only the response time criterion on both sets of *P*-trials. As Smedslund (1966e) points out, however, response time is a very sensitive measure and is probably very efficient in tapping the number and complexity of transformations involved in performing a cognitive task. In addition, most of the *z* scores interpreted as indicating a shift in the basis of a child's responses are well above the arbitrarily selected criterion and some represent dramatic increases in response time.

The fact that the only subject to give an acceptable explanation in the three additional verbal trials attained the response time criterion on both *P*-trials and the verbal criterion on neither provides further support for the identification of such significant increases in response time with the use of transitive inferences. The failure of the other subjects who attained the verbal and/or response time criteria on both types of *P*-trial to provide acceptable explanations in the verbal trials is not inconsistent with the possession of genuine transitivity. There is ample evidence (e.g. Gonzalez and Ross, 1958; Kendler and Vineberg, 1954) that the development of successful conceptual performances need not be paralleled by the ability to verbalize their bases. The number of correct responses which they achieved also supports their claim to possess genuine transitivity since, if we regard three correct responses as indicating a pass on the verbal trials, they performed significantly better than the ten children who did not attain the verbal or response time criterion on both types of *P*-trial ($\chi^2 = 4 \cdot 54$, d.f. $= 1$, p $< \cdot 05$, Yates' correction applied).

For the reasons already outlined, it also appears justifiable to assert that the children who attained the verbal and/or response time criterion on a single type of *P*-trial did employ the $A > B: \supset A > C$ or $A < B: \supset A < C$ non-transitive hypothesis. The data, however, throw no light on the basis of performance in the subjects who failed to achieve the criterion on either type of *P*-trial. Parsimony suggests that they should be regarded as being capable of employing either type of non-transitive hypothesis as the initial measurement on each trial ($A > B$ or $A < B$) demands. It could, also, be argued with less apparent justification, that they have genuine transitivity and realize that a valid judgement is not possible on the *P*-trials but, wishing to provide the experimenter with a response, switch to the use of guessing or a non-transitive hypothesis without verbal comment or a detectable increase in response time.

Import of Results for the Smedslund–Braine Controversy

In view of the very limited size of the sample of children used in this pilot study tentative comments on the findings seem to be more appropriate than definite conclusions. As far as the continuing transitivity controversy is concerned (Murray and Youniss, 1968; Smedslund, 1969) the results afford partial support to both Smedslund and Braine. On the methodological issue they support Smedslund's contention that it is possible for children to attain the pass level on Braine's non-verbal test of transitivity by employing non-transitive hypotheses. On the question of the age of emergence of genuine transitivity, in contrast, they are to some extent in accord with Braine's position. Smedslund (1966a) maintains that five-year-old children who pass genuine measurement tests employ pre-logical patterns which differ from genuine transitivity in two important ways. First, they depend on absolute judgements, determined by the momentary adaptation level ('long', 'short'), as distinguished from the more developed relative judgements with explicit reference to a specific comparison object ('A is longer than B'). Second, the pre-logical pattern as distinguished from genuine transitivity has no intrinsic necessity and can be extinguished like any learned response. The present study provides no basis for comment on the latter point. The performance of the children who attained the verbal and/or response time criteria on both types of pseudomeasurement trial, however, supports the view that these five-year-olds employed relative, as opposed to absolute judgements in their performance on the genuine measurement trials. At the most, this finding can be interpreted as support for Braine's assertion that genuine transitivity develops in some children about the age of five years, although the proportion (33 per cent) may be somewhat smaller than he indicates. At the least, it provides grounds for doubting Smedslund's conclusion that the earlier pre-logical inferences tapped by Braine's non-verbal procedure have nothing in common with transitivity proper except an unfortunate superficial resemblance.

Demerits and Merits of the Non-Verbal Approach

Despite the qualified success achieved in the pilot study in detecting the use of two non-transitive hypotheses, the results obtained do little to suggest that this approach affords a solution to the general difficulties presented by the adoption of non-verbal methods or to the particular problem posed by the fact that efforts to exclude empirical rule working by refining test procedures to a point at which success can only be achieved by means of the conceptual ability being assessed inevitably result in an increase in the likelihood of an under-estimate of the subject's conceptual status. The strategy of employing trials aimed at detecting the adoption of specific empirical rules appears to be as open to criticism as attempts at excluding empirical rule working on the grounds that it results in a considerable increase in the complexity of the test procedure. The two strategies are, also, alike in that there is no means of determining if the child is achieving success by employing an empirical rule other than those anticipated by the experimenter. These two shortcomings constitute a vicious circle since the inclusion of new types of detection trial aimed at discovering further modes of empirical rule working inevitably leads to further complications in test procedure and, thus, to the provision of further cues which may provide the children with the basis for new empirical rules.

So much for the shortcomings of the non-verbal approach. What of its merits and the failings of the alternative verbal methods? As indicated in Chapter One, Braine (1964) has dealt with both of these topics. In his view the goal of determining the earliest ages at which conceptual processes can be unequivocally elicited can only be attained by employing the simplest possible experimental situations devoid of ambiguities of presentation. This involves eschewing verbally posed problems since their use confounds assessment of the subject's level of linguistic development with that of his conceptual ability. Although this line of argument in favour of the adoption of non-verbal methods is open to criticism on the grounds that extreme simplification may result in an experimental task ceasing to demand functioning at a conceptual level, the attack made on the short-comings of verbal methods appears to be well founded. The work of Braine and Shanks (1965) on children's interpretation of conservation questions is the most recent of a number of studies, alluded to in Chapter One, which have produced evidence of the misconceptions and ambiguities accompanying the verbal approach.

A Compromise Solution to the Verbal or Non-Verbal Methods Problem
     In view of the shortcomings of both the non-verbal and verbal methods and the practical necessity of establishing a methodological modus vivendi, a search for a compromise solution appears to be the appropriate course of action. The approach adopted by Smedslund (1964) seems to possess a substantial degree of merit. On the one hand

he takes pains to avoid the pitfalls of the non-verbal approach by ensuring that his subjects perceive the relevant events and remember the relevant information while, on the other, the weakness of the verbal approach is combated by requiring them to operationally demonstrate their comprehension of the verbal terms used in the presentation of the experimental problems. The adoption of this technique and an extension of it to take account, for example, of Braine and Shanks' (1965) findings concerning the presumptions which children bring to the task of interpreting the experimenter's questions, may constitute the desired compromise.

Could the methodological compromise outlined above be adopted in dealing with all developmental levels?

The appearance of new techniques for assessing young children's comprehension of verbal terms and syntactic structure is consistent with the view that wider application may be possible. Slobin and Welsh (1967), for example, have successfully employed imitation in investigating comprehension. Children, as young as 2:6 years, are asked to repeat sentences read by an experimenter. Comprehension is indicated by the extent to which the children's responses constitute repetitions of the meaning of the presented sentences and there is no insistence on verbatim reproduction.

Promising methodological leads in the study of verbal comprehension do not, however, represent progress towards answering the fundamental question posed by Braine (1964). Does conceptual structure exist at a point in development before a child is able to exhibit his possession of it in a verbal test situation even of the carefully controlled type advocated above? The answer to this question awaits the resolution of the controversies surrounding the functions of language in cognitive development (Bruner, Olver and Greenfield, 1966; Piaget, 1967; Staats, 1968; McNeill, 1970a, b). The Geneva–Harvard debate has already been alluded to in Chapter Four but further discussion of this issue lies without the scope of the present study. Sufficient be it to say that, at present, any prospects of such a resolution appear remote, to say the least.

This gloomy prognosis completes the treatment of the thorny problems presented by the verbal and non-verbal methods issue. The focus will now be shifted once again, to the question of stages in conceptual development which brings equally vexing methodological problems in its train. Chapter Six constitutes a pioneering attempt to put into practice the main recommendations which emerged from the extended consideration in Chapter One of the existing work on the topic of stages.

The Stages Issue and the Analysis of Qualitative Data

ON THE QUESTION of ends as opposed to means the fact that the data obtained in the present study was entirely confined to the topic of number conservation dictated that the problem of stages in the process of acquisition of concepts should be the focus of attention rather than the related question of whether stages are characteristic of the development of persons. This concentration on the nature of the process of acquisition of conservation of number is consistent with Flavell's (1963) recommendation that a practical way of catching hold of some of the developmental reality at the process level is to look for the expression and exemplification of general developmental principles in a few selected individual processes having a measure of developmental richness, that is, producing a sufficient amount of variation in individual performance to enable the detection of stages, if they exist. The criteria adopted for the identification of developmental stages are of the more flexible nature outlined in Chapter One and involve acceptance of the inevitibility of inconsistencies and individual variations in subjects' responses. A substantial degree of agreement in the qualitative features of the performance of a number of children would be regarded as indicative of the presence of a stage. The question of how to decide when the degree of agreement is sufficiently substantial to justify positing a stage introduces the topic of means.

On the methodological plane the short-term longitudinal nature of the present study is in line with the overwhelming case for the adoption of the longitudinal approach to the problem of stages. The use of parallel verbal and non-verbal tests permits a comparison of the relative merits of verbal and non-verbal responses as data contributing to the stages issue and an investigation of the claim that the use of non-verbal responses diminishes the influence of the experimenter's preconceptions by reducing the need for subjective interpretation of the data. The crucial feature in the search for the maximum degree of objectivity is the nature of the method adopted for analysing the subject's responses. As indicated above Smedslund

(1964) is of the opinion that it should be possible to devise a set of completely objective rules for interpreting verbal responses based exclusively on a pattern of direct judgements while Dienes (1959), in the same vein, has stressed the pressing need for a statistical technique which would make it possible to find the patterns or groupings of responses which are essentially determined by a set of qualitative data, without invoking a preconceived theoretical bias in any particular direction. Such a method would allow the confirmation or denial of the existence of stages without the necessity for the researcher to adopt any preconceived scheme as a guide. The writer has been fortunate in being permitted to use a technique for the classification of qualitative data, devised by M. A. Brimer of the Bristol University School of Education, which goes far towards satisfying these criteria of objectivity. An account of this method of analysis (Brimer, 1967), is available and is recommended to the mathematically sophisticated reader. This statement should not, however, deter the reader of more modest mathematical pretensions from proceeding further in the present chapter. The description which follows of the results of applying the analysis to the stages problem demands no more than a nodding acquaintance with standard statistical techniques while an appreciation of the general orientation adopted and of the salient features of the discussion should be within the compass of even the numerophobic reader.

Limitations of the data

Before a description is offered of how the Brimer analysis was employed, two limitations of the data available in the present study must be emphasized. Both stem from the attempt made to tackle the acceleration and stages problem concurrently. Since repeated administration of the *same* test or tests is, of course, an essential feature of any longitudinal study, the procedural changes in the verbal and non-verbal pre-tests, necessary to fit them for use as post-tests in a meaningful attack on the acceleration issue, reduce the data relevant to a longitudinal approach to the problem of developmental stages to the results obtained in the two verbal and non-verbal post-tests. This, in turn, has the effect of reducing the extent to which the material to be analysed exhibits the developmental richness which Flavell (1963) advocates as enabling the detection of stages, if they exist, as the amount of variation in individual performance between the first and second post-tests is clearly much less than that between the pre-tests and first post-tests. In addition, the fact that the majority of the subjects underwent an experimental treatment vitiates, from the outset, any claim that stages detected by the analysis are characteristic of the course of the 'normal' development of conservation of number or possess any degree of generality beyond groups treated as specified in the present study. In view of these limitations the goal of the remainder of this chapter will be an attempt to explore the potential of the Brimer analytical technique in the developmental area rather than to produce an authoritative account of the entire process culminating in the appearance of number conservation and, accordingly, the analysis will include the results of both the conservation and addition-subtraction test items.

Description of method of analysis

The first step in the preparation of the post-test data for processing by the Brimer analysis was the categorization of the subjects' responses to the individual test items on the basis of whether they were the same or different. The responses of the first child considered defined an initial set of categories and this was added to whenever a subsequent child's response on an item was judged to be different from any of those encountered before. The carrying out of this task on the results of the non-verbal post-tests involved little labour since there were only three possible responses on each item and these were of a clear-cut, unambiguous nature. Coping with the verbal post-test data demanded a more protracted procedure. The fact that the subjects' verbal explanations had to be considered as well as the accuracy of their responses rendered it a much more complex operation. Initially the writer went through all of the records of the children's performance on the first verbal post-test assigning the individual responses on items to categories according to whether they were pass or fail responses and to whether the verbal explanations offered appeared to be the same or different from those already categorized. No distinction was made between conservation and addition-subtraction items in carrying out this operation. As in the case of the non-verbal data a new category was created whenever an unprecedented response was encountered. The first verbal post-test results were then passed to a second experimenter who proceeded to carry out an independent categorization. A comparison of the results of this independent assessment and the writer's classification revealed 95 per cent agreement. The individual responses on which there was disagreement were reconsidered and categorized by the two assessors in concert.

The scheme of categories derived from the first verbal post-test was used as the initial set of categories in considering the results of the second verbal post-test. Once again, two independent classifications of the individual responses were carried out and this yielded a similarly high percentage of agreement to that obtained in the first post-test. As before, conflicting assignments were resolved before a final classification was produced. The final scheme of categories was, in fact, identical with that derived from the first-post-test results. It was not found necessary to create new categories to accommodate the second post-test data and, indeed, a number of the categories required for first post-test responses remained void during the processing of the second post-test data. A description of the 17 categories comprising the final scheme follows:

(a) *Categories of explanation of pass responses on conservation and addition-subtraction items:*

1. A *pass* response accompanied with an '*I don't know*' or no explanation.

2. An explanation based on *accurate counting*, e.g. 'You have six and I have six' or 'I counted'.

3. A correct response founded on an appreciation of the effects of *addition and subtraction*. This includes explanations such as 'You didn't put one down or take one away', 'Because they are all left', and 'We've still got the same'.

4. Responses supported by explanations of a descriptive type, e.g. 'You moved them', or 'You put a paper on top'. The use of the term '*reversibility*' to designate this category carries none of the logical implications involved in Piaget's use of the expression. It is prompted simply by the fact that responses of this type appeared to indicate that the child was able to reconstruct the sequence of events culminating in the situation in which the scored questions were posed.

5. A pass response founded on *co-ordination* of the spatial *relations* in the test situation. The subject demonstrates an appreciation of the compensatory nature of the changes produced in the spatial distribution of the elements in the two collections by advancing an explanation such as 'We have the same because yours are spread out and mine are close together'.

6. A pass response justified by an erroneous assessment of the number of objects in the two collections, e.g. 'You have five and I have five' or, much less frequently, 'You have six and I have five' when there are six objects in both collections. This category will be referred to for convenience as '*inaccurate counting*' although such explanations could clearly arise from other causes.

7. Explanations involving a reference to the *one to one corres-pondence* between the elements in two collections. In Item 5, for example, which involved two rows of counters, a subject asserted continuing equality on the grounds that 'We put them one after the other in the same place and so they are the same.' Another child supported a similar verdict on the provoked correspondence Item 18 by stating that 'You (the experimenter) put the eggs by the egg cups'.

8. A pass response accompanied by a nonsense explanation, e.g. 'Because I am a big girl'.

(b) Categories of explanation of fail responses:

9. A *fail* response with an '*I don't know*' or no explanation.

10. This category is defined by the classic non-conservation type of explanation, e.g. 'I have more because mine are all spread out'. It will be referred to as the *global-perceptual* category.

11. A *fail* response based on *inaccurate counting*. The subject, for example, asserts that he has more 'because I have six and you have five', when both collections contain six elements.

12. This category corresponds to Gréco's (1962) distinction between 'quotité' and 'quantité'. The subject gives a fail response but asserts correctly that 'You have six and I have six', or 'There were five before'. For convenience the category will be described as '*fail but evidence of accurate counting*'.

13. This is the fail counterpart of pass category 4, above. By way of explanation the subject gives an accurate account of the experimenter's actions. To distinguish it from the reversibility category, this type of response will be described as '*fail + descriptive explanation*'.

14. A relatively infrequent type of response in which the subjects' *failure* appeared to be *due to verbal features* of the test situation. It is best defined by offering two examples. On Item 1 a subject initially stated correctly that there were four blocks in the single collection. The blocks were spread out and he was asked 'Are there more now?' To this he gave a correct negative reply but, on being asked 'Are there the same number of blocks?' his rejoinder was 'No, there are still four.' Another child readily agreed that there were the same number of counters in the two rows at the commencement of Item 5. The experimenter proceeded to spread out the counters in his own row and posed the question 'Have I got more than you?' This elicited an erroneous, positive reply accompanied by the global-perceptual explanation 'Because you stretched yours out'. The subsequent question 'Have we got the same number?' was, however, answered

correctly and justified on the grounds that 'They're still the same number'.

15. A *fail* response was supported by a *co-ordination of relations* type of explanation exactly similar to that described in 5 above.

16. A *fail* response followed by an *addition and subtraction* justification as defined in 3 above.

17. A *fail* response with a nonsense explanation as illustrated in pass category 8.

The relative importance of these 17 response categories can be gauged from the details, presented in Table 19 of their frequency of occurrence in the first and second verbal post-tests.

With the preliminary categorization operations completed, the process of carrying out the Brimer analysis was identical for both the non-verbal and verbal data. It was implemented by means of three computer programs written by R. H. Thomason of the Bristol University Computer Unit. The results of each of the post-tests were processed separately. Initially each set of data was drawn up in a form which revealed the frequency of occurrence of each item-category pair. This was accomplished by allocating an identifying number to each of the subjects and listing the numbers of the subjects who made each response under the appropriate item-category heading. The numbers of subjects who underwent the first and second verbal post-tests were 85 and 81 respectively. Due to the exclusion of the children who failed to pass the initial training series the corresponding figures for the first and second-non-verbal post-tests were 52 and 49. In the non-verbal post-tests the combination of 36 items and three possible response categories to each of them yielded a possible total of 108 item-category pairs. Subjects made responses under all of these headings in the first non-verbal post-tests but under only 106 of them in the second post-test. The possible total of item-category pairs in the verbal post-tests was 272 since there were 16 items (four addition-subtraction and 12 conservation) and 17 possible response categories. In the first verbal post-test 171 of them were required to cover the variety of subjects' responses and in the second post-test the number fell to 118.

The first program in the package accepted the data in the form described above and produced a matrix in which each column represented an item-category pair and each row an individual subject. Each child's performance profile took the form of a row of 1's and 0's indicating whether or not he made a response under each item-

TABLE 19: *Relative frequency of occurrence of categories of response on the verbal post-tests*

First post-test

ITEMS	1	2	3	4	5	6	7	8	9	10	11	12	13	14	15	16	17
									CATEGORIES								
1	18	6	25	17	1	0	0	0	13	1	1	0	1	2	0	0	0
2	10	2	47	1	1	0	1	0	15	0	2	2	0	3	0	1	0
3	10	3	52	2	1	1	0	0	10	0	2	1	1	1	0	1	0
4	11	7	24	16	1	3	0	0	14	0	1	1	2	0	0	5	0
5	9	6	23	17	1	0	1	0	15	3	0	1	3	4	1	1	0
6	7	9	18	22	1	0	0	0	16	4	0	1	2	4	1	0	0
7	7	3	58	0	1	1	0	0	11	3	0	0	0	1	0	0	0
8	6	7	24	24	0	0	0	0	16	3	1	2	1	1	0	0	0
9	5	7	22	28	0	0	0	0	13	4	0	1	1	2	1	1	0
10	6	2	57	1	0	0	0	0	12	1	1	0	1	1	1	2	0
11	5	3	26	28	1	1	0	0	15	2	1	0	1	0	1	1	0
12	11	7	25	21	1	0	0	0	13	2	0	1	2	1	1	0	0
13	8	4	26	19	0	1	0	0	13	5	2	1	2	2	2	0	0
14	13	6	24	22	0	0	0	0	13	0	0	0	2	1	0	4	0
15	22	16	17	20	0	2	4	1	2	0	1	0	0	0	0	0	0
16	9	9	22	24	0	1	0	0	13	1	0	2	1	2	0	0	1
Total	157	97	490	262	9	10	6	1	204	29	12	13	20	25	8	16	1

Second post-test

ITEMS	1	2	3	4	5	6	7	8	9	10	11	12	13	14	15	16	17
									CATEGORIES								
1	10	5	26	32	0	0	0	0	8	0	0	0	0	0	0	0	0
2	2	0	67	0	0	0	0	1	9	0	1	0	0	0	0	1	0
3	4	1	68	1	0	0	0	0	6	0	0	0	0	0	0	1	0
4	3	1	29	32	0	0	0	0	10	0	0	0	1	0	0	4	0
5	6	2	19	38	0	0	3	0	10	2	0	0	0	0	0	1	0
6	4	3	19	38	1	0	2	0	10	2	0	0	1	0	0	1	0
7	1	1	71	0	0	0	0	0	7	1	0	0	0	0	0	0	0
8	2	2	23	35	1	1	2	0	13	1	0	0	0	0	0	1	0
9	6	1	24	38	0	0	0	0	10	1	0	0	1	0	0	0	0
10	2	0	68	0	0	0	0	0	7	0	0	0	2	0	0	2	0
11	9	2	22	34	0	0	0	0	9	0	0	0	2	0	0	2	0
12	4	3	34	24	4	0	1	0	8	1	0	0	2	0	0	0	0
13	4	2	33	21	4	0	1	0	13	1	0	0	2	0	0	0	0
14	13	6	27	25	1	0	0	0	5	0	0	0	3	0	0	1	0
15	10	13	27	12	0	0	17	0	1	0	0	0	0	0	0	1	0
16	4	2	22	36	2	0	7	0	7	0	0	0	2	0	0	1	0
Total	84	44	579	366	13	1	33	1	133	9	1	0	16	0	0	16	0

category heading. The resulting matrix of 1's and 0's was submitted to a second program which initially produced a symmetrical matrix of the frequency of co-occurence of item-category pairs. In the case of the verbal post-tests, for example, one cell of this matrix contained the number of subjects who gave a pass response with an addition and subtraction explanation on Item 3 and a fail response with a description explanation on Item 4. With a view to avoiding bias stemming from variations in the frequencies of occurrence of item-category pairs, the cell entries in the matrix were then converted to standardized relative frequencies. The frequencies of co-occurrence of item-category pairs to be expected on a chance basis were now computed, converted to standardized relative frequencies and subtracted from the corresponding standardized relative frequencies already calculated on the basis of the subjects' test performance. The standardized differences between the observed and expected frequencies of co-occurence obtained formed the data for a third program which carried out the analysis proper.

The process of detecting groupings of responses (item-category pairs) began with an examination of the matrix to discover the item-category pairs with the highest, positive standardized difference of co-occurrence. The two item-category pairs in question formed the nucleus of the first group. All of the item-category pairs having positive standardized differences of co-occurence with both of the item-category pairs included in the group were now detected and the one with the highest sum of these values was added to the group. This process was continued until the point was reached when no further item-category pairs had positive values with all those already included in the group. The group was now regarded as complete but to ensure the detection of any other item-category pairs which, although not qualifying for group membership, were strongly associated with it the sums of values with those included in the group were calculated for all the remaining item-category pairs. All item-category pairs for which the sum was positive were regarded as being associated with the group.

The analysis continued with an examination of the standardized differences of co-occurrence of the item-category pairs not included in the first group. The two item-category pairs exhibiting the highest, positive value were selected as the basis for a second group which was duly completed in the fashion already outlined. The process of group formation was continued until all the item-category pairs having a positive standardized difference of co-occurrence with another item-category pair had been assigned to a group. That is to say groups were formed until every item-category pair had been considered for its contribution to a group and had either been assigned to a group or identified as having no frequency of co-occurrence with any other item-category pair which was greater than chance.

The complete results obtained by submitting the four sets of data to the Brimer analysis are available for inspection (Wallace, 1967) but practical considerations of bulk dictate that they cannot be included in the present volume. It is not inappropriate in a pioneering study, however, to concentrate on outlining the main features of the findings to the exclusion of more detailed considerations since the latter can, all too easily, obscure the focal issues. Accordingly, in the account which follows the emphasis will be placed on an examination of the nature of the groups which emerged and the additional complexities introduced by associated categories, for example, will not be considered.

The nature of the groups detected by the analysis dictates that the verbal post-test data should be the focus of attention. In the case of the non-verbal data the relative distribution of the alternatives falling under the four dimensions of procedural variation constitute the principal means of determining the nature of the 29 and 31 groups derived, respectively, from the first and second post-tests. It will be recalled that the dimensions comprised the basic procedural differences between addition, subtraction and conservation trials, variations in the initial number of elements employed, the adoption of perceptual or numerical initial correspondence between the elements in the collection and the dots on the card and, finally whether the collection was covered over or left uncovered after the addition, subtraction or conservation phase of each trial. These procedural variations prove to be broken reeds in this context, since, in general, each of the groups includes item-category pairs embodying all of the alternatives on each dimension. As the position of the door chosen by the subject on each item appears to be similarly unrelated to the nature of the groups this leaves the pass-fail dichotomy as the only remaining basis for interpretation. This is more productive in the sense that, with the exception of two groups in the first post-test and five in the second, all of the groups can be designated as being of a purely pass or fail nature. In view of the lack of relationship between the procedural variations and group divisions, however, this knowledge does nothing to illuminate the course of development.

The seven inconsistent groups are of much greater interest as they exhibit a relationship between the pass-fail dichotomy and the 'covered' or 'uncovered' procedural variation which appears to be relevant to the related issues of the power of the perceptual dimension and the possibility of accelerating conceptual development by removing the influence of irrelevant perceptual cues discussed in Chapter Four. Five of the groups (Group 20 on the first post-test and Groups 20, 24, 27 and 28 on the second) are characterized by the linking of fail responses on 'uncovered' items with pass responses on 'covered' items while in the remaining two (Group 25 on the first and second post-test) fail responses on the 'covered' items are linked with pass responses on the 'uncovered' items. The predominance of the groups suggesting that 'covered' items are more easily coped with is in accord with the results based on the verbal post-test scores and contrasts with the significantly superior performance on the 'uncovered' items consistently found in the scores on the non-verbal post-tests.

With the exception of this single aspect relevant to one specific problem, the results of the analyses of the non-verbal post-tests appear to have nothing to contribute to the resolution of developmental issues. That this disappointing outcome is to be attributed to the qualitatively limited data derived by employing the non-verbal approach and that it in no way constitutes a censure on the method of analysis adopted is clearly revealed by a consideration of the results obtained by analysing the two sets of verbal data.

Once again, as in the case of the non-verbal results, the dimensions of procedural variation provide minimal assistance in the search for the bases which have determined the constitution of the 32 groups obtained in the analysis of the first verbal post-test data and the 26 groups which emerged from the results of the second post-test. In contrast to the non-verbal situation, however, the availability of the subjects' explanations of the reasons underlying their responses goes far towards resolving this difficulty. An inspection of the fashion in which the Brimer analysis has grouped the item-category pairs, as exemplified in the listing of Groups 1, 3, 4 and 5 from the first verbal post-test data presented in Table 20 (pages 153–5), suggests, without further processing of the results, that the general basis for the groups is the subjects' preferred mode of approach to the solution of the problems. This appears in many cases, to be constant over the pass response-fail response division as the constitution of Groups 1 and 4 in the first post-test, for example, indicate. There are also Groups such as 5 in the first post-test, which seem to represent points at which a transition from one mode of approach to another is taking place and are, thus, suggestive as far as the course of development is concerned.

TABLE 20: *Examples of groups obtained by analysis of verbal post-test one*

	Item No.		Response Category	Pass (P) Fail (F)	+, − or C	Covered or Un-covered	Sum of Dif-ferences
Group 1	1	Co-ordination of relations	5	P	C	U	13·02
	2	Co-ordination of relations	5	P	+ −	U	13·02
	3	Co-ordination of relations	5	P	+ −	U	13·02
	4	Co-ordination of relations	5	P	C	C	13·02
	5	Fail + evidence of co-ordination of relations	15	F	C	U	13·02
	6	Fail + evidence of co-ordination of relations	15	F	C	U	13·02
	7	Co-ordination of relations	5	P	+ −	U	13·02
	9	Fail + evidence of co-ordination of relations	15	F	C	U	13·02
	10	Fail + evidence of co-ordination of relations	15	F	+ −	U	13·02
	11	Fail + evidence of co-ordination of relations	15	F	C	C	13·02
	12	Fail + evidence of co-ordination of relations	15	F	C	U	13·02
	19	Fail + descriptive explanation	13	F	C	U	13·02
	13	Fail + evidence of co-ordination of relations	15	F	C	U	9·64
	18	Reversibility	4	P	C	U	3·63
	16	Reversibility	4	P	C	C	3·50
	8	Reversibility	4	P	C	C	3·25

Continued over

	Item No.		Response Category	Pass (P) Fail (F)	+, − or C	Covered or Un-covered	Sum of Dif-ferences
Group 3	1	Inaccurate counting	11	F	C	U	12·22
	3	Correct answer based on inaccurate counting	6	P	+ −	U	12·22
	7	Fail, hinging on verbal features	14	F	+ −	U	12·22
	8	Fail, hinging on verbal features	14	F	C	C	12·22
	10	Fail, hinging on verbal features	14	F	+ −	U	12·22
	11	Correct answer based on inaccurate counting	6	P	C	C	12·22
	12	Fail, hinging on verbal features	14	F	C	U	12·22
	9	Fail, hinging on verbal features	14	F	C	U	9·46
	19	Fail, hinging on verbal features	14	F	C	U	9·46
	13	Fail, hinging on verbal features	14	F	C	U	8·96
	18	Correct answer based on inaccurate counting	6	P	C	U	8·96
	2	Fail, hinging on verbal features	14	F	+ −	U	8·00
	4	Correct answer based on inaccurate counting	6	P	C	C	7·42
	6	Fail, hinging on verbal features	14	F	C	U	7·26
	5	Fail, hinging on verbal features	14	F	C	U	7·26
	16	Addition-subtraction wrongly adduced	16	F	C	C	6·47

Continued

	Item No.		Response Category	Pass (P) Fail (F)	+, − or C	Covered or Un- covered	Sum of Dif- ferences
Group 4	1	Fail + descriptive explanation	13	F	C	U	8·53
	2	Reversibility	4	P	+ −	U	8·53
	8	Fail + descriptive explanation	13	F	C	C	8·53
	12	Co-ordination of relations	5	P	C	U	8·53
	6	Fail + descriptive explanation	13	F	C	U	6·56
	3	Reversibility	4	P	+ −	U	6·26
	4	Fail + descriptive explanation	13	F	C	C	6·83
	13	Fail + evidence of co-ordination of relations	15	F	C	U	6·42
	16	Fail + descriptive explanation	13	F	C	C	6·70
	5	Fail + descriptive explanation	13	F	C	U	5·61
	18	Reversibility	4	P	C	U	3·68
	19	Reversibility	4	P	C	U	3·55
	11	Reversibility	4	P	C	C	3·12
	9	Reversibility	4	P	C	U	3·03
Group 5	2	One-to-one correspondence	7	P	+ −	U	8·06
	10	Pass 'Don't know' or 'No'	1	P	C	U	8·06
	19	Global-perceptual	10	F	C	U	8·06
	12	Global-perceptual	10	F	C	U	7·05
	8	Global-perceptual	10	F	C	C	6·24
	7	Global-perceptual	10	F	+ −	U	5·99
	11	Accurate counting	2	P	C	C	6·48
	6	Global-perceptual	10	F	C	U	5·37
	5	Fail + descriptive explanation	13	F	C	U	4·95
	13	Global-perceptual	10	F	C	U	4·80
	16	Accurate counting	2	P	C	C	5·40
	4	Accurate counting	2	P	C	C	4·44
	9	Accurate counting	2	P	C	U	4·36
	18	Accurate counting	2	P	C	U	3·25

Investigation of the relationship between groups

Such subjective pronouncements seem out of place in a study allegedly aimed at attaining the maximum degree of objectivity possible in the processing of qualitative data. In assessing the potential of the Brimer analytical technique in the developmental area the paramount problem is that of objectively determining the nature of the interrelationships between the groups detected by the analysis. A satisfactory technique for this purpose should be capable of simplifying the structural picture by detecting key groups possessing a number of 'satellite' groups and pinpointing cases in which the degree of association between groups is such that one can take the place of a number of others without materially affecting the general structure. More important in the present context, it should be able to cope with the relationship between the groups on the developmental dimension and to determine whether this is of a sequential, parallel or other nature.

It was decided in the present study to explore initially the possibilities of correlational analysis as a technique for attaining these objectives. The first step in the procedure was to derive a score for each of the subjects on each of the groups. This was accomplished by means of a computer program which used the matrix of 1's and 0's and the sums of values for each item-category pair on each group which were already available. The row of 1's and 0's representing each subject's performance profile was compared with the list of sums of values for a group and wherever a value coincided with a 1, the subject's score on the group was incremented by that value. This procedure was repeated until sets of scores were derived for all of the groups. Product-moment correlation coefficients for all possible pairs of groups were then computed separately for the first and second verbal post-tests. The results obtained are presented in Table 21.

The basic assumption underlying the adoption of correlational analysis as an approach to the problem of determining the nature of the interrelationships between groups was that a high positive correlation between the sets of scores for two groups would indicate a close, qualitative association which might justify the use of the procedure suggested above for simplifying the general group structure. Values greater than ·283 and, thus, significant at the ·01 level with 79 degrees of freedom were regarded as high positive correlations for this purpose. An examination of the pairs of groups indicated as being closely associated on this basis casts doubt on the adequacy of a straightfoward correlational approach to the problem of group relationships. On the first verbal post-test, for example, Groups 4 and

TABLE 21A: *Intercorrelations of individuals' scores on groups: first verbal post-test*

With 79 degrees of freedom ·217, ·256 and ·283 are the values for significance at the 5%, 2% and 1% levels respectively

	1	2	3	4	5	6	7	8	9	10	11
1		−·002	·13	·36	·08	−·06	·34	·2	·01	−·05	·08
2			−·06	·13	·03	·81	·18	·15	·12	·02	−·07
3				·55	·52	·03	·11	·38	·07	·24	·23
4					·51	·12	·39	·5	·003	·09	·08
5						·11	·03	·53	·05	·17	·15
6							·03	·17	·01	·1	−·04
7								·31	·33	−·02	−·04
8									·45	·18	·27
9										·29	·39
10											·29

	12	13	14	15	16	17	18	19	20	21	22
1	·02	·03	·11	·13	·01	−·19	·12	−·12	·04	−·12	−·02
2	−·03	·13	·07	·23	·03	−·02	·05	·04	·07	·05	·17
3	−·01	·13	−·03	−·14	·12	−·13	·29	·04	−·16	−·06	−·12
4	−·16	·05	·08	·04	−·06	−·11	·15	−·15	·07	−·02	·08
5	−·20	·19	−·12	−·01	−·01	−·13	·08	·04	−·17	−·08	−·12
6	−·01	·03	·001	·13	−·05	−·09	−·02	·05	·06	−·15	−·04
7	−·14	·1	·29	−·08	·06	−·09	−·05	−·01	·3	·07	·19
8	−·11	·28	·06	·02	·03	−·04	·23	·21	·02	·11	·17
9	·13	·38	·34	·17	·29	·01	·01	·19	·15	·19	·19
10	·33	·18	·41	·14	·10	·09	·07	−·03	·05	−·1	−·2
11	·15	·35	·5	·4	·47	·23	·27	−·01	·06	·33	·09
12		−·06	·28	·21	·39	·29	·2	·003	−·08	−·12	−·07
13			·12	·15	·14	·11	·03	·08	·02	·29	−·01
14				·34	·29	·1	·02	−·11	·24	·23	·11
15					·39	·14	·13	−·08	−·07	·17	·13
16						·21	·31	·06	−·16	·24	·24
17							·31	·51	·32	·39	·29
18								·44	·13	·43	·46
19									·40	·41	·51
20										·23	·37
21											·64

	23	24	25	26	27	28	29	30	31	32
1	−·11	−·03	−·13	·12	−·01	·08	·33	·22	−·004	·26
2	·02	−·22	·26	−·02	·36	·08	·21	·37	−·22	·12
3	−·07	·09	−·02	·04	·01	·02	−·04	·05	·17	·05
4	·03	·001	·002	·18	·08	·06	−·09	·29	−·07	·22
5	·03	−·05	−·13	·14	·12	−·04	−·08	·22	−·03	·03
6	−·01	·01	·14	·03	·23	−·002	·08	·25	·3	·02
7	−·03	−·01	·03	·02	·13	·03	·17	·16	−·16	·28
8	·14	·09	−·01	·19	·23	−·1	·11	·38	·14	·33
9	·13	−·08	·06	−·02	·26	−·1	−·05	·35	−·04	·07
10	−·05	·13	−·10	·1	·20	−·1	−·18	−·03	·08	−·19
11	−·07	·07	·05	·3	·21	−·08	−·09	·14	−·11	·03
12	−·01	·01	−·33	−·17	−·22	−·23	−·22	−·25	−·13	−·21
13	·23	·03	−·06	·23	·44	·15	−·07	·43	·18	−·02
14	−·05	−·07	·07	·19	·26	−·07	·02	−·03	−·21	·04
15	·04	−·22	·04	·26	·18	·15	·29	·27	−·01	·26
16	·33	−·02	·12	−·15	·12	·1	−·02	·07	−·08	·04
17	·29	·15	·14	−·05	·02	−·06	−·2	−·11	−·1	−·09
18	·24	·05	·3	−·18	−·02	·11	·05	·01	·17	·01
19	·56	·4	·44	−·1	·13	·14	−·06	·27	·2	·02
20	·21	·15	·27	·10	·05	·03	−·09	·02	−·12	−·12
21	·39	·05	·54	−·01	·39	·22	·09	·03	−·13	·2
22	·66	·16	·61	−·001	·28	·25	·29	·22	·09	·3
23		·42	·5	·02	·32	·33	·04	−·38	·2	−·07
24			·25	·24	·11	·02	−·003	−·04	−·24	−·06
25				−·004	·46	·35	·33	·2	−·19	·11
26					·18	·05	·43	·26	·07	·22
27						·57	·17	·29	·24	·41
28							·13	·18	·3	·41
29								·31	·23	·43
30									·31	·23
31										·23

TABLE 21B: *Intercorrelations of individuals' scores on groups: second verbal post-test*

With 79 degrees of freedom ·217, ·256 and ·283 are the values for significance at the 5%, 2% and 1% levels respectively

	1	2	3	4	5	6	7	8	9
1		·08	·08	·16	−·02	·01	−·02	−·004	·03
2			·72	·36	·33	·38	·44	−·004	·03
3				·5	·36	·47	·48	·03	·06
4					·72	·73	·76	·47	·38
5						·85	·82	·49	·51
6							·88	·54	·51
7								·56	·55
8									·59

	10	11	12	13	14	15	16	17	18
1	·01	·03	·04	−·1	−·09	−·05	−·12	−·12	−·12
2	·16	·1	·07	−·08	·07	−·002	−·03	·06	−·02
3	·18	·05	·02	−·06	·06	−·02	−·09	·09	−·06
4	·22	·07	·23	−·08	·06	·07	·06	·08	·01
5	·28	·1	·23	·02	·02	·05	−·001	·04	·06
6	·33	·15	·28	·07	·09	·04	·1	·13	·002
7	·3	·19	·3	−·01	·1	·05	·08	·11	·01
8	·08	·14	·24	·16	−·02	·03	·02	·06	−·02
9	·26	·08	·14	·04	·02	−·08	−·05	−·03	·03
10		−·02	−·01	−·05	·07	·04	−·09	·13	−·02
11			·72	·27	·42	·4	·37	·09	·06
12				·34	·45	·51	·49	·12	·08
13					·71	·70	·69	·62	·54
14						·85	·82	·72	·66
15							·77	·64	·56
16								·68	·68
17									·71

	19	20	21	22	23	24	25	26
1	−·14	·02	−·003	·01	·002	−·01	·12	·02
2	−·02	·04	·03	·0005	−·07	−·03	−·12	−·07
3	−·06	·12	·09	·01	−·09	−·05	−·15	−·13
4	−·03	·05	·08	−·05	−·04	−·03	−·16	·11
5	−·01	·08	·08	−·08	−·15	−·12	−·16	·05
6	−·03	·23	·08	−·1	−·08	−·08	−·19	·04
7	−·02	·12	·05	−·11	−·08	−·08	−·23	·03
8	−·06	·1	−·01	−·02	−·02	−·0001	−·12	·09
9	−·03	·06	·06	−·11	−·08	−·09	−·19	−·01
10	−·03	·14	·13	−·02	−·05	·07	−·14	−·07
11	·2	·21	·14	·01	·07	−·02	−·14	−·06
12	·34	·2	·07	·05	·16	−·01	−·11	·11
13	·22	·15	·34	·14	·16	·09	−·004	·03
14	·32	·27	·44	·09	·1	·11	·03	−·01
15	·31	·2	·28	·05	·04	·05	−·02	·01
16	·29	·32	·4	−·01	·08	·02	·01	·01
17	·21	·38	·54	·13	·14	·19	·07	·06
18	·15	·34	·6	·25	·15	·17	·15	·12
19		·11	·17	·02	·05	·09	−·1	·01
20			·56	·22	·19	·15	−·08	·05
21				·24	·25	·14	·03	·01
22					·86	·85	·66	·7
23						·8	·64	·68
24							·71	·74
25								·53

1 which are patently qualitatively similar, are selected but so too are Groups 4 and 3 which, as Table 20 indicates, are, just as clearly, qualitatively dissimilar. The sets of scores from which these apparently discrepant significant relationships were derived were examined with a view to detecting the source of these anomalies. As the scores

for Groups 4 and 3 presented in Table 22 illustrate, this proved to be the large number of subjects with negative scores on both groups. A correlation coefficient significant at the ·01 level can, thus, indicate that groups have common negative, rather than positive, characteristics. Since shared negative characteristics are irrelevant to the task in hand, methods must be sought for counteracting their effect.

A possible solution to the difficulty would be to use a much higher criterion level in the search for close, qualitative associations between groups. A positive correlation of ·7 or greater suggests itself since this is the point at which 50 or more per cent of the variance is accounted for. There is, however, no guarantee that this expedient would result in the rejection of all positive correlations founded on common negative scores and it is, also, of an undesirably arbitrary nature. An alternative, less arbitrary procedure which could be adopted at an earlier stage in the calculation of the correlation coefficients would be to remove from the covariance, Σxy, the portion derived from pairs of negative scores. This however, involves tampering with a standard statistical procedure. A third approach to the problem which avoids this pitfall and, also, has the merit of comparative simplicity could be based on the sums of values available for all item-category pairs on each group rather than on the individual subjects' scores on the groups. The first step in this procedure would be to count the number of item-category pairs with a positive sum of values on each group separately. The number of item-category pairs with a positive sum of values on both groups would then be calculated and expressed as a proportion of these totals. If either or both of the proportions exceeds 0·5, the group yielding the smaller proportion (i.e. the group which accounts for the greater proportion of the other) would be regarded as subsuming the other group and the structural picture would, accordingly, be simplified by discarding the 'satellite' group.

To clarify the procedure involved and to demonstrate its superiority to the straight correlational approach for this purpose, it will be applied to the case of Groups 4 and 3 already adduced as an illustration of a significant positive correlation based on negative scores. The total number of item-category pairs with a positive sum of values is 59 in Group 4 and 39 in Group 3. The total number of item-category pairs with a positive sum of values on both groups is six. These totals yield proportions of 0·102 (6/59) for Group 4 and 0·15 (6/39) for Group 3 and, accordingly, the degree of qualitative association between the groups would not be regarded as sufficient to justify structural simplification by dropping one of them. The relative simplicity and apparent effectiveness of this approach to determining

TABLE 22: *Subjects' scores on Groups 4 and 3 illustrating the effect of pairs of negative scores on the correlation coefficient*

		GROUPS			
4	3	4	3	4	3
1·98	−5·93	−7·00	−15·41	29·26	−13·93
15·61	−14·06	−12·28	−16·33	19·36	−14·31
−15·44	−8·05	−12·28	−16·33	9·72	−11·28
−18·79	−8·40	·41	−16·32	17·89	−5·92
−17·11	15·95	14·22	−13·93	24·55	−14·59
−7·00	−12·63	−8·07	−13·11	19·60	−14·67
19·63	−7·85	−11·35	−15·81	30·47	−13·91
−13·23	−11·45	−12·28	−16·33	15·52	1·13
6·54	−10·54	12·88	−14·94	−·48	4·34
10·88	−14·07	−12·28	−16·33	5·58	−12·24
19·73	−12·80	8·62	−15·67	19·56	−5·90
−19·65	−7·66	−1·17	−16·14	−18·88	−8·74
−19·61	−6·84	−8·18	−14·65	−20·35	−8·86
−9·38	6·51	12·71	−15·49	−20·36	−8·55
−17·67	−8·00	−12·28	−16·33	−11·18	−11·98
−15·39	−7·05	14·14	−15·13	23·37	−12·42
−13·11	−13·62	−12·28	−16·33	−4·54	−9·65
−7·59	−1·65	−12·28	−16·33	−18·18	−8·15
−7·34	−2·58	−12·03	14·33	−19·16	·11
16·27	−14·22	−11·79	−14·05	−20·62	−8·91
−15·78	−6·48	19·92	−15·32	−19·10	−9·23
−6·44	3·63	5·21	−3·90	−18·40	−8·51
10·04	21·08	16·68	−14·89	16·55	−13·80
−11·11	−15·70	−10·27	−16·09	7·04	−6·35
15·01	−4·84	10·41	−11·52	−6·19	158·81
−11·09	−4·80	19·38	−13·68	87·54	−8·61
−9·29	−13·83	21·95	−14·66	−8·87	−3·92

the nature of the interrelationships between groups seem to justify further exploration of its potential in later work.

Investigation of the sequence of development

Three main assumptions underlay the decision to adopt correlational analysis as a means of exploring the relationship between groups on the developmental dimension. It was assumed that a significant positive correlation ($p < ·01$) between the sets of subjects' scores on any two groups would indicate that the responses comprising the groups were developmentally aspects of the same level. A similarly significant negative correlation, on the other hand, would suggest that one of the groups followed the other in the developmental sequence. In such cases it was hoped that a comparison of their pattern of relationships with the remaining groups would indicate the order of their occurrence. A zero order correlation could be interpreted in two ways. It could either indicate that groups occur in the same developmental sequence but are not adjacent to each other or that they belong to separate, parallel 'strands' of development. Here again it was hoped that the overall structural picture would indicate which of these alternatives appeared to be the more plausible.

In practice, the truth or falsehood of these assumptions became academic questions as the nature of the results derived from the correlational analysis (see Table 21) did not permit them to be tested. The above discussion of the shortcomings of correlational analysis as an approach to the problem of structural simplification has already dwelt on the dangers of regarding significant positive correlations as indications of a close, qualitative association between groups. The deleterious effect of the common negative scores is no less fatal to the usefulness of positive correlations as indicators that groups belong to the same developmental level. The total absence of significant negative correlations ($p < ·01$) from both the first and second verbal post-tests results, also, removes any possibility of detecting developmental sequences on this basis. This dearth, like the spurious high positive correlations, may be attributable to the effect of common negative scores. It is, therefore, possible that the adoption of the procedure involving the exclusion of the portion of the covariance attributable to pairs of negative scores would result in the appearance of significant negative correlations between groups which previously yielded non-significant negative, zero order or even positive correlations. This approach again involves tampering with a standard statistical procedure and rather than expending effort in an attempt to produce a viable method based on correlational analysis it was decided that a more worthwhile aim for the present study would be to attempt to devise an entirely new technique for assessing the developmental implications of the Brimer analysis.

The starting point for the new procedure was not, as in the case of the correlational analysis, ·the groups obtained by applying the Brimer analysis separately to the results of the two verbal post-tests. It was hypothesized that, rather than detecting groups and then attempting to divine the developmental relationships between them, a more promising line of attack would be to try to derive groups which were themselves indicative of lines of development. To this end the

F

records of the subjects' responses on the first and second verbal post-tests were combined. The resulting block of data comprising a profile of the responses of 81 children on 283 possible item-category pairs was submitted to the Brimer analysis and passed through the stages outlined above. The analysis of the combined data produced 40 groups.

Lines of Development Underlying Groups

The groups obtained were in accord with the hypothesis underlying the line of approach adopted in that all but two of them contain item-category pairs from both post-tests and, thus, can be regarded as indicative of lines of development. An overall picture of the sequence and structure of development could be derived from the grouped data on a subjective impression basis, but in view of the large number of groups and the complex nature of many of them, such a procedure would inevitably result in conflicting interpretations. The adoption of this approach would also be completely opposed to the emphasis in the present study on the need to devise objective methods wherever possible. Accordingly, a generally applicable technique must be sought which is capable of objectively divining the main lines of development underlying the detailed composition of a large number of groups. The remainder of this chapter will be devoted to an account of one attempt to cope with this task.

Like the Brimer analysis itself, the basic concern of the technique adopted is the frequency of co-occurrence of item-category pairs. Two types of such co-occurrence within groups are regarded as being of particular significance in detecting the course of development. If A1 and B1 are two item-category pairs on the first post-test and A2 and B2 are item-category pairs on the second post-test belonging to the same two response categories, the co-occurrence of A1 and B2 in a group is regarded as an instance favouring the view that the response category of which B2 is an example supercedes the response category of which AI is a member in the course of development. If there are no groups in which B1 and A2 co-occur, the developmental sequence A———→B is accepted. If, however, contradictory instances favouring a B———→A sequence are found, recourse is had to a quantitative procedure.

The total number of co-occurrences of the type A1 and B2 and of the type B1 and A2 are calculated. The manner in which this is done is best illustrated by an example. In Group 3, as Table 23 indicates, there are six Fail + Descriptive Explanation item-category pairs from the first post-test and a single Pass: Reversibility item-category

TABLE 23: *Group from analysis of combined verbal post-test one and verbal post-test two data* (A bracketed number 2 under the Item heading indicates responses from the second post-test.)

ITEM No.	RESPONSE CATEGORY	PASS (P) FAIL (F)	+, − OR C	COVERED OR UNCOVERED	SUM OF DIFFERENCES	DIAGONAL ELEMENT
1.	Fail + descriptive explanation	F	C	U	9·53	·99
2.	Reversibility	P	+	U	9·53	·99
8.	Fail + descriptive explanation	F	C	C	9·53	·99
12.	Co-ordination of relations	P	C	U	9·53	·99
6.	Fail + descriptive explanation	F	C	U	7·39	·98
3.	Reversibility	P	+	U	7·04	·98
4.	Fail + descriptive explanation	F	C	C	7·04	·98
13.	Fail + evidence of co-ordination of relations	F	C	U	7·39	·98
16.	Fail + descriptive explanation	F	C	C	7·04	·98
4 (2).	Addition–subtraction wrongly adduced	F	C	C	5·94	·95
5.	Fail + descriptive explanation	F	C	U	5·84	·96
16 (2).	Fail + descriptive explanation	F	C	U	6·20	·96
11 (2).	Fail—'Don't Know' response	F	C	C	3·60	·89
18 (2).	Reversibility	P	C	U	3·17	·85

Group 3

pair from the second post-test. This is regarded as providing six instances supporting the view that the Fail + Descriptive Explanation response category is succeeded by the Pass: Reversibility response category in the sequence of development. The group also contains two Pass: Reversibility item-category pairs from the first post-test and one Fail + Descriptive Explanation item-category pair from the second post-test. There are, thus, two contradictory instances favouring a Pass: Reversibility——→Fail + Descriptive Explanation sequence. The simple rule adopted for deciding the issue is that the sequence of categories with the larger total of co-occurrences over all of the groups (i.e. more than 50 per cent of the occasions on which the categories are grouped together favour this order) is accepted as being likely to be closer to the developmental reality. In the event of the two co-occurrence totals being equal, this is regarded as an indication that the response categories in question may be linked aspects of the same developmental level.

These simple working rules may seem to ignore plausible alternative interpretations of the results. It could be argued, for example, that a sequence of categories with a lower total of co-occurrences represents the true course of development and that the lower total is simply due to the two tests being carried out at points in the period of transition before the ultimate predominance of the more advanced category becomes apparent. Similarly, equal co-occurrence totals could be regarded as representing the mid-point in a transition phase leading to the supercession of one response category by another rather than as indicating that they belong to the same developmental level. The adoption of the two rules outlined as a working basis does not seem unreasonable, however, when it is remembered that the relationship between two categories is not viewed in isolation but must fit into a wider network of relationships with a number of other categories. If this process of reconciliation indicates that one of the alternative hypotheses outlined above appears to be more in keeping with the overall structure of relations, appropriate modifications can be made. A set of longitudinal data without the shortcomings of the results of the present study would, also, normally comprise records of subjects' responses derived from more than two occasions of testing and this would diminish the likelihood of misinterpreting the outcome of a transition phase of development.

When the technique described above was applied to the forty groups detected by the analysis of the combined first and second verbal post-test data the co-occurrence totals presented in Table 24 were obtained. The frequencies in brackets represent the corres-

TABLE 24: *Co-occurrence totals derived from 40 groups obtained by analysing combined first and second verbal post-test data*

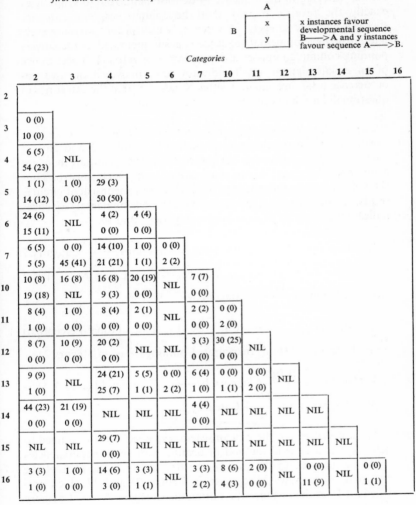

	2	3	4	5	6	7	10	11	12	13	14	15	16
2													
3	0 (0) / 10 (0)												
4	6 (5) / 54 (23)	NIL											
5	1 (1) / 14 (12)	1 (0) / 0 (0)	29 (3) / 50 (50)										
6	24 (6) / 15 (11)	NIL	4 (2) / 0 (0)	4 (4) / 0 (0)									
7	6 (5) / 5 (5)	0 (0) / 45 (41)	14 (10) / 21 (21)	1 (0) / 1 (1)	0 (0) / 2 (2)								
10	10 (8) / 19 (18)	16 (8) / NIL	16 (8) / 9 (3)	20 (19) / 0 (0)	NIL	7 (7) / 0 (0)							
11	8 (4) / 1 (0)	1 (0) / 0 (0)	8 (4) / 0 (0)	2 (1) / 0 (0)	NIL	2 (2) / 0 (0)	0 (0) / 2 (0)						
12	8 (7) / 0 (0)	10 (9) / 0 (0)	20 (2) / 0 (0)	NIL	NIL	3 (3) / 0 (0)	30 (25) / 0 (0)	NIL					
13	9 (9) / 1 (0)	NIL	24 (21) / 25 (7)	5 (5) / 1 (1)	0 (0) / 2 (2)	6 (4) / 1 (0)	0 (0) / 1 (1)	0 (0) / 2 (0)	NIL				
14	44 (23) / 0 (0)	21 (19) / 0 (0)	NIL	NIL	NIL	4 (4) / 0 (0)	NIL	NIL	NIL	NIL			
15	NIL	NIL	29 (7) / 0 (0)	NIL	NIL	NIL	NIL	NIL	NIL	NIL	NIL		
16	3 (3) / 1 (0)	1 (0) / 0 (0)	14 (6) / 3 (0)	3 (3) / 1 (1)	NIL	3 (3) / 2 (2)	8 (6) / 4 (3)	2 (0) / 0 (0)	NIL	0 (0) / 11 (9)	NIL	0 (0) / 1 (1)	

Diagram legend (top right):

A

B | x
B | y

x instances favour developmental sequence B———>A and y instances favour sequence A———>B.

Categories

ponding totals obtained by considering only the conservation items in the two post-tests. To facilitate interpretation of the developmental structure derived from these totals by applying the working rules already discussed, the system of coding adopted in Tables 23 and 24 has been devised. If read by columns, the presence of a one in a cell indicates that the row response category appears to succeed the column category in the sequence of development. A zero symbolizes exactly the reverse, namely that the column response category succeeds the row category. A category which occurs comparatively late in the developmental sequence is easily identified as the corresponding column comprises a large number of zeros. The occurrence of an equals sign in a cell indicates cases in which the two co-occurrence totals are equal. A letter N indicates that the categories in question did not co-occur in any of the groups.

Problem of Apparently Inconsistent Developmental Sequences

The picture of development presented by Tables 25 and 26 is a comparatively complex one but before discussing its import there are a number of internal inconsistencies within it which must be considered. These are indicated by the presence of inconsistent circular triads. As the following examples of circular developmental sequences indicate these appear to stem from Categories 7 and 10.

1. Category 3 (Pass: Addition and Subtraction) $\xrightarrow{0/45}$ Category 7 (Pass: One to One Correspondence) $\xrightarrow{5/6}$ Category 2 (Pass: Accurate Counting $\xrightarrow{0/10}$ Category 3.

2. Category 2 $\xrightarrow{10/19}$ Category 10 (Fail: Gobal-Perceptual) $\xrightarrow{0/2}$ Category 11 (Fail: Inaccurate Counting) $\xrightarrow{1/8}$ Category 2.

3. Category 2 $\xrightarrow{10/19}$ Category 10 $\xrightarrow{0/1}$ Category 13 (Fail + Descriptive Explanation) $\xrightarrow{1/9}$ Category 2.

The antecedents of these inconsistent sequences were examined to determine if a general method of dealing with such inconsistencies could be devised. In the case of the first example the root of the apparent anomaly was discovered in Groups 23 and 29 which provided all 45 of the instances favouring the Category 3——→Category 7 sequence. An examination of these groups indicated that the relationship between the categories was not of the A1——→ B2 type as the co-occurrence totals might suggest, but took the form A1——→ B2 A2. Both groups comprised as many Category 3 responses from the second post-test as from the first post-test and, accordingly, although the relationship might indicate the beginning of the replacement

TABLE 25: *Developmental relationship between response categories based on combined first and second verbal post-test data*

	2	3	4	5	6	7	10	11	12	13	14	15	16
2		0	0	0	1	1	0	1	1	1	1	N	1
3	1		N	1	N	0	N	1	1	N	1	N	1
4	1	N		0	1	0	1	1	1	0	N	1	1
5	1	0	1		1	=	1	1	N	1	N	N	1
6	0	N	0	0		0	N	N	N	0	N	N	N
7	0	1	1	=	1		1	1	1	1	1	N	1
10	1	N	0	0	N	0		0	1	0	N	N	1
11	0	0	0	0	N	0	1		N	0	N	N	1
12	0	0	0	N	N	0	0	N		N	N	N	N
13	0	N	1	0	1	0	1	1	N		N	N	0
14	0	0	N	N	N	0	N	N	N	N		N	N
15	N	N	0	N	N	N	N	N	N	N	N		0
16	0	0	0	0	N	0	0	0	N	1	N	1	

Key to tables 25 and 26

2. Pass: accurate counting.
3. Pass: addition and subtraction.
4. Pass: reversibility.
5. Pass: co-ordination of relations.
6. Pass: inaccurate counting.
7. Pass: one-to-one correspondence.
10. Fail: global-perceptual.

11. Fail: inaccurate counting.
12. Fail, but evidence of accurate counting.
13. Fail, + a descriptive explanation.
14. Fail, due to verbal features.
15. Fail: co-ordination of relations.
16. Fail: addition and subtraction.

TABLE 26: *Developmental relationship between response categories based on conservation items only in combined first and second verbal post-test data*

	2	3	4	5	6	7	10	11	12	13	14	15	16
2		N	0	0	0	=	0	1	1	1	1	N	1
3	N		N	N	N	0	N	N	1	N	1	N	N
4	1	N		0	1	0	1	1	1	1	N	1	1
5	1	N	1		1	0	1	1	N	1	N	N	1
6	1	N	0	0		0	N	N	N	0	N	N	N
7	=	1	1	1	1		1	1	1	1	1	N	1
10	1	N	0	0	N	0		N	1	0	N	N	1
11	0	N	0	0	N	0	N		N	N	N	N	N
12	0	0	0	N	N	0	0	N		N	N	N	N
13	0	N	0	0	1	0	1	N	N		N	N	0
14	0	0	N	N	N	0	N	N	N	N		N	N
15	N	N	0	N	N	N	N	N	N	N	N		0
16	0	N	0	0	N	0	0	N	N	1	N	1	

of Category 3 responses by Category 7 responses, this cannot be asserted on the basis of the available evidence which could, equally well, be regarded as indicating that the categories are linked aspects of the same developmental level. The problem remains unsolved.

The inconsistent circular triads emanating from Category 10 do not qualify for the same comments as those stemming from Category 7 since the crucial group in both examples, Group 10 does not conform to the $A1 \longrightarrow B2\ A2$ pattern. In an attempt to detect the source of the inconsistency all the item-category pairs which were not members of Group 10 but had a positive sum of values on it were included in a re-calculation of the co-occurrence totals. The margin of 112 to 90 in favour of the Category 2 $\longrightarrow$ Category 10 developmental sequence was narrower than that of 19 to 10 obtained when only the responses in the group were considered but still perpetuated the existence of the inconsistent circular triads. The scores of the individual subjects on Group 10 were, also, examined. It was found that only 15 children had a positive score on the group and only three had a score greater than the sum of the three highest sums of values of item-category pairs in the group. This indicates that the line of development represented by Group 10 is only followed by a small minority and can, up to a point, be regarded as idiosyncratic. It does not, however, provide a solution to the problem of coping with the inconsistent developmental sequences.

Overall picture of development provided by analysis

As it is extremely difficult to derive a conception of the complex network of interrelationships between categories which constitutes the overall developmental picture, Figures XIII and XIV (see the inside front and back covers of this book) represent an attempt to translate the data represented in Tables 25 and 26 into a graphical form. Before any discussion of the resulting graphs it must be reiterated that there is no implication that any tentative conclusions reached have any relevance to the 'normal' course of development of conservation of number or to the behaviour of subjects other than those treated in a fashion similar to the children in the present study.

In constructing these graphical representations of the developmental structure which emerges from the analysis, the unsolved problem of dealing with the circular inconsistent triads was tackled at a superficial level by applying a simple working rule. This operated on the two categories from whose inconsistent relationship the circular triad sprang, e.g. Categories 2 and 10 in the second and third examples quoted above. The numbers of inconsistent relationships produced with the other 11 categories when the sequences Category 2———→ Category 10 and Category 10———→ Category 2 are adopted, were computed and compared. The sequence producing the smallest total of inconsistent relationships was then incorporated into the structure. In the example, the respective totals were 3 and 0 and, accordingly, the sequence Category 10———→ Category 2 was preferred.

Despite the 'ad hoc' nature of the procedure the developmental structures produced by this expedient are consistent with a number of general and detailed comments in the literature on the course of development. They do, for example, have much in common with von Bertalanffy's (1960, pp. 74-6) suggestion that the psychobiological development of the child may be of an equifinal nature in which equifinal phases are reached from different starting points and in different ways, and maintained over a time till a change in conditions —external or internal— causes a new development in the system and brings it on the way by diverse routes towards another equifinal phase. The position occupied in both graphs by Categories 2, 4 and 7, for example, is consistent with this hypothesis. This viewpoint is obviously related to Piaget's concept of successive equilibria stages or levels but departs from it in introducing the idea of a variety of routes, rather than a single path, from level to level.

In commenting on the results of her acceleration study of number concepts, Churchill (1958) maintained that Piaget's theory of stages in the growth of mental operations was too rigid to accommodate the individual differences among the children. Her evidence suggests that experience of an appropriate kind may result in the acceleration of the growth process and, also, that what makes a significant contribution to mental structure in one child may not do so for another for whom another kind of experience seems to be more formative. Qualitative correspondence, founded on the perceptual features of the situation, could be as fully operational in character as numerical correspondence. Linking this finding with the fact that some of the children at the fully operational 'stage three' tended to use numerical correspondence and others qualitative correspondence throughout the tests, Churchill suggests that this may not be a chance difference but may, rather, reflect a fundamental personality difference. The structure of the graphs in the present study are consistent with Churchill's views on the complex nature of the variations in development between individuals and, also, lend support to her suggestion that some children consistently adopt a perceptual or numerical approach throughout the developmental sequence. The Category 15———→ Category 4———→ Category 5 and the Category 11———→ Category 2———→ Category 3 'routes' are two of a number of threads of development in Figures XIII and XIV which can be unequivocally assigned to the perceptual and numerical approaches respectively.

If these aspects of the graph structures can be viewed as representing departures from the Piagetian account of development, the finding that the Pass: Addition-Subtraction category is the culmination of all the routes in both graphs, including those of a perceptual nature, is in accordance with his stated expectations (Piaget, 1960b, p.112). He contends, however, that the addition-subtraction explanation is founded on a prior appreciation of reversibility and cannot appear without this underlying factor. If, despite the notorious unreliability of verbal report at this age level, the explanations of the children in the present study are accepted as indications of their methods of tackling the problems posed, there would appear to be no inevitability about the Reversibility———→ Addition-Subtraction sequence. Piaget, however, would undoubtedly maintain that the reversibility stage is undergone regardless of the type of verbal explanations offered and, in any case, as was clearly stated in the definition of the Pass: Reversibility category, there is no claim that it has the same logical implications as Piaget's concept of reversibility.

The assertion that the reversibility stage may be undergone without the emergence of any observable verbal evidence, once again, raises the question of Piaget's view of the relationship between the operative, structural and the symbolic, mediational aspects of thought. As indicated in Chapter Four, he makes an important distinction between them and emphasizes the predominance of the former over the latter. This viewpoint suggests a line of argument which might go some way towards reconciling the Genevan account of intellectual development with the developmental picture derived from the graphs obtained in the present study and from Churchill's findings. The alternative developmental routes characteristic of the graphs could be attributed to variations between individuals in their preferred symbolic modes. This expedient is consistent with Piagetian theory since, unlike the Harvard group, he has never asserted that the figurative, symbolic aspect of thought exhibits a unified sequence of development with a set progression of clearly differentiated stages. These features are confined to the development of the operative, structural aspect and although there is constant interaction between the operative and figurative, symbolic functions the latter lacks the continuous development characteristic of the former. The various types of symbolic activity cannot be said to develop one from the other in the fashion of the successive, operative levels of thought. From this orientation the alternative perceptual and numerical threads of development depicted in Figures XIII and XIV, for example, can be viewed as belonging purely to the figurative, symbolic aspect and as being typical of its lack of unified development. If, in contrast, the structural, as opposed to the figurative, aspect of thought is regarded as following the rigid sequence of development which Piaget has outlined the apparent conflict of the experimental evidence with the Genevan position is resolved. It should be mentioned that at the time of writing in 1971 there are indications that Piaget is engaged in a major revision of his theory. The available evidence (Celérier, 1972) suggests that the modifications are introducing a much greater flexibility into his account of development and bringing it closer to the 'liberal' view of the concept of stages and the multilinear picture of development presented in the present study. A more detailed discussion of the on-going modifications in Piaget's theoretical position will be offered in the next chapter.

The discussion of the implications of the two graphs will be terminated at this point. It must be reiterated that the suspect nature of the data on which they are founded renders the speculations which have been based on them perilous to say the least. The general approach to the problem of stages of which they form a part is also, clearly, crude. A description of it has been offered in the present chapter purely on the grounds that it may assist in highlighting some of the problems involved in interpreting the developmental import of the results obtained by submitting sets of longitudinal data to the Brimer analysis. It has, also involved gross simplification of the issues since, for example, it has not considered the significance of response categories which are not full members of a group but have a high degree of association with it or attempted to determine the number of children who appear to follow each of the developmental routes.[1] The challenge of applying the full power of graph theory to this type of data, also, remains to be accepted although there are indications in the work of Kiss (1968, 1969), for example, that the prognosis for such an approach in this area is good. It can only be hoped that if these features are considered in further work on this theme, the results may be the discovery of solutions to

[1]Since the completion of the present study, a modified version of the Brimer analysis has been produced. It includes an additional procedure to prevent the proliferation of closely associated, independent groups.

the difficulties already encountered rather than the further proliferation of unsolved problems.

In short, it is evident that the construction of a procedure for
divining the developmental significance of results obtained by means
of the Brimer analysis presents many unsolved problems. This is
inevitable in an approach directed at dealing with longitudinal
data in its full, qualitative richness. The extent to which the Brimer
method appears to be successful in finding the patterns or groupings
of responses essentially determined by sets of qualitative data
without invoking preconceived theoretical biases in any direction,
certainly renders further studies to explore its potential in the
developmental area imperative. The first aim of such enterprises
should be the collection of longitudinal data on the course of development free from the shortcomings imposed on the results of the present
tudy by its attempt to tackle the acceleration issue.

CHAPTER SEVEN

Present Trends and Future Prospects

As INDICATED at the outset, the present volume had its genesis in a wide ranging survey of research on conceptualization in the period 1955-63. Although there is no intention of attempting to emulate this breadth of coverage it seems appropriate to devote this concluding chapter to viewing the results of the experimental investigation which has been described against the broader canvas of the research scene at the time of writing in 1971. At an organizational level this objective is relatively easily attained since both the general orientation of the experimental work and the specific issues tackled in it continue to attract the attention of research workers. Their retention of relevance despite the passage of time is to be attributed to the continuing dominance of Piaget in European developmental psychology, now undisputed for a decade, and to the dramatic rate of increase during the last five years in the volume of American research studies stimulated by his work. Since the twin problems of the existence of stages and the nature of the transition rule still provide the themes for the vast majority of experimental studies stimulated by aspects of Piaget's formulations, a successive treatment of these two issues will be adopted as the framework for a consideration of the import for the contemporary research scene of the experimental findings obtained in the present study.

The problem of stages in development
It will be recalled that a review of the theoretical and experimental literature in the period up to 1964 on the topic of stages was presented in Chapter One. The conclusion reached was that, confronted with the inconsistency and difficulty of the experimental data, there seemed to be two possible lines of action. The pursuit of exact developmental relations between inference patterns could be rejected, the inevitability of inconsistencies and individual variations in subjects' responses accepted and a consequent adjustment made in the criteria employed in identifying developmental stages. This was, of course, the starting point adopted in designing the experimental

approach to the problem in the present study. The alternative course of action involves the retention of the Piagetian view of stages with its emphasis on rigidly predictable developmental sequences and its disregard for individual differences. The goal of research conducted from this point of view is to definitively establish the truth or otherwise of Piaget's scheme by progressively refining methods until all variation in the data due to extraneous factors has been removed. The practical implications of this approach are exemplified in Smedslund's (1964) study aimed at determining the nature of the interrelations within a set of test items regarded as tapping specific aspects of Piaget's level of concrete reasoning. Since Smedslund has continued to figure among the trend setters in this research area a brief account of the major changes in his approach during the last five years will provide a convenient perspective from which to view the current situation.

The results of the 1964 investigation revealed that not one of the fourfold tables covering the relations between pairs of items contained an empty cell and, thus, none of the pairs of items exhibited the exact relationship with no exceptions which Smedslund regards as an important direct indication of the nature of the underlying psychological processes. Similarly there was no support for the hypothesis that there is a regular order of acquisition within the set of items. In interpreting these findings Smedslund did not regard them as evidence against the unitary nature of concrete reasoning but rather as indicative of the narrow situational scope of its acquisitions. Exact relations between inference patterns, he concluded, could only be discovered if goal objects (what the subject is instructed to attain) and percepts (processes depending on the momentary stimulus-inputs) were held rigidly constant.

His next series of experiments (Smedslund, 1966 b, c, d) utilized a task which was designed to do just this. Briefly, the technique involved the presentation of two collections with an equal number of elements. The child was told that the two collections were equal and his acceptance of their equality was checked and reinforced. The collections were hidden from his view under two equal boxes, and then one piece was added to or taken away from one of the collections. The child was asked whether the left collection now had more, whether the two collections were equal, or whether the right collection had more. The experimenter pointed to the boxes and the terms 'left' and 'right' were not used. Then the experiment proceeded with another addition or subtraction, the child's judgment was again requested, and so on. No item contained more than three successive operations and no difference larger than two elements was allowed between the two collections.

Contrary to Smedslund's expectations, even with this narrow task, exact relations between items proved to be a chimera. The results demonstrated that the same logical task-structure, with identical perceptual and conceptual contents, may yield radically different solution frequencies depending, for example, merely on position in the series of tasks or on the preceding relative frequency of operations on the two loci. The lesson to be learned from these and other findings, Smedslund (1966d) believes, is that the task must be analysed in much more detail than is provided by a mere description of its conventional logical structure. The consequences of the particular instructions given, the place of the item in the sequence of tasks, and the perceptual context at least, must be considered. The general problem involved is to determine exactly how the input is encoded by the subject, and what transformations occur between encoding and decoding. The objective task structure alone does not yield a valid description of the solution performance and it is necessary to diagnose the actual psychological processes in great detail, to obtain minute descriptions or well supported inferences about the actual sequence and content of the thinking processes.

The considerable intra and inter-individual variability encountered, even in the most well-controlled situations, is a great obstacle to making this exact diagnosis. The differences in error pattern from subject to subject indicate that the inter-individual variability stems partly from differences in processing routines. It is, therefore, clear that nothing meaningful will come out of a detailed analysis of average error frequencies. Consequently the research strategy must be shifted to an analysis of the performance of individual subjects. At this point the problem of intra-individual variability is encountered. Irrespective of the extent to which this variability stems from fluctuations in concentration or from continuous changes in processing routines it would seem appropriate to study the same individual for prolonged periods, in order to average out non-systematic variations and to reach some kind of asymptotic level, with stabilization of a particular set of routines. This, in Smedslund's opinion, appears to be the only passable route for future research, staying within the given type of deductive tasks and the given conceptual framework and it, undoubtedly, squarely confronts the researcher with the immense complexity of the human being as an intellectual instrument.

Smedslund's prescription for future action brings us face to face with the current situation. The desire to get to grips with the fine

grain of intellectual development as, for example, in intensive, longitudinal studies of the same individuals is spreading and there are indications that this movement is having two extremely important
results. It is leading workers in the Piagetian tradition to search for
instruments capable of representing the highly complex structures
likely to be derived from such detailed analysis. This in turn, is
stimulating a healthy 'anti-compartmentalist' interest in techniques
which have hitherto largely been confined to other specialist areas
within the psychological field, such as graph theory, information
theory, various forms of set theory and the methods of structural
linguistics. This tendency is in evidence at a time when there is an
equally healthy trend for workers outside the developmental orbit to
become increasingly intrigued by problems posed by the development
of thought processes. In the writer's opinion the most exciting and
potentially valuable example of this broadening of outlook is the
mounting interest in cognitive development being evinced by some of
the protagonists of the information processing approach since they
have at their disposal techniques well suited to dealing with complex
and detailed data. Some indication of the major features of their
position appears to be in order. The brief introduction which follows
is based on Reitman's (1965) excellent account of the information
processing approach and any reader desirous of a clearer and more
detailed exposition should refer to this source.

In recent years American psychologists have been spending an
increasing amount of time in examining the representations and
processes involved in cognitive activity. One of the most interesting
developments to date has been the emergence of the information
processing school led by Allan Newell and Herbert Simon (1961,
1972) and centred on Carnegie-Mellon University at Pittsburgh. In
its simplest terms, if one considers that each of us consists of receptors,
effectors and a control system for joining them, the information
processing approach involves concentrating on the control system
and avoiding most questions dealing with sensory and motor activities. Its protagonists attempt to explain the content and direction of
thought by postulating a control system consisting of a number of
memories which contain symbolized information and are inter-
connected by various ordering relations, a number of primitive
information processes which operate on the information in the
memories, and a well-defined set of rules for combining these primitive processes into whole programmes of processing. Typically they
collect extensive data from human subjects asked to 'think aloud'
while solving problems under laboratory conditions, submit the

protocols to a close analysis, then produce a flow chart and subsequently a computer program that will account for the behaviour observed in the data. Such a program is regarded as a theory of the system of psychological processes and structures underlying the behaviour and is held to have a status comparable to that of a theory framed in words or mathematical symbols.

It should be pointed out that the assertion that the appropriate way to describe thought is in terms of elementary information processes has nothing directly to do with computers. Indeed, the psychological literature can provide several examples of theorists who have produced explanations of thought which have much in common with the information processing approach and yet have made no reference to computers at all. One of the most interesting is de Groot's (1965) analysis of problem solving by chess players. His theory is based on the thought psychology of Selz, one of the successors of the Wurzburg school (Humphrey, 1963). More recently, Bruner (1965) in his work on concept attainment, used the term 'strategy'—derived from the theory of games—to describe a construct very similar to the Carnegie group's conception of a program.

Why do Newell, Simon and the others, then, trouble to write their programs in a computer language? What benefits are to be derived from running such programs on a computer? An answer to these questions has been provided by Reitman (1965). Three main advantages are claimed. In a theory stated verbally or mathematically it is all too easy to omit possibilities which ought to have been included and to produce mutual contradictions and ambiguity. Such inattention to detail is easily detected in a theory expressed as a computer program since any such internal inconsistencies will prevent the program from running.

The use of a computer program as a vehicle enables systems of psychological constructs to be stated and explored in a manner not possible with theories framed in words or mathematical terms. With verbal or mathematical models it is practically impossible to be sure that conclusions follow only from explicit assumptions and in no way depend on implicit assumptions entering informally into the argument. There can be no doubt that the conclusions obtained by running a computer program—however unexpected they may be— are founded exclusively on explicit assumptions. In addition, the computer will provide a complete trace of every step in the processing of the data. As a means of assessing the adequacy of the simulation, this can subsequently be compared with human protocols obtained in the same situation.

Above all, the adoption of computer simulation techniques by harnessing the immense potential of the computer as a symbol manipulating device enables the complex processes of thought to be tackled with a theorizing instrument capable of equal complexity. One of the most interesting effects of information processing research to date has been to make us revise upward our estimates of the intrinsic complexity of the psychological systems being studied. For example, the more important features of Newell's General Problem Solver program (Newell, 1963; Ernst and Newell, 1969) which fairly successfully simulates the behaviour of individuals in tackling logical and algebraic problems, require a description of over 100 pages. This revision may, in turn, lead us to reconsider just what we are after in our efforts to provide theories or models of psychological functions. We tend to set our goals in terms of the physical sciences and seek elegant general laws. We may be better advised to turn to the biological sciences for our model and think in terms of theories involving the description of complex structures and functions.

To sum up, information processing models enable us to think about and represent functions involved in extremely complex human activities in a form that is precise, objective and as detailed as we wish to have it. They also allow us to generate behavioural consequences from a computer, and thus to study the strict implications of our theories. No previous approach is remotely comparable in any of these respects.

Information processing and developmental problems

The application of the information processing approach to the developmental problems posed by Piaget's work could well provide the methodological breakthrough which the area so badly needs. There are numerous indications that this potentially fruitful combination is being achieved. Simon has read widely in Piaget's work and a few of the ablest of his young disciples are devoting a considerable proportion of their time to devising possible applications of information processing techniques to intellectual development issues. A reciprocal interest in computer simulation and information processing methodology is currently being evinced by some of the leading research workers in the area of cognitive development. One of the most interesting examples of this trend is to be found in a recent paper by Flavell and Wohlwill (1969). Since they also outline a potentially valuable new approach to the problem of dealing with the apparently inconsistent data characteristic of studies of intellectual development, their views will be accorded an extended treatment.

Flavell and Wohlwill maintain that the distinction between competence and performance employed by Chomsky in his work on psycholinguistics may prove to be useful in considering some of the major issues in cognitive development. The nature of the distinction is illustrated by means of a comparison of the performance of three hypothetical subjects on a range of tasks involving transitive inferences of the type $X < Y$ and $Y < Z$ logically implies $X < Z$. Child A (age four) fails to exhibit anything resembling transitive inference on any of the tasks even with the help of brief training or prompting. Child B (age eight) gives clear evidence of transitive inference on some of the tasks but not on others. Training produces success on some of the tasks previously failed but no improvement in performance on the more complex tasks. Child C (age 14) applies the transitivity rule correctly, without any training, in almost all of the problems presented to him. In terms of the competence-performance distinction child A is viewed as differing from both B and C in that there is no evidence that a transitivity rule is, as yet, part of his cognitive competence whereas it must be included in the competence descriptions of B and C. The difference between B and C, in contrast, is explained in terms of the performance system, i.e. the processes by which the subject transforms the task data into suitable coded form, accesses and utilizes the functional equivalent of the transitivity equation, and so on. Child B has the transitivity rule in his competence repertoire but his performance system is unable to access and use it in all of the situations where it is appropriate. Child C's performance system is not characterized by these deficiences and, consequently, he does not exhibit such limitations on the transfer and generalization of the transitivity rule. In short, the competence-performance approach does not ignore or underplay the evident difference between B and C but asserts that it is not the same *kind* of capacity difference as that which distinguishes A and B.

Competence-performance analysis is not presented by Flavell and Wohlwill as an immediate panacea for the current difficulties of research on cognitive development. They are well aware that it brings its own quota of problems in its train. The assessment of the state of a child's competence system at any given point in development is, for example, fraught with difficulty. Since any conclusions must be reached on the basis of overt performance, how can we be sure that we are confronted with a genuine instance of the application of a particular cognitive algorithm like the transitivity rule? This raises, in a new context, all the unresolved methodological questions posed in the consideration of the relative merits of the verbal and non-verbal approaches in Chapters One and Five. In seeking to detect that a child possesses a specific competence item efforts must be made to remove any 'noise' from the performance system which may mask its presence by causing the child to fail the task. This, however, introduces the danger that the process of simplifying the demands of the task on the performance system may result in an overestimate since it ceases to demand functioning at the appropriate competence level and is, thus, useless for the purpose in view. The relative faults and failings of the non-verbal pre-test and the non-verbal post-tests in the present study provide ample evidence of how attempts to avoid over-estimation of subjects' competence by increasing the procedural complexity of tasks may raise the demands on the children's performance systems to a level at which an underestimate of their competence is highly likely.

Despite these methodological problems, Flavell and Wohlwill assert that the competence-performance distinction is a real one which may provide new and profitable ways of looking at traditional issues in cognitive developmental theory. An analysis of cognitive development, in their view, must be guided by some conception of what this development successively precipitates and any such conception should incorporate a competence-performance distinction. They believe that an abstract competence description of what the child knows and can do, at any level of maturity, will be an extremely long and complicated affair. Similarly, the performance model representing how this knowledge is actually stored, accessed and used by a human subject will be at least as complex in structure and function as the most powerful and flexible computer system currently envisaged. In general, simple models of human cognition just will not do since, regardless of their seeming advantages when it comes to explanation and operational definition, they appear certain to be at best incomplete and at worst erroneous.

Viewed from this standpoint, intellectual development essentially consists of ontogenetic change in the content and organization of highly intricate 'programs'. Flavell and Wohlwill seek to amplify this statement by listing some of the contents and characteristics which must be attributed to these programs. Most importantly they must comprise the child's stored information about self and world. This may be as well defined as the early concept of object permanence and the later conservations or as nebulous and non-specific as the fact that other minds exist and that this implies a multiplicity of cognitive-perceptual perspectives. The information in the child's program can be as specifiable as a concrete concept and as ineffable as a pervasive world-view. An adequate model of what he is and has at a given point in cognitive growth must take account of both kinds of information. It must, also, specify what the child knows and how this information is represented and organized. Finally, the program must incorporate the child's innate and acquired procedures for extracting, processing and utilizing information from both the permanent-store and the current environmental input.

Flavell and Wohlwill's model of the formation of stages

What are the implications of the competence-performance distinction and of Flavell and Wohlwill's general orientation for the stages problem? They have attempted to make these explicit by providing a general model for the analysis of the formation of stages of intelligence. This is based on a distinction made between two determinants of the child's performance in a cognitive task. These, in turn, are clearly derived from the competence-performance distinction and comprise, on the one hand, the rules, structures, or 'mental operations' embodied in the task and, on the other, the actual mechanisms required for processing the input and the output.

Three parameters which, it is asserted, jointly determine a child's performance are specified. The first of these, P_a, is the probability that a given operation has become fully established and is functional in a particular child. To account, for example, for children vacillating between conservation and non-conservation and for the abundance of alternative evidence of instability in their performance it is assumed that, during the period of transition from preoperational to operational thought, operations have a probabilistic character. This is expressed by according to P_a a range of values changing from 0 in the preoperational period to 1·0 when the operation has become established.

P_b, the second parameter, is an attribute of the task. It represents the likelihood for any given task that the necessary operation, if functional in the child, will in fact be called into play and its end product translated into the desired output. The value of this factor, which is also regarded as varying between 0 and 1·0, is determined by a large number of factors related to task difficulty. These comprise, for example, the amount of irrelevant information from which the relevant information has to be abstracted and the size of the information load placed on the child in dealing with the problem.

The influence of these task-related variables clearly varies with the age of the child. This is the reason for introducing the third parameter k, or more particularly its complement, $1-k$, as a power to which P_b is raised. The parameter expresses the weight that the P_b corresponding to a particular task carries for a given child, depending on his ability to abstract the information required to utilize a particular operation and to code and process information generally. It is assumed that k varies from 0, at a relatively early phase in the establishment of an operation, to an ideal of 1·0 when the stage has become fully consolidated. The influence of P_b, when raised to the power of $(1-k)$, is, accordingly, expected to decrease progressively during this period.

Flavell and Wohlwill summarize the form of the interaction of the three parameters in the following equation

$$P(+)=P_a \times P_b{}^{(1-k)}$$

This indicates the probability of a given child, characterized by particular values of P_a and k, solving a task with a particular value of P_b. On the basis of this equation, they describe the formation of a new cognitive structure in terms of a four phase process. In the initial phase the child lacks the operation in question, $P_a=0$, and he fails all of the problems which require it for their solution. This gives way to a transitional stage during which P_a changes from 0 to 1·0 while k is assumed to remain equal to 0, or close to it. As a result $P(+)=P_a \times P_b$ and the child still fails most of the tasks based on the operation. If, for example, $P_a=0·5$, for a task of medium difficulty for which $P_b=0·5$ then $P(+)=0·25$. The child must still be considered pre-operational and his performance will display the oscillations and intermediary forms of reasoning characteristic of this transitional period. The third phase is one of stabilization and consolidation. The operation has now become functional and $P_a=1·0$ but success still varies with the demands placed on the child by the particular task, i.e. the value of P_b for that task. The contribution of this factor progressively decreases during the phase as $1-k$ diminishes from 1·0 towards an ideal state of 0. With the advent of the final period $P_b=1·0$ and $k=1·0$ and the child is able to bring the operation to bear on the problem successfully, regardless of the situational and task variables involved. In practice Flavell and Wohlwill presume that k always falls short of 1·0, even at the most advanced levels. Unless P_a is very low, however, due to the task difficulty being very high, the expectation of success, $P(+)$, will still be close to 1·0.

With this four-phase model of development Flavell and Wohlwill offer a new way of coping with the apparently inconsistent performance data obtained in studies of the stages issue. Instead of attributing the inconsistency to extraneous factors and attempting to remove it by further refinement of experimental methods they have incorporated the situational and individual variables from which it springs into their theory by means of the P_b and k parameters. The four phases outline the changing nature of the inter-task relations to be expected during the course of the development of a stage and consistency in performance across tasks takes on the rôle of an ideal end product.

The extent to which this new approach represents a real advance as opposed to a mere 'paper' gain will be determined by the success of Flavell and Wohlwill's theory in producing accurate predictions of subjects' performances on specific tasks. Their account concludes with an initial evaluative attempt based on data relevant to the four phase model obtained by Uzgiris (1964) in an investigation of the attainment of conservation of substance, weight and volume in children aged from six to eleven years. The aim of the study was not only to verify the progression from substance to weight to volume by questioning the same children about the three types of conservation but, also, to examine the situational generality of conservation responses across different materials and varied transformations. Flavell and Wohlwill tackled the task of determining the degree of fit between their model and the data by initially examining each child's pattern of passes and fails on the tasks and then dividing the patterns into five categories representing respectively phases 1, 2, 2/3, 3 and 4. On the basis of crudely estimated values for P_a, P_b and k predicted mean numbers of passes for children in each of the phases were calculated. These were compared with the corresponding observed means obtained from the scores of the children whose response patterns fell within the appropriate categories. Over all the degree of agreement was, in Flavell and Wohlwill's opinion, sufficient to warrant further research specifically designed to test the adequacy of their model. Such an investigation would require a larger number of tasks of varying difficulty and a substantial number of judgments on the same or equivalent forms of these tasks to provide direct estimates of P_a for any given child.

Critical discussion of Flavell and Wohlwill's approach

Since the confines of a summary overview will not permit a detailed discussion of Flavell and Wohlwill's position only two points which seem to have broad implications for research strategy will be mentioned. It appears likely that, even with the assistance of experimental data acquired specifically for the purpose, deriving values for the parameters P_a and k for individual children will be an extremely difficult task. A convincing attack on the problem will involve a close and detailed analysis of the performance of individual children conducted over prolonged periods of time. This is, of course, exactly the type of experimental strategy advocated by Smedslund (1966d). As already indicated, the information processing approach and computer simulation techniques are particularly well suited to dealing with the complex and detailed results obtained in such studies and offer a promising medium for theory construction on the basis of fine-grained data. The attractiveness of the information processing approach in this area highlights an inconsistency in Flavell and Wohlwill's research strategy. As we have seen, they have a predilection for discussing cognitive development issues in information processing terms. 'Intellectual development is essentially a matter of ontogenetic change in the content and organization of highly intricate "programs". . .' (Flavell and Wohlwill, 1969, p.74). It is, also, their opinion that the cognitive developmental theorist of the future will need to be well trained in computer simulation lore, in addition to possessing good intuitions about how children think. 'Our ideal would be a combination of Herbert Simon and Piaget, with perhaps a bit of Chomsky added for writing the competence model.' Despite their liking for information processing terminology, however, Flavell and Wohlwill present their major hypotheses in the form of a stochastic theory.

There appear to be good grounds for questioning the wisdom of abandoning the information processing approach when it comes to the task of detailed theory construction since it is precisely at this level that its greatest potential lies. Theoretical statements couched in information processing terms when these are employed at the metaphorical level favoured by Flavell and Wohlwill are characterized by the same deficiencies as the major existing theories in the developmental area. It is extremely difficult to derive clear, differential predictions from them which can provide a basis for critical experiments. There is, also, no objective method of demonstrating that they are sufficient to account for the range of behaviour which they purport to explain. These shortcomings can, however, be avoided if full use is made of the potentialities of the information processing approach. This involves moving from the metaphorical level to the construction of detailed process models of the method of solution of specific tasks. The work of Simon, Newell and their followers, described by Reitman (1965), has clearly demonstrated the promise of a combination of information processing analysis and computer simulation techniques as a theorizing medium providing ease of detection of mutual contradictions and ambiguity and a foolproof method of examining the exact behavioural consequences of theoretical statements.

There is a good case for the contention that Flavell and Wohlwill should have attempted to express their theoretical viewpoint in the shape of process models geared to specific tasks and formalized as computer simulation programs rather than in the form of a stochastic theory. The major arguments which could be adduced in support of this assertion have been outlined by Gregg and Simon (1967) in a discussion of the criteria that might be used in choosing between relatively detailed process models, on the one hand, and highly aggregated stochastic theories, on the other, as vehicles for explaining concept attainment. They demonstrated that, in the case at hand, process models are to be preferred as being stronger and more readily falsified than stochastic theories. Process models are, also, more precise since they generate more definite predictions, and predictions about many aspects of the subjects' behaviour which are abstracted away in stochastic theories. Finally, they are simpler and more parsimonious, in allowing fewer degrees of freedom to fit them to the data. There seems to be no *prima facie* reason why the advantages claimed for information processing models as a means of theorizing about concept attainment should not, also, accrue in the wider area of concern selected by Flavell and Wohlwill.

Relationship of two approaches to the stages problem

It will be recalled that at the outset of the present chapter a distinction was drawn between two broad lines of approach to the stages problem. The first of these was adopted in the experimental work in the present study and involved the rejection of the pursuit of exact developmental relations between inference patterns and the adjustment of the criteria employed in identifying developmental stages to take account of children's inconsistent performance. The basic tenets of the alternative approach were a continuing emphasis on the search for rigidly predictable developmental sequences in the Piagetian tradition and a disregard for individual differences. Flavell and Wohlwill's general model for the analysis of the formation of stages of intelligence prompts some speculation on the nature of the future relationship between these two strategies. Their work has its genesis in Piaget's theory. This is abundantly clear since, for example, phases 1, 2 and 3 are said to correspond respectively to the stages designated by Piaget as that of preoperational thought, IIA and IIB, and IIIA. By including parameters to account for the effect of individual and situational variables as an integral part of their theory, however, they go well beyond Piaget's concessions to these sources of variation. These comprise the concept of horizontal décalage and an admission that tasks involving the application of the same operations to heterogeneous objects (e.g. conservation of a quantity of water and conservation of a quantity of plasticene) may give rise to 'slight décalages' explainable 'by the difference in the perceptual or intuitive conditions' (1941, p.266). Flavell and Wohlwill's approach, thus, represents a closing of the gap between work in the Piagetian tradition and the more flexible approach to the stages problem adopted in the present study.

The trend towards liberalizing the conception of a cognitive-developmental stage to accommodate individual and situational variables has continued in a more recent paper by Flavell (1970) in which he discusses stage-to-stage development in terms of the child's repertoire of cognitive 'items', defined as cognitive skills, rules or strategies. In his view the items that define a stage develop gradually rather than abruptly. Moreover the typical item probably does not achieve its final level of 'functional maturity', defined in terms of the item's evocability and utilizability as a solution procedure until *after* the conventional termination age of the stage in which it is supposed to begin its development. For example, a concrete-operational item like transitive inference probably continues to be perfected as an instrument of reasoning well after the generally accepted end point of the concrete-operational stage at 10 to 11 years. The effect of this addition to the Flavell and Wohlwill stages model outlined above is clearly to increase the emphasis on the importance of individual and situational variables.

There are indications that a closer relationship between the two orientations may produce valuable results. It may assist in answering some of the questions posed and left unsolved by Flavell and Wohlwill in outlining their model. They ask, for example, whether it is reasonable to attribute to the parameter k the status of a constant over all types of tasks. This, it will be recalled, is intended to reflect a child's ability to abstract the information required to utilize a particular operation and to code and process information generally. It may well be, they suggest, that through training and experience, or conceivably even as a function of purely endogenous factors, some children may be better able to process information for one type of problem while others will find some other type easier. If so, it would mean that k will have to be defined relative to a particular domain or type of information-processing problem.

Despite the imperfections of the data, the results of the Brimer analysis presented in Chapter Six suggest that although the value of k will vary between problem domains these fluctuations may be determined by a constant factor in the child's information processing. This is the particular mode of mediation which he seems to prefer in constructing internal representations of problems. The alternative perceptual and numerical developmental 'routes' detected in the graphs presented in Figures XIII and XIV are respectively consistent with a preference for a concrete visual and an abstract symbolic mode of internal representation. In the case of conservation of number children appear to be able to attain competence and a fair measure of performance on the basis of either of these representational modes. Churchill's (1958) finding that throughout her tests some of the children at the fully operational 'stage three' tended to use numerical correspondence and others qualitative correspondence, founded on the perceptual features of the situation, suggests that this assertion may be applicable to a broad range of number concepts. In some areas a preference for one or other type of representation may make the difference between success or failure in attaining competence or, at least, between relative ease and extreme difficulty in performance.

A good illustration of this effect is provided in Paige and Simon's (1966) study of the behaviour of American high school and college students confronted with the task of setting up equations for algebra word problems. They found a great deal of individual variation in the extent to which their subjects attacked the problems by making a direct translation from the initial verbal presentation to abstract mathematical symbols and in the degree to which they made use of physical representations of the problem such as diagrams. A set of 'contradictory' problems were used to detect the relative incidence of these two approaches. It was possible to set up an equation for these problems as they were stated literally but, as in the following example, they represented physically impossible situations:

A board was sawed into two pieces. One piece was two-thirds as long as the whole board and was exceeded in length by the second piece by four feet. How long was the board before it was cut?

On the basis of their performance on problems of this type Paiget and Simon were able to classify their subjects into those who were primarily 'physical' in their responses, and those who were primarily 'verbal'. The differences between the two groups showed up quite consistently in, among other things, the extent to which they detected the contradictions. The verbal solvers failed to do so while the subjects who employed physical representations sometimes did.

Another intriguing example which illustrates the advantages and handicaps of extreme reliance on a single type of internal representation, in this case the concrete visual mode, is provided by Luria (1969) in his account of the methods employed by the late S. V. Shereshevskii who possessed an amazing talent for memorizing and retaining vast quantities of material. His mnemonic virtuosity was founded on two techniques both of which involved the use of vivid concrete images. He either continued to 'see' series of words or numbers which had been presented to him or he translated these elements into a linked sequence of elaborate visual images. This extreme dependence on a concrete, visual mode of representation enabled Shereshevskii to faultlessly recall the details of memorized material even after the passage of years but rendered him relatively unable to cope with abstractions and frequently placed him at a disadvantage in problem solving and even in understanding meaningful language since single words or phrases were all too liable to give rise to elaborate images contradicting the intended meaning.

Acceptance of the suggestion that a preference for a particular mode of representation may be a constant factor in individual children's information processing would have considerable implications for the educational enterprise. It would, for example, be necessary to view the task of facilitating the solution of a particular class of problems by children as essentially involving three dimensions. These comprise the structure of the content area being dealt with (Gagné, 1965), the current status of the operative, structural aspect of the child's thought (Piaget, 1969) or, in Flavell and Wohlwill's (1969) terms, the library of 'programs' which he has at his disposal and, thirdly, the nature of his preferred representational mode. If due attention is paid to the last dimension there should be an appreciable increase in the likelihood of the input to the appropriate programs proving to be couched in an acceptable form. Some support for this assertion is provided by the varying degrees of generalization of the conservation of number principle revealed by the two experimental groups in the present study. In the nonverbal technique, which appeared to be more conducive to generalization, the children were left to derive the principle for themselves and, thus, to devise their own personalized form of representation of it. The less successful verbal acceleration method, in contrast, presented the children with the principle represented in a particular combination of verbal and imaginal terms which would clearly be more consistent with some children's representational preferences than with those of others.

The problem of the transition rule in development

It appears appropriate to end this discussion of the stages issue with the above consideration of an aspect of particular educational relevance since we must now turn to the problem of the nature of the transition rule governing the child's movement from state to state through the developmental sequence. This topic is closely linked to the question of the possibility of accelerating the course of intellectual development. As indicated at the outset of Chapter One, the availability of a well-defined and accepted transition rule would vastly simplify the task of designing acceleration techniques. Not only is no such rule currently available but, somewhat paradoxically, acceleration studies have continued to be the most popular method of approach to the transition problem in the period under review (Sigel and Hooper, 1968; Rothenberg and Orost, 1969). The last three years, however, have, also, seen the raising of some fundamental questions concerned with research strategy in this area. Flavell and Wohlwill (1969, pp.70–71) have raised the question of priorities. In their view we should be as precise and explicit as the state of science permits about the cognitive make-up of children at critical points in development before attempting to construct a model of the evolutionary process. This emphasis on the production of stage descriptions before tackling the problems of transition is consistent with Simon's (1963) prescription for action.

Difficulties in an experimental approach to the transition issue

Regardless of the attitude adopted towards the assertion that the time is not yet ripe for tackling the transition issue, there can be no denial that the numerous, laboratory based acceleration studies conducted to date have dismally failed to provide any illumination. The position has been succinctly described by Laurendeau and Pinard (1966) who assert that in the light of the available evidence two attitudes are possible. The first consists of simply admitting the impracticability of demonstrating either the insufficiency of the factors invoked by learning theories to explain transition or the necessity of having recourse to the factor of internal equilibration. Any attempt to demonstrate the importance of the process of equilibration by means of an experimental analysis seems doomed to failure because of the temporal dimension which is one of its essential characteristics. If the impossibility of experimentally inducing the process of equilibration is accepted, this appears to leave two possible courses of action both of which are unsatisfactory. One can assume that equilibration is the only factor underlying the development of logical structures and seek to demonstrate the necessary nature of its rôle by showing that recourse to any other factor is never effective. This approach is misconceived, however, since such an exclusive rôle has never been part of the equilibration hypothesis: the preponderance of the internal factor of equilibration has, certainly, been insisted upon, but, although the sufficiency of other factors is rejected, their necessity is recognized. Piaget himself, as indicated in Chapter One maintains that learning 'in the strict sense' (that is on the basis of external reinforcement) cannot account for the stability of intellectual structure. He does not assert that equilibration should replace learning 'in the strict sense' as the transition rule in intellectual development but rather that equilibration is a necessary addition or complement to it, and he advocates a search for the laws common to both of them and their amalgamation as learning 'in the wider sense'.

Another, equally unsatisfactory, approach is to admit that external factors can lead to certain partial acquisitions and then seek to demonstrate the imperfection and limitations of such acquisitions in comparison with those resulting from the natural and spontaneous equilibration of structures. This strategy gives rise to an interminable debate since those who champion the necessity of factors distinct from equilibration can always argue that the transitory nature of acquisitions produced by such external factors is due to deficiencies in the way in which they have been handled in the experimental situations.

Laurendeau and Pinard themselves reject the postulate that the process of equilibration is entirely unamenable to systematic analysis and have engaged in attempts to devise experimental situations aimed at determining the conditions and limits of its action. They accept that the equilibration model is hard to put into concrete form as soon as the frame of reference is extended beyond the hypothetical and somewhat artificial situation where a given subject must resolve a particular problem in a limited period of time. Their experimental approach is, accordingly, based on liberalizing the pattern a bit by disregarding the aspects of equilibration that are too specific or limited to a particular type of cognitive structure (for example, necessary conflict between the opposing dimensions of an object) and returning to Piaget's fundamental position that the evolution of behaviour within any cognitive sector is characterized by the progressive coordination of actions (overt or interiorized) that are at first isolated from one another. This less strict formulation, in Laurendeau and Pinard's view, conserves the essentials of the equilibration model and provides a suitable starting point for empirical analysis. The adoption of a 'weak' theoretical statement as a basis inevitably leads to the presence of an embarrassingly high number of degrees of freedom when the time comes for the designing of practical studies. The diversity of the techniques advocated by Laurendeau and Pinard (1969, pp.157–9), in a discussion of actual and possible training experiments, as methods of stimulating the equilibratory mechanism amply bears this out and provides little ground for optimism that a clear and unambiguous account of the process of equilibration will be produced by this line of approach.

The present discussion of the difficulties of a laboratory experimental approach to the transition rule issue has been confined to learning and equilibration. It should, however, be pointed out, parenthetically, that they are not the only transition rules currently giving rise to experimental work. The influence of Chomsky-inspired research in psycholinguistics has produced a revival of interest in nativism as a possible explanatory principle in cognitive development. Mehler and Bever (1967), for example, administered what they claimed to be a test of conservation of discontinuous quantity to 200 children ranging in age from 2:4 to 4:7 years. On the basis of the results they concluded that children of 2:6 and 4:6 years show more conservation than children of 4:2 years and, therefore, that the inability to conserve quantity is a temporary phase in the developing child. The child does not gradually acquire quantity conservation during his fourth year; rather, he reacquires it. The fact that the very young child successfully solves the conservation problem shows that he does have the capabilities which depend on the logical structure of the cognitive operations.

Mehler and Bever believe that what they regard as the temporary inability to solve the conservation problem reflects a period of over-dependence on perceptual strategies. Eventually, the child develops a more sophisticated integration of the logical operation with his perceptual strategies which allow him to count the individual members of an array. He then has the capacity to ignore his perceptual expectancies in those critical instances in which they are not confirmed. The intermediate age 'nonconserving' child cannot disengage his perceptual strategies in this way. Thus, in their view, nonconservation behaviour is a temporary exception to human cognition, not a basic characteristic of man's native endowment.

These conclusions, not surprisingly, have given rise to controversy on both the theoretical and empirical planes (Piaget, 1968; Beilin, 1968; Bever, Mehler and Epstein, 1968).[1]

No less potentially contentious are the claims for an increase in the importance of maturation as a transition rule advanced by Pascual-Leone (1969, 1970). He conceptualizes Piaget's cognitive-developmental variables as a quantitative construct, the central processor M. The set measure of M, defined as the maximum number of discrete 'chunks' of information or schemes that M can control or integrate in a single act, is assumed to grow in an all-or-none manner as a function of age in normal subjects. The M measure is taken as the quantitative characteristic of each developmental stage. M values for the Piagetian stages were inferred from Piagetian data and postulated as experimental hypotheses which, as Pascual-Leone (1970, pp. 309, 339–41) freely admits, are difficult to test.

Although the confines of the present study will not permit a fuller appraisal of their work, the proposals of Mehler and Bever and of Pascual-Leone represent a healthy broadening of the area of research activity concerned with transition. In the context of this discussion, however, the most relevant feature of their studies is that there is no indication that an experimental approach to the transition problem predicated on either of their viewpoints is less fraught with methodological difficulties than an approach from a learning or equilibration orientation.

Alternatives to the experimental approach

In general, it would be true to say that the attitude of disillusion with the efficacy of an experimental approach to the problem of the transition rule in development is more widespread than continuing faith in its ultimate success. This trend is having interesting and significant effects on the direction of research. Disenchantment with the highly artificial problems and non-human environments characteristic of laboratory experiments is leading researchers to concern themselves with speculations on the nature of the generalized changes in children's codes and strategies as a result of their spontaneous extra-laboratory activities which, presumably, underlie the changes noted with increasing age in the performance on the logico-mathematical laboratory tasks. More particularly, there is an increasing conviction that social interaction is a crucial factor in cognitive development which has been under-emphasized due to the pre-

[1]Appendix B comprises further discussion of this topic in the light of recent work reported by Bryant (1971a, b) after completion of this report.

dominance of the individual subject, laboratory experiment approach. This point of view has been strongly argued by Smedslund (1966a) in a theoretical paper on the social origins of decentration and, more recently, (Smedslund, 1968) in a discussion of his earlier attempts to accelerate the appearance of conservation of substance and weight by producing cognitive conflict. He believes that confronting individual children with the apparently contradictory effects on objects of addition, subtraction and perceptual deformation is too neutral a procedure to create conflict and suggests an organism-organism conflict, that is, a confrontation of different points of view among children, as a necessary condition for modification of intellectual structures.

Efforts to redress the balance on the empirical level are, also, already underway. Wohlwill (1966) asserts that research efforts should be concentrated on a search for the essential 'ingredients' for 'cognitive growth'. Such a search at the outset demands some sort of ecological approach with a view to examining the set of conditions, determined by the environment, in which cognitive development remains essentially unvarying, as well as the diverse experiential factors which seem to be linked to variations in the rate of development. At the conclusion, the list of experiential conditions obtained ought to lead to the discovery of the fundamental common factors to which one could attribute the determination of the process of cognitive development.

Numerous studies would clearly be necessary to attain this objective but, as a first step, Wohlwill provides a description of a design for a pilot study incorporating his main methodological suggestions. The subjects, a randomly selected group of children, would be followed up during the years from five to seven, a sufficiently protracted period of time to permit observation of the important changes taking place in their cognitive processes. They would be tested, at the outset, on a group of tests aimed at tapping concrete operational ideas and retested at the end of the first and second year. The question posed would be to discover the characteristics of the children who reveal the most marked changes and the most consistent performance in contrast to those who display less marked or less consistent changes. In attempting to answer this question, the changes observed in the children's performance on the cognitive tasks would be related to information obtained on such aspects of their behaviour as the development of their conceptual language, the degree to which they spontaneously engage in the operations of classification, measurement, seriation and counting, the nature of their interest in

G

games and the extent to which they participate in 'problem solving' activities. This information would be obtained by direct observation of the child in his home and by questioning his parents.

Any success achieved in identifying aspects of children's every-day experience with objects and persons in the environment which are critical for cognitive change will clearly represent a major break-through in the study of transition. As even a cursory examination of the outline of Wohlwill's proposed investigation indicates, however, the path to this goal is fraught with unresolved methodological difficulties.

The information processing approach and the transition issue

Although of major importance, the study of children's everyday experience and their social interaction does not represent the only alternative to group acceleration studies currently being explored. The difficulty of designing critical laboratory experiments can be largely attributed to the prevalent type of experimental approach which exemplifies a point made repeatedly by Bartlett (1958) about the study of both cognitive and motor skills, and, more recently, emphasized by Jeeves (1968). It is that confining measures of sub-jects' performance to totals of successes or failures on particular tasks leads to an over-estimation of the adequacy of explanations derived from theoretical models. The truth of this observation is clearly demonstrated, for example, in the increasing number of acceleration studies in which variations produced by different training sequences in the number of conservation responses derived from subjects who at the outset were non-conservers are, in accord-ance with the theoretical predilections of the experimenters, regarded as being consistent with the claims of learning or equilibra-tion theory.

Can this criticism be avoided without abandoning the experimental approach? The answer offered to this question is consistent with the recommendations of Jeeves (1968) and, also, with the prescription for action already outlined in our discussion of the stages issue. If light is to be thrown on the nature of the mechanisms underlying intel-lectual development and a realistic assessment made of the relative merits of the conflicting explanations of the transition from state to state, researchers must undertake intensive longitudinal studies of changes in the cognitive performance of individual children. In con-trast to the prevailing emphasis on the degree of success or failure on particular tasks it is only by concentrating on the close and detailed analysis of the component parts of individual subjects' performances that we can hope to begin to get to grips with the process of change. This assertion, once again, highlights the problems involved in coping with complex, fine-grained data. The solution advocated in the discussion of the stages issue, namely the application of information processing analysis and computer simulation techniques, appears to be equally promising in this context.

The contribution of this methodological approach to the resolution of the problems of transition need not be confined to coping with data from intensive, longitudinal studies. The competing theoretical accounts of the transition from state to state in the process of intellectual development are at one in their overall vagueness and in being characterized by a degree of generality which renders them compatible with an alarmingly wide range of experimental results. This lack of specificity gives rise to uncertainty as to whether they are sufficient to account for the behaviour which they purport to explain. The failure of the theories of Piaget and Berlyne to deal with the transition from probabilistic to stable structure has been highlighted elsewhere (Wallace, 1967) and it seems likely that any attempt to use them as the basis for the construction of a functioning system would result in the detection of further lacunae where the omission of fundamental operational features has been glossed over. If our attempts to produce a theoretical account of the transition rule in intellectual development are based on information processing analysis and expressed in terms of a computer program several advantages accrue. It is impossible to simulate vague models on a computer. The discipline of actually making the computer behave in the way that we hypothesize children behave compels us to be completely rigorous in the specification of our model. By carrying out appropriate experiments with the computer model, we can discover whether the type of structure proposed really does give rise to the type of behavioural development which we are trying to explain. Moreover, we may find that a given model gives rise to behaviour unforeseen when the model was proposed. If this happens, we can test the model further by performing new experiments to see if children also behave in the new ways predicted.

One possible approach to the problem of transition and the stages issue based on this rationale is currently being explored by the writer in collaboration with Dr. David Klahr of Carnegie-Mellon University. The initial line of attack adopted has involved focussing on a specific set of related tasks whose successful completion is considered to be indicative of a certain stage in cognitive development. The specific set of seven classification tasks considered were selected from

G*

a set of eleven tasks employed in a single study by Kofsky (1966) of the performance of four- to nine-year-old children and belong to those which in Piaget's view require functioning at the level of concrete operations for successful performance. They were chosen because of the complex structural interrelationships which they exhibit and because they constitute a representative subset of the wide range of concrete operational tasks.

In contrast to the Piagetian paradigm of analysing behaviour in terms of the logical and algebraic properties of the experimental situation, the approach involves analysing the information processing requirements of the tasks. Accordingly, the initial question posed is 'What routines for processing information would a child need in order to perform these tasks?' A partial answer to this question has been devised in the case of the classification tasks (Klahr and Wallace, 1970a, 1972) and work is currently underway directed at expanding this process model to cover the wider range of tasks included in Smedslund's (1964) monograph on concrete reasoning.

It is evident that the major relevance of the work to date is to the problem of stages. It does, however, have methodological implications for the transition rule issue. The decision to concentrate initially on a state description of one point in intellectual development before tackling the problem of the transition rule determining the passage from state to state in development is consistent with the line of approach advocated by Simon (1963) and Flavell and Wohlwill (1969). It is, also, consistent with the approach adopted by the writers in studying the very specific skill of series completion (Klahr and Wallace, 1970b). In terms of delineating the requirements for sufficiency, the criteria which a transition mechanism must fulfil are likely to be much clearer if a sufficient state description is already in existence before the question of self-modification of structure is tackled. Although the present model of cognitive performance in the narrow area of the classification tasks totally lacks processes which would enable it to engage in self-modification of structure it does, however, include aspects through which such self-modification could be introduced.

It has already been indicated that one of the main difficulties in tackling the transition issue is the level of generality at which the major theoretical accounts of transition have been presented. Wohlwill (1966b), for example, has pointed out that Piaget's descriptions of the functioning of equilibration do not deal with the particular mechanisms governing developmental changes or specify the conditions under which they take place. As a method of tackling the problem of transition, information processing analysis would appear to have the twin merits of commencing by focussing on specific task situations and of constantly demanding a completely specific statement of the processes which are hypothesized to under-lie performance. These features should ensure that any theory of transition produced by this approach will, at least, comprise a detailed description of a mechanism which is demonstrably sufficient to account for developmental change and of its mode of functioning in a range of completely specified situations.

The Genevan attitude to the information processing approach

It might be anticipated that the attitude of the Genevan group to the information processing approach would be one of polite, but detached, interest. As Wohlwill (1966b) has pointed out, the focus of change is, in general, imperfectly developed in Piaget's formulation of intellectual development since, for all its formal elaboration and complexity, his system remains at base a structural analysis of children's performance in cognitive tasks at different levels of their development. His treatment of the functional side of the problem, the nature of the processes by which these changes take place, is much less complete. There are indications, however, of greatly increased Genevan interest in the process as distinct from the structural aspect of intellectual development and in the information processing approach in particular.

This change of emphasis is clearly illustrated in a recent paper by Celérier (1972), one of the younger members of Piaget's group. The theme of the paper, symptomatically, is the question of what aspects of Piaget's theory are relevant to the information processing approach. Celérier believes that Piaget's interest in the structure and evolution of concepts and the 'state of the art' in mathematical formulization at the time when he was doing his main work on groups and groupings account for what has been called his 'sublime disregard of process' in his epistemological analyses. It would be grossly misrepresenting his theory, however, to say that process has no place in it. His characterization of intelligence as an extension of biological adaptation, and of schemes as the organs of this adaptation afford an obvious counter-example. Piaget's recent experiments on conceptualization of schemes and on conflicts between schemes, also, show a significant trend towards a more detailed observation and representation of processes and, in Celerier's view, a formulation of these observations in a completely specified algorithmic form is a necessary condition for the realization of this goal. Such a statement emanating from Geneva is sweet music to the ears of the protagonists of the information processing approach.

An increased concern with process is evidenced in Piaget's recent reformulation of the equilibration model (Celérier, 1972). This is based on the idea that a child's functioning in a problem environment is determined by a process that produces new rules and concepts by decomposing and recombining those which he already possesses. The new combinations are evaluated on the basis of their effects on the external problem environment and the outcome gives rise to a new recombination sequence. A cyclic chaining of external observations and internal combinations is, thus, established, By generating the extension of certain rules new properties of the environment can be discovered and these new properties serve to invent new rules that can then be used to discover new properties. The cycle stops when nothing new is generated, under a given definition of the problem environment.

The consequences of this new emphasis on process for the general course of development have been outlined by Celerier: 'This type of analysis gives rise to a picture of cognitive development as a parallel evolution of cognitive categories, each composed of a neat "filiation" of progressively stronger structures. It has been recently complicated by the discovery that many different schemes and concepts may be applied by the child to the same problem, also that this seems to be a general rule, and that the different cognitive categories seem to evolve at slightly different rates. The net result is that lateral inter-actions . . . appear at the decomposition and recombination level. These inter-actions (Piaget describes them as reciprocal assimilations between schemes, resulting in new coordinations) take place between elements that are heterogeneous in two ways: they originate from different categories and their degrees of completion are not necessarily the same. Thus, Piaget's picture of development now incorporates vertical relations (intra-category filiations) horizontal ones (inter-category lateral interactions) and oblique ones (interactions between elements of different "operatory levels").' This picture of cognitive development has much in common with the liberalized view of the concept of stage advocated by Flavell (1970).

The ongoing series of learning experiments conducted by the Genevan group (Inhelder and Sinclair, 1969; Inhelder, 1972) stand in the relation of both cause and effect to the revision of Piaget's theory. Their results were partly responsible for the changes. It is, also, hoped that the experiments will permit the observation of 'not the coordination process itself, but a close series of snapshots of its effects: how the schemes are decomposed, what are the successive recombinations that are generated and tried out, what are the guiding constraints their generation is subjected to' (Celérier, 1972). An excellent illustration of this last aspect is provided by the 'compromise' solutions to the line matching tasks produced by Inhelder and Sinclair's (1969) subjects. It will be recalled that some of the children broke one of the matches in the line they were constructing in order that the conflicting numerical equality and end alignment criteria might both be satisfied.

What, in summary, is the current relationship between Piaget's theoretical position and the information processing approach. As an exponent of the latter technique, the writer concurs with Celérier's statement that Piaget's central concepts even in their present revised form are still not sufficiently specified to be programmable.

Are accelerating studies worthwhile?

In view of the ineffectiveness of acceleration techniques as an approach to the problem of transition, is any useful purpose served by conducting acceleration studies of the type reported in the present volume? In seeking to answer this fundamental question it must first be pointed out that the major objective of the experiment was not the theoretical one of illuminating the transition issue but the severely practical aim of devising a method *sufficient* to produce acceleration in the process of concept formation. Its *raison d'être* must, therefore, be evaluated on empirical, educational criteria.

Piaget (1964) has posed the question Why do we wish to accelerate development? A possible rejoinder to this question is to highlight the contemporary information explosion and assert that this places a high premium on swift cognitive development. This line of argument, however, misses the heart of the issue. Accelerating development and pushing it downwards, in terms of age, to its maturational limits does not constitute the main educational objective of acceleration studies. The principal aims are, first of all, to devise methods which are sufficient to produce the attainment of particular landmarks in cognitive development and then, by shifting the focus from sufficient to necessary conditions, to refine the successful techniques and increase their efficiency by eliminating inessential features and discovering the most effective combination of the necessary components. This work has obvious relevance to the education of slow learning children but the return from it is by no means confined to this area. It appears likely that where environ-

mental demands are left to dictate the course of cognitive development important aspects of it may be omitted. Elkind (1961), for
example, found that only 47 per cent of a group of 469 American 12-
to 18-year-olds had attained conservation of volume. There is, also
no reason to suppose that the way in which children in general
arrive at particular cognitive attainments constitutes the acme of
efficiency.

Viewed from this angle it is clear that acceleration is employed
as a method not as an objective. Its adoption is dictated by the fact
that the search for sufficient techniques can only be conducted by
using as subjects children who have not yet spontaneously reached
the cognitive landmarks in question. The end in view is, then, the
production of adults possessing a comprehensive range of cognitive
tools, as Flavell and Wohlwill (1969) have put it 'not at first but at
last, not the "fustest" but with the "mostest" '.

If the case for conducting acceleration studies on educational
grounds is to be based initially on the search for sufficient treatments,
two questions raised by Wohlwill (1966a) must be considered before
any pronouncement on its validity can be made. What has the child
learned at the end of training—a particular response, a group of particular responses, a more general notion resting on the understanding
of the principle implicit in the experience or an 'operation' in the true
Piagetian sense of the term? If we allow that the learning produced
is real and lasting, does the process by which it comes about have anything in common with the processes which determine the normal
acquisition of these notions by a child? These questions will be
considered in turn.

**How authentic are changes in performance produced by acceleration
techniques?**

An appropriate way of treating the question of the authenticity
of the changes in cognitive performance produced by acceleration
treatments appears to be to consider the results obtained in the present study in relation to the criteria suggested by Piaget (1964) himself for assessing authenticity. When confronted with an apparently
successful case of induced acquisition of logical structures Piaget
maintains that we must always ask ourselves about the persistence of
the acquisition over time and in the face of counter-suggestion, the
initial operational level of the subjects trained, and the extent to
which it shows transfer and generalization. The delayed post-test
results in the present study indicate that the improvements in conservation performance produced by both experimental treatments

persisted over time. Indeed, in the case of the non-verbal method it will be recalled that there was a significant improvement in the subjects' performance between the first and second post-tests.

The subjects who attained the pass criterion on the verbal post-tests, also, did so despite the strong counter-suggestion included in the wording of the crucial questions. It could be argued, however, that the counter suggestion employed was not sufficiently strong to test the logical necessity of the children's grasp of the conservation principle and that the experimental paradigm provided by Smedslund (1963) should have been followed. This involved the use of what Smedslund has termed an 'extinction' procedure although the term is not used in the sense in which it is customarily employed in conditioning studies. Eleven children, who had acquired conservation of weight during a series of trials in which the invariance of the weight of an object over deformations was empirically demonstrated on a balance, and thirteen children, who acquired conservation prior to the study, were shown some instances of apparent non-conservation. All the children in the first or trained group easily gave up their concept of conservation and reverted to more primitive perceptual strategies. About half of the subjects in the second group resisted the attempt at 'extinction' and interpreted the apparent non-conservation as meaning that something had been added or taken away. These results are viewed by Smedslund as being consistent with his hypothesis that a concept of conservation acquired by means of external reinforcement does not have the functional properties of a normally acquired 'logically necessary' concept and, thus, as revealing the predicted difference between empirical learning and genuine insightful acquisition founded on equilibration. Although Wohlwill (1966a) has advocated the wider application of the resistance to 'extinction' criterion in assessing the outcome of training studies, the failure of an increasing number of investigations to successfully replicate the results of Smedslund's experiment (Kingsley and Hall, 1967; Hall and Kingsley, 1968; Smith, 1968) and the highlighting of methodological difficulties implicit in the endeavour (Hall and Kingsley, 1968; Wallace and Leigh-Lucas, 1970) are not conducive to confidence in its efficacy.

Piaget's insistence on considering the initial operational level of the subjects trained is consistent with Flavell and Wohlwill's (1969) account of the formation of cognitive structures in terms of a four-phase process, in which transitional and stabilization phases intervene between the initial preoperational phase and the final fully-fledged establishment of the operation. This formulation suggests that very different effects of learning are to be expected, according to the phase in which the child is located at the outset. Children in the preoperational phase should show little evidence of acquisition of concrete-operational concepts—and this is in accordance with the lack of success of most Piaget-inspired acceleration studies below the age of five. Children in the transitional stage should be variably receptive to influences aimed at speeding up the initial emergence of concrete operations, and for those that do learn, the extent of transfer exhibited should be fairly limited. Children in the stabilization phase would presumably show effects mainly of a consolidation or generalization nature—i.e. the extension of previously established operations to new domains. Finally, those in the final phase cannot give evidence of any learning effects.

As indicated in Chapter Three, the initial level of the children's performance exhibited in the pre-tests formed the main basis for the selection of the subjects in the present study. The three categories of performance employed were much more specific than the broad bands comprising Flavell and Wohlwill's four phase process. It appears reasonable, however, to view Type 1 pre-test performance, the inability to appreciate the numerical equivalence of two rows of six counters, as belonging to the preoperational phase and both Type 2 and Type 3 pre-test performance as being representative of the second or transitional phase. If these assignments are accepted, it would be predicted that the children in the Type 1 sub-groups would show little evidence of acquisition of conservation while varying amounts of improvement would be revealed by those in the Type 2 and Type 3 sub-groups. Since the results obtained conform with these predictions the application of the initial level of performance criterion appears to support the authenticity of the changes in cognitive attainment produced by the acceleration treatment.

There are strong indications that more precise assessment of subjects' initial levels of performance is becoming an increasingly important aspect of research on cognitive development. The results of the relatively successful acceleration studies conducted by Sigel and his associates (Sigel *et al.*, 1966; Sigel, 1968), for example, support the view that conservation can be induced if the training procedures employed embody the prerequisite operations of multiple classification, multiplicitive relations, reversibility and seriation. A logical development of this approach would appear to be the compilation of an operational profile of each subject at the outset to enable the adoption of a training procedure specifically designed to encourage the operations which he seems to lack.

This initial profile strategy has similar relevance in the context of the very different account of development presented by Gagné (1965, 1968). He maintains that a child has to learn a number of subordinate capabilities before he will be able to learn how to perform a task such as judging equalities and inequalities of volumes of liquids in rectangular containers. Investigators who have tried to train this final task have often approached the job by teaching one or two, or perhaps a few, of the subordinate capabilities, but not all of them in the appropriate sequential manner. According to Gagné's model, the incompleteness of the learning programs employed accounts for the lack of success in having children achieve the final task. The compilation of an accurate profile of a child's initial performance repertoire is clearly essential to determine which subordinate capabilities must be learned and to enable a decision to be made on an appropriate training sequence.

There are, also, indications that initial profiles may have an important part to play in the application of information processing analysis to the problems of stages and transition in development. This can be illustrated in terms of the study of classification tasks (Klahr and Wallace, 1970a) outlined above. One of the most fundamental issues raised by this work concerns the evaluation of the extent to which the information processing model presented constitutes a valid description of the intellectual processes of children solving Kofsky's range of classificatory tasks. A promising line of approach would involve the construction of test items corresponding to each of the processes included in the model to enable the compilation of a process profile of individual children. Versions of the model incorporating the details of the profiles could then be used to predict the individual performance of the children on the range of classificatory tasks and the accuracy of the predictions would be assessed by comparison with actual performance data.

The compilation of process profiles could, also, be used as the initial step in an attempt to evaluate the model by means of a training study. The experimental group would consist of a random sample of four year olds and the scope of the training provided would be determined by the process profiles of the individual children revealing the processes which they seemed to lack. Each child would, if necessary, be trained to criterion on all of the fundamental processes which the model suggests underlie successful performance on the classificatory tasks. When all of the members of the experimental group had attained criterion levels of performance on the processes which they appeared to lack, they would be given Kofsky's group of classificatory tasks. The Kofsky tasks would, also, be given to groups of seven-, eight- and nine-year-olds. The results obtained by testing all four groups would be combined for purposes of analysis. This would enable the validity of the model to be evaluated by investigating the extent to which the individual response patterns of the trained children could be distinguished from those of the control group.

The last of Piaget's criteria for assessing the authenticity of changes in cognitive performance produced by training is the extent to which they show transfer and generalization. The production of generalization was a declared objective of both of the acceleration treatments employed in the present study and was the main reason for the inclusion in them of an extended series of relevant learning experiences involving the use of a wide variety of materials. The relative degree of generalization of the concept of number conservation produced by the verbal and non-verbal acceleration treatments was discussed at length in Chapter Four. The apparent efficacy of the non-verbal treatment in producing generalization of the conservation principle across the range of verbal and non-verbal post-test items does not satisfy the Genevan generalization criterion of the authenticity of cognitive acquisitions. This is founded on Piaget's contention that all of the groupings underlying the stage of concrete operations 'appear at the same time without our being able to seriate (them) into stages' (1941, p. 246). From this viewpoint generalization of the effect of conservation training to performance, for example, on transitivity tasks would be necessary to establish authenticity.

The status of this extremely demanding generalization criterion is, however, itself currently a focus of controversy. On the theoretical plane there are differences of interpretation as to whether the principle of synchronism of operations is an indispensable feature of Piaget's model. Pinard and Laurendeau (1969) adopt the view that any empirically-established asynchronism among the constituent groupings of a given concept would seriously jeopardize Piaget's conception of stage because it would deny one of its most essential characteristics, and because it would be difficult to reconcile with the very nature of groupings with their theoretical interdependence on both the psychological and the epistemological level. Flavell and Wohlwill (1969), in contrast, assert that 'Piaget has placed a quite unnecessarily heavy burden of proof upon himself, by stipulating that *all* of the various concrete operations (i.e. all of the several groupings) develop in unison. There appears to be no reason that the *structures d'ensemble* could not be looked at as a family of separate structures, each following its own developmental timetable.' Wohlwill (1966a) believes that the adoption of this substitute hypothesis in no way weakens Piaget's system.

More recently, Flavell (1970) reached the following two conclusions after an interesting discussion of the notion of developmental synchrony or concurrence. 'First, items from the same stage may often emerge in an invariant or near-invariant sequence rather than concurrently, although important methodological problems cloud the research evidence on this point. Second, a stage theory such as Piaget's does not in any event logically require or predict anything but a very loose sort of item concurrence at most, and research attempts at establishing strict concurrences have been accordingly misguided in rationale.'

These conflicting interpretations on the theoretical plane are paralleled by the results obtained in empirical studies. A review of the research aimed at evaluating Piaget's assertion that all of the groupings underlying the stage of concrete operations appear at the same time (Pinard and Laurendeau, 1969, pp. 138–45) provides an inconsistent picture with some of the results supporting synchronism while others reveal asynchronisms. The designing of experiments on this theme is clearly an extremely difficult task.

Until theoretical and experimental work produces a more coherent picture of the developmental relationship between concrete operational tasks any attempt to apply a generalization criterion appears, at best, premature. To enable detailed predictions of the generalization to be expected from particular training procedures to be made, a detailed analysis of all of the tasks falling within the concrete operations area will be necessary. Two approaches which appear to operate at an appropriate level of detail for this purpose are represented in the work of Gagné (1968) and in the type of information processing analysis exemplified in the Klahr and Wallace (1970) study of classification tasks.

The controversial status of some of the criteria applied makes it extremely difficult to reach an overall verdict on the authenticity of the changes in cognitive performance produced by the acceleration treatment in the present study. All that can be said by way of a summary statement is that on relatively unambiguous criteria, such as persistence over time and consistence with the initial operational level of the subjects, the changes in performance produced by the non-verbal acceleration treatment give considerable evidence of being authentic.

Relationship of the processes produced by acceleration to 'normal' development

If we accept, on the strength of two favourable and two not proven verdicts, that the learning produced seems to have been real and lasting, the second question raised by Wohlwill (1966a) remains. Did the process by which the learning came about have anything in common with the processes which determine the normal acquisition of conservation of number by a child? In terms of justifying the conducting of acceleration studies on educational grounds, it can be argued that this issue is considerably less important than the question of the authenticity of the learning outcomes. If the learning produced is real and lasting there is no necessity for the processes which give rise to it to be identical with those which prevail in the normal course of development. The nature of the 'normal' course of development is, in any case, obscure to say the least. The logical conclusion to this line of argument would be, that the process question need not be considered further since it is irrelevant to the consideration of the educational value of acceleration studies. To adopt this conclusion, however, is to ignore the important and closely related topic of the effect on a child's general level of cognitive development of treatment aimed at accelerating a specific aspect of his performance.

It has been argued by Wohlwill (1966b) that the effects of training in producing vertical progression tend to be inversely proportional to the extent of horizontal transfer achieved. Flavell and Wohlwill (1969) suggest that this inverse relationship quite possibly represents the key to the difference between the effects of training and controlled experience and those of the child's spontaneous, unprogrammed experience. 'The latter results in vertical progress that is undoubtedly slower and more haphazard, but in compensation it takes place on a much broader scale horizontally.' The value of acceleration treatments must certainly be called in question if the more successful they are the more lopsided becomes the child's general level of cognitive development. The rapid acquisition of a single adult finger would be disastrous for the coordinated activities of a child's hand. If the rapid development of a particular aspect of his cognitive equipment has a similarly disruptive effect the use of acceleration treatments is clearly counter-productive.

A final decision on the validity of this line of argument must await the emergence of a generally accepted theory of cognitive development expressed at a similar level of detail to that necessary to make predictions of the degree of generalization to be expected from training procedures. In the absence of such a theory all that will be presented are a few comments based on the Klahr and Wallace (1970) study of classification tasks since, although being narrow in scope, it has the merit of operating at the requisite level of detail. It will be recalled that the initial question posed was 'What routines for processing information would a child need to perform these tasks?' The information processing model which has emerged in answer to this question includes three broad types of processes. These comprise processes which are confined to a single, specific task routine, processes which figure in several task routines and a third group of processes that are included in all of the classification task routines. There are relatively few single routine processes. Since the vast majority of the processes are relevant to several or all of the task routines it appears a reasonable assumption that any training sequence aimed at inculcating the processes required for successful completion of a single classification task should result in much wider and more powerful additions to a child's process repertoire than would be predicted purely on the basis of a consideration of the superficial features of the specific classification task constituting the focus of the training procedure. If the extension of the information processing approach from the topic of classification to the wider area of concrete operations as a whole reveals the same preponderance of processes with multiple task relevance over those confined to single tasks, and there seems to be no *prima facie* reason for regarding this as unlikely, the danger of impeding a child's general level of cognitive development by submitting him to an acceleration treatment geared to a particular task routine will not appear to be great.

The most cogent statement of the view that the processes tapped by acceleration treatments are so far removed from those involved in children's cognitive development in everyday life that training studies represent valueless enterprises has been presented by Smedslund (1966d). He asserts that the fact that various training methods have been shown to lead to acquisitions does not prove that similar processes occur outside the laboratory. It is very hard to find, in children's daily life, any observations, conflicts and reinforcements directly relevant for the acquisition of concepts like conservation, transitivity, class inclusion and the multiplication of classes. In Smedslund's opinion, this strengthens the suspicion that Piaget's concrete operational tasks represent unique and highly atypical experiences to the children, and that acceleration studies, employing training items closely related to the criterion task, are on the wrong track. The indications are that the improvement in performance on the concrete operational tasks with increasing age derives, not from specific related experiences, but in highly complex and indirect ways from some kind of generalized changes in children's codes and strategies.

In the current state of ignorance of the determinants of cognitive development in children's everyday lives it is impossible to positively confirm or refute Smedslund's contention that a gulf exists between the processes tapped in training studies and those concerned in 'normal' development. There are, however, grounds for asserting that it is likely that he is exaggerating the extent to which training studies are unavoidably divorced from everyday experience. Accepting the basic artificiality of the laboratory situation which applies to all training studies, acceleration treatments vary considerably in the extent to which their procedure is akin to a child's everyday life. A treatment involving a high degree of experimenter direction and training directly on the criterion task with a single set of materials is clearly considerably further removed from a child's free interaction with his environment than the relatively undirected procedure involving an indirect approach to the criterion task and the employment of a great variety of everyday materials which characterized the non-verbal training sequence in the present study.

Although not of negligible importance, the procedural question constitutes a relatively superficial aspect of the issue highlighted by Smedslund. The nub of the argument centres on the nature of the routines necessary to cope successfully with the concrete operational tasks. The view was advanced above that processes with multiple task relevance are likely to predominate over those relevant to only a single task in the routines necessary for successful performance on concrete operational test items. This affords some support to Smedslund's assertion that generalized changes in children's codes and strategies underlie improvement in their performance on concrete operational tasks. Due to their considerable degree of generality of application, processes with multiple task relevance may presumably be added to a child's repertoire in the total absence of interaction with any situations resembling Piaget's tests of concrete operations. Care must be taken, however, to avoid underestimating the extent to which the demands of everyday life may call upon children to construct and employ the particular sequences of general and specific processes which constitute the concrete operational routines.

It is unquestionably true that the administration of concrete operational tasks, such as conservations and transitivity in their laboratory form is not a feature of children's everyday experience. It is not a necessary conclusion from this fact that improvement in children's performance over time in these tasks comes about in the total absence of specific related experience. If the structural relations and sequences of processes involved in the concrete operational tasks are adopted as the yardstick it seems likely that children may undergo a considerable amount of experience likely to foster the formation of the sequences of processes which constitute sufficient routines for coping with these tasks. In the case of number conservation, for example, it seems likely that the sequence of processes underlying appreciation of constancy of number over perceptual transformations will become part of the child's repertoire of routines as a result of interacting with his home environment. As Bunt (1951) has pointed out, in the course of play experiences and daily activities involving collections of discrete items, such as beads, shoes and the people in his family, he has ample opportunity to satisfy himself that a number undergoes no change in the absence of addition or subtraction. 'This experience, gained at first with small numbers of relatively large objects, is gradually extended to large numbers of smaller objects until the time comes when this property of a quantity of remaining constant, at length is regarded as a matter of course.'

It is conceivable, also, that experience specifically related to concrete operational tasks may come about as a result of social inter-action between children. A single child may not present himself with a conservation test but the necessary structural relations demanding the sequence of processes constituting conservation may be produced in the course of interaction with other children. The writer has recently been carrying out a pilot study of the activities indulged in by pairs of children when left without supervision to play freely with a cafeteria-like variety of materials including water and a selection of containers. Analysis of videotapes of these sessions has revealed that in the course of water play pairs of five- and six-year-old children typically function in either an imitative fashion, with one child slavishly copying the other in a sequence of transfers of water from container to container, or in a competitive fashion in which they vie with one another to have the greater amount of water. In the former mode, sequences of transformations constituting confirmations of conservation of quantity, in the sense of conservation of identity, were very frequent since the children repeatedly transferred the entire contents of one container to another and then returned it to the first container. The competitive climate produced a number of examples of tests of conservation of equivalence as children grudg-ingly shared the water equally between them in similar receptacles at the outset and then apparently proceeded to try to make their share look 'more' by transferring it to another shape of container. Although these results were not obtained in a completely 'normal' setting they do seem to suggest that an analysis of children's everyday activities may reveal that specific as well as generalized experience plays an important part in the development of the sequences of processes underlying performance on concrete operational tasks.

Overview

It is evident from the conflicting viewpoints reviewed above that a definitive answer to the question of the nature of the relationship between the processes evoked by training sequences and those which figure in 'normal' development is still a considerable way off. Taken in conjunction with the only slightly more clear cut evidence on the question of the authenticity of the changes in performance produced by training, this assessment supports the conclusion that the case against the educational utility of acceleration studies remains to be proved. In the interim, their potential practical contribution in the search for methods sufficient to produce the attainment of particular landmarks in cognitive development appears to make the continuation of acceleration studies worthwhile. The balance of the evidence suggests that future studies should conform to certain guidelines if they are to make the maximum contribution possible on both the empirical and theoretical planes. The acceleration treatments used should be based on task or process analyses at the level of detail exemplified in the work of Gagné (1968) or Klahr and Wallace (1970). They should, also, include an extended series of relevant learning experiences involving the use of a wide variety of materials and presented in a sufficiently non-directive fashion to allow children to employ their own preferred modes of mediation.

The foregoing discussion has ranged widely and is not amenable to a neat concluding summary. This is probably as it ought to be since the overall impression of research in the area is one of 'open-endedness'. This is particularly marked in the sphere of methodology where the search for new orientations and instruments suitable for tackling the intractable problems of stages and transition has produced several possible lines of inquiry which are themselves challenging but, also, distinctly promising.

It would be a rash reviewer who would suggest that solutions to these problems lie just around the corner. The road to the cognitive researchers' hell is paved with such optimistic prognoses.

Sufficient be it to say that the present tendency to tackle complex issues with complex instruments is sufficiently encouraging to tempt the writer to conclude with the assertion that in 1971 the outlook for research on conceptualization and in the wider area of cognitive development appears to be considerably brighter than in 1963.

Additional details of the tests

(*a*) *The Verbal Pre-Test*—The complete procedure item by item is as follows:

'I want you to help me to find out some things about numbers. Would you like to do that? We'll play some games and see what we can find out about numbers.'

1. 'First of all, can you tell me how many fingers are there here?' (Show one hand.)   Right ☐   Wrong ☐

   (If answer is 'four')—'Point to the four fingers'.

---

2. 'Now, can you tell me how many hands you have?'   Right ☐   Wrong ☐

---

3. 'How many blocks are there here?' (Show four.)   Right ☐   Wrong ☐

   'How many are there now?' (After adding one more.) If no response ask again.   Right ☐   Wrong ☐

---

4. Beads and beakers. Let child count six beads into each beaker, in pairs.

   'Are there the same number of beads in each glass?'   Yes ☐   No ☐
                    Don't know ☐

   Other answer:

   'How do you know?'   They look the same ☐
                    Same height ☐
                    I counted them ☐
                    Don't know ☐

   Other answer:

---

5. Pour beads from one beaker into a narrow beaker.
   'Are there the same number of beads in
   each glass now?' Yes ☐   No ☐
   Don't know ☐

   If child answers 'Yes', ask 'How do you know?'
   Answer:
   If child answers 'No', ask 'Which has more? 'Why?'

   Looks higher here ☐
   Looks more here ☐
   Don't know ☐

   Other answers:

---

6. Let the child count eight beads, in pairs, into the standard beaker
   and the narrow beaker used in subtest 5.
   'Are there the same number in each
   glass?' Yes ☐   No ☐
   Don't know ☐

   If 'Yes', ask 'How do you know?' Answer:
   If 'No', ask 'Which has more? Why? Looks higher here ☐
   Looks more here ☐
   I counted them ☐
   Don't know ☐

   Other answer:

---

7. Pour beads from narrow beaker into a second standard beaker.
   'Are there the same number in each
   glass now?' Yes ☐   No ☐
   Don't know ☐

   If 'Yes', ask 'How do you know?' Answer:
   If 'No', ask 'Which has more? Why?' Answer:

---

8. Eggs and egg-cups. Arrange six egg-cups in a row (2″ apart).
   Ask the child to put one egg in each cup.
   'Are there the same number of eggs and
   cups?' Yes ☐   No ☐
   Don't know ☐

   If 'No', ask 'Are there more eggs or more cups? Why?

9. Remove the eggs from the cups and place them in a row close to the cups.

'Have we got the same number of eggs and cups now?'

Yes ☐   No ☐
Don't know ☐

'How do you know?'

There's one for each ☐
We counted them out ☐
Don't know ☐

Other answer:

---

10. Push the row of eggs together into a bunch and ask again 'Are there the same number of eggs and cups now?'

Yes ☐   No ☐
Don't know ☐

If 'Yes', ask 'How do you know?' Answer:
If 'No', ask 'Are there more eggs or more cups? Why are there more eggs (or cups)?'

More eggs ☐   More cups ☐
Looks more here ☐
Don't know ☐

Other answer:

---

11. Ask the child to put eggs back *in* cups. 'Are there the same number of eggs and cups now? (Yes.) Were there as many eggs as cups when the eggs were all bunched up *here*?'

Yes ☐   No ☐
Don't know ☐

If 'No', ask 'Why not?'

There were more here ☐
The eggs were all together ☐
Don't know ☐

Other answer:

---

12. Arrange six counters in a row (about 1″ apart). Offer six counters and ask child 'Can you put out another row like this one?'

Right ☐   Wrong ☐

'How many coloured pieces are in my row?'

Right ☐   Wrong ☐

'How many are there in your row?'

Right ☐   Wrong ☐

'So are there as many in your row as there are in my row?'

Yes ☐   No ☐

13. Spread out the first row of counters (about 2″ apart).
    'Has one row more pieces in it now?'   No ☐
                                          Both same ☐
                                     First row more ☐
    Other answer:
    'Why?'   This row is longer ☐
                                            Looks more ☐
                                            Don't know ☐
    Other answer:

---

14. 'Can you make as many in your row as there are here?'
                                    Puts out more counters ☐
                                      Moves own counters ☐
    Other approach:

---

15. Put the first row of counters back in their original positions
    (about 1″ apart).
    'Are there the same number in each
    row now?'   Yes ☐   No ☐
    If 'Yes', ask 'How do you know?' Answer:
    If 'No', ask 'Why are there more in this row?'
                                          Looks more ☐
                                       Row is longer ☐
                                      Counted them ☐
                                        Don't know ☐
    Other answer:

---

16. 'Can you make these two rows the same again, with the same
    number of pieces in each?'
                                     Moves counters ☐
                                   Removes counters ☐
    Other approach:

---

17. 'Are there the same number in each
    row now?'   Yes ☐   No ☐

H*

(*b*) *The Verbal Post-Test*—The complete procedure item by item
                        was as follows:

    'I want you to help me to find out some things about numbers.
We'll play some games and see what you can tell me about
numbers.'

1. Lay out four blocks close together in a row.
    'How many blocks are there?'   Right ☐ Wrong ☐
    Spread out the blocks in a much longer row.
    'Are there more blocks now?'   Right ☐ Wrong ☐
    'Are there the same number of blocks?' Right ☐ Wrong ☐
    'Can you tell me why?'

---

2. Lay out five blocks in a widely spaced row.
    'How many blocks are there?'   Right ☐ Wrong ☐
    Add another block in full view of S to the row and push the
    row close together.
    'Are there the same number of blocks
    now?'   Right ☐ Wrong ☐
    'Are there more blocks?'   Right ☐ Wrong ☐
    'Can you tell me why?'

---

3. Lay out six blocks in a tightly packed row.
    'How many blocks are there?'   Right ☐ Wrong ☐
    Take one block away in full view of S and spread out the row.
    'Are there more blocks now?'   Right ☐ Wrong ☐
    'Are there the same number of blocks?' Right ☐ Wrong ☐
    'Can you tell me why?'

---

4. Lay out six blocks in a widely spaced row.
    'How many blocks are there?'   Right ☐ Wrong ☐
    Push the row close together and, immediately, cover it over to
    prevent S from recounting it.
    'Are there more blocks now?'   Right ☐ Wrong ☐
    'Are there the same number of blocks?' Right ☐ Wrong ☐
    'Can you tell me why?'

---

5. Place a pile of counters on the table.

   'I am going to make a row with some of these coloured pieces and I want you to make a row just like mine. You put one in your row each time I put one in mine.'

   Arrange six counters in a row about $\frac{1}{2}$ " apart.

   'Have we the same number of pieces in
   our rows?'   Right ☐ Wrong ☐

   (If S doesn't agree all the counters should be returned to the pile and the rows should be reconstructed with S being asked the above question after the placing of each pair of counters.)

   E spreads out his counters about 1 " apart.

   'Have we got the same number of pieces?' Right ☐ Wrong ☐
   'Have I got more pieces than you?'   Right ☐ Wrong ☐
   'How do you know?'

---

6. Two rows with six counters are again arranged as in 5.

   'How many pieces are there in your row?' Right ☐ Wrong ☐
   'How many pieces are there in my row?'   Right ☐ Wrong ☐
   'Have we the same number of pieces in
   our rows?'   Right ☐ Wrong ☐

   E spreads out S's counters about 1 " apart.

   'Have you got more pieces than me?'   Right ☐ Wrong ☐
   'Have we got the same number of pieces?' Right ☐ Wrong ☐
   'How do you know?'

---

7. Two rows with six counters are arranged again. On this occasion the counters are about 1 " apart.

   'Have we the same number of pieces in
   our rows?'   Right ☐ Wrong ☐

   E adds a counter to his row in full view of S and pushes his row close together.

   'Have we got the same number of pieces?' Right ☐ Wrong ☐
   'Have I got more pieces than you?'   Right ☐ Wrong ☐
   'How do you know?'

---

8. Two rows with six counters are arranged again. The counters are, again, about 1″ apart.

'Have we the same number of pieces in
our rows?'   Right ☐ Wrong ☐

E pushes his row close together and, immediately, covers it over to prevent S from recounting it.

'Have you got more pieces than me?'   Right ☐ Wrong ☐
'Have we got the same number of pieces?'   Right ☐ Wrong ☐
'How do you know?'

---

9. Place 14 beads in a tight row on the table.

'How many beads are there?'   Right ☐ Wrong ☐

Spread out the row.

'Are there more beads now?'   Right ☐ Wrong ☐
'Are there the same number of beads?'   Right ☐ Wrong ☐
'How do you know?'

---

10. 14 beads again in a tight row.

'How many beads are there?'   Right ☐ Wrong ☐

E removes one bead in full view of S and spreads out the row.

'Are there more beads now?'   Right ☐ Wrong ☐
'Are there the same number of beads?'   Right ☐ Wrong ☐
'How do you know?'

---

11. 14 beads in a wide, irregular formation.

'How many beads are there?'   Right ☐ Wrong ☐

Push the beads together into a bunch and cover them over immediately.

'How many beads are there now?'   Right ☐ Wrong ☐
'Are there the same number of beads?'   Right ☐ Wrong ☐
'How do you know?'

---

12. Pile of beads on table. E places two glass beakers of the same size in front of himself and S.

'We are going to put some beads in these glasses. You put one in your glass each time I put one in mine.'

Seven beads are placed in each glass.

'Have we the same number of beads in our glasses?' Right ☐ Wrong ☐

(If S doesn't agree the beads are removed from the glasses and replaced in them with S being asked the above question after the placing of each pair of beads.)

E pours his beads into a tall, narrow cylinder.

'Have I got more beads than you?' Right ☐ Wrong ☐

'Have we got the same number of beads?' Right ☐ Wrong ☐

'How do you know?'

---

13. Procedure same as for 12 but 14 beads are placed in each glass.

'Have we the same number of beads in our glasses?' Right ☐ Wrong ☐

E pours S's beads into the tall, narrow cylinder.

'Have you got more than me?' Right ☐ Wrong ☐

'Have we got the same number of beads?' Right ☐ Wrong ☐

'How do you know?'

---

14. E places six eggs on the table in a tight bunch.

'How many eggs are there?' Right ☐ Wrong ☐

The eggs are spread out and immediately covered over.

'Are there more eggs now?' Right ☐ Wrong ☐

'Are there the same number of eggs?' Right ☐ Wrong ☐

'How do you know?'

---

15. Arrange six egg-cups in a row about 1″ apart.

Ask S to put the eggs into the egg-cups.

'Are there the same number of eggs and egg-cups?'

Right ☐ Wrong

---

16. Remove the eggs from the cups and place them in a row close to the cups.

'You have the eggs and I'll have the cups. Have we got the same number of things?' Right ☐ Wrong ☐

'How do you know?'

17. Push the row of eggs together into a bunch.

'Have I got more than you now?' Right ☐ Wrong ☐
'Have we got the same number?' Right ☐ Wrong ☐
'How do you know?'

(c) The Non-Verbal Post-Test

The instructions for administration and complete sequence of items were as follows:

Initial practice trial. When S enters the first set of choice cards are in position over the three doors in the presentation apparatus. They comprise, from S's left to right, six black dots, seven black dots and purple concentric circles. The sample card, which is placed on the table in front of the apparatus, also shows two purple concentric circles.

E tells S that he wants to play a game with him: E will hide a bead behind one of the 'doors' and S is to try to find it and string it with the other beads on a lace with which he has been provided. E further informs S that he will be able to find the bead every time if he looks first at the choice cards and then carefully at the sample card which will indicate the correct 'door'. E invites S to make a choice and to open one of the 'doors'. If the choice is correct, S takes the bead and strings it on the lace. In the event of an incorrect choice, S is allowed to correct it until he finds the bead. He is urged to look very closely at the card on the table, since there is something on this card which tells him which of the doors has the bead behind it. This correction procedure applies only to this single practice trial.

Training series. Following the practice trial, the choice card with the concentric circles is replaced with one showing eight black dots. The three choice cards, thus, represent the numbers six, seven and eight, respectively, arranged initially from left to right above the 'doors'. The relative positions of these cards are altered after every three trials throughout the training series.

The series involves the use of a set of 12 sample cards, featuring six, seven or eight dots in varying configurations, none of which is identical to any of the choice cards above the 'doors'. As in the practice trial, the sample cards are placed, one at a time in random order, on the table directly in front of the apparatus. S is not given the opportunity, however, to correct wrong choices. The criterion of learning is six consecutive correct responses; if this criterion is not met in 48 trials, S is discarded from the test population.

1. *Unprovoked Correspondence (Part I)*. This test consists of a series
of conservation, addition and subtraction trials in the sequence
outlined in the table below. The choice cards from the Training
Series, representing the numbers six, seven and eight, are retained.
Instead of the sample cards a number of small counters are used.
In two-thirds of the trials these are initially arranged in a pattern
exactly duplicating the configuration of dots on the corresponding
choice card; in the remainder of the trials the correspondence is
purely numerical. S is told to look at the counters as they will
indicate the correct 'door', and he then makes his choice. Since the
purpose of this preliminary choice is only to inform S of the choice
card whose dots are in numerical correspondence with the set of
counters, E prevents S from carrying out an incorrect choice by
stopping him short if he moves to open a wrong 'door'. S is asked to
try again and urged to look carefully at the cards and counters.
These preliminary choices are not scored.

After the information portion of the trial, the relative positions of
the cards above the doors are altered on all trials. In addition and
subtraction trials E now adds one counter or takes one away from
the collection in front of S, taking care to alert S to the action which
he is taking, and, then scrambles the counters by hand in full view of
S. In conservation trials only the action of scrambling is required.
On half of the trials the counters are, after a short pause, now
covered over to prevent S from recounting them; on the remainder
no such action is taken. All trials are concluded by E inviting S to
respond anew to one of the doors.

Trial	+, − OR C	Initial Number of Objects	Perceptual or Numerical Initial Correspondence	Covered or Uncovered After +, − or C
1	C	8	PC	UC
2	+	6	PC	UC
3	C	7	PC	UC
4	+	6	PC	C
5	C	7	PC	C
6	C	6	PC	C
7	−	8	NC	C
8	+	7	NC	C
9	C	6	NC	C

2. *Provoked Correspondence*. This test is identical in administration to Test I but the choice cards depict six, seven and eight egg-cups and the counters are replaced by eggs. It consists of 18 trials following the sequence below.

TRIAL	+, − OR C	INITIAL NUMBER OF OBJECTS	PERCEPTUAL OR NUMERICAL INITIAL CORRESPONDENCE	COVERED OR UNCOVERED AFTER +, − OR C
1	C	8	PC	UC
2	+	6	PC	UC
3	C	7	PC	UC
4	−	8	PC	C
5	+	7	PC	C
6	C	6	PC	C
7	−	8	PC	UC
8	−	7	PC	UC
9	C	8	PC	UC
10	+	6	PC	C
11	C	7	PC	C
12	C	6	PC	C
13	C	8	NC	UC
14	+	6	NC	UC
15	C	7	NC	UC
16	−	8	NC	C
17	+	7	NC	C
18	C	6	NC	C

3. *Unprovoked Correspondence (Part II)*. This is a continuation of Part I and exactly corresponds to it in administration. It consists of the following sequence of nine trials.

TRIAL	+, − OR C	INITIAL NUMBER OF OBJECTS	PERCEPTUAL OR NUMERICAL INITIAL CORRESPONDENCE	COVERED OR UNCOVERED AFTER +, − OR C
1	−	8	PC	C
2	+	7	PC	C
3	C	6	PC	C
4	−	8	PC	UC
5	−	7	PC	UC
6	C	8	PC	UC
7	C	8	NC	UC
8	+	6	NC	UC
9	C	7	NC	UC

The Development of Conservation of Discontinuous Quantity in the Light of Recent Experimental Findings

As INDICATED on p. 191, results obtained by Mehler and Bever (1967) with the sequence of situations presented in Figure XV led them to suggest that the inability to conserve discontinuous quantity is a temporary phase in the developing child. They propose a developmental sequence in which dependence on inappropriate perceptual strategies temporarily undermines an existing conservation performance capability. This dependence is terminated by the development of a counting approach which permits the reappearance of conservation. In view of the notorious methodological difficulties involved in gathering data from subjects in the two- to four-year-old range it is hardly surprising that the validity of the experimental results on which Mehler and Bever base their proposed sequence has been questioned. Studies by Achenbach (1969), Beilin (1968), Piaget (1968) and Rothenberg and Courtney (1968) have failed to replicate their findings while Bever, Mehler and Epstein (1968) and Calhoun (1971) have obtained results broadly supportive of the outcome of the original investigation.

A view similar to that of Mehler and Bever of the causation of non-conservation performances in the classic Genevan test situation has been recently advanced by Bryant (1971a, b). He argues that non-conservation in these circumstances is due to a misleading but compelling perceptual strategy which prevents existing conservation competence from being carried over into performance rather than to the absence of conservation competence. Three-year-old children understand that the quantity of elements in a collection remains unaltered when it undergoes a perceptual transformation. This conclusion is based on the finding that when the first situation depicted in Figure XV is changed into the second almost all of the children continued to assert that the top row still had more counters than the bottom row. Bryant believes that the children carried out the initial quantitative comparison in the first situation on the basis of one-one correspondence. All the counters were paired off except one. That the children's correct responses in the second situation were based on a

FIGURE **XV**: *Transformations used in recent experiments on conservation of discontinuous quantity*

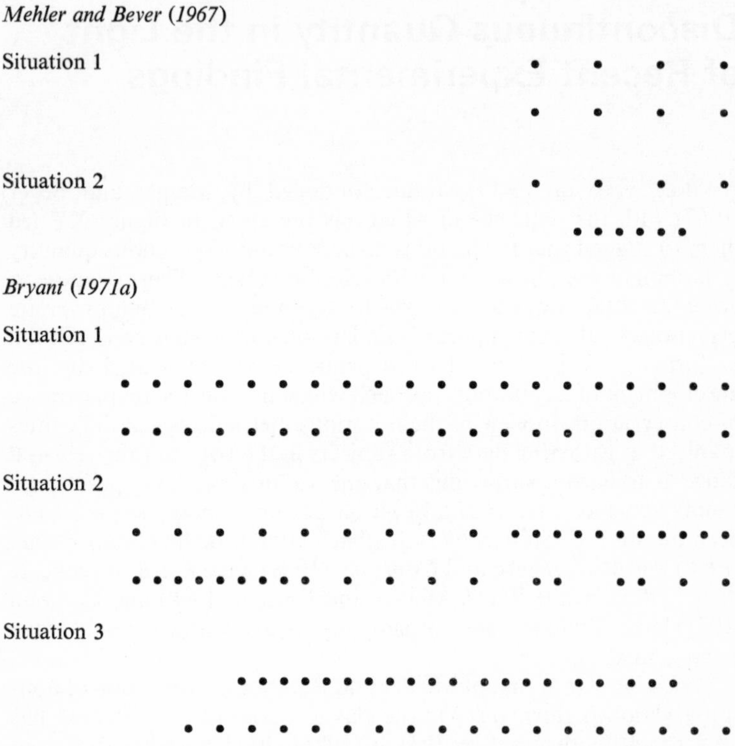

Mehler and Bever (1967)

Situation 1

Situation 2

Bryant (1971a)

Situation 1

Situation 2

Situation 3

---

grasp of the conservation principle is supported by the fact that the numerical level of both rows of counters exceeded the subjects' counting competence. It also appears exceedingly unlikely that their success was achieved by comparing either the length or density of counters of the rows after the perceptual transformation since, when the same subjects were confronted with the second situation without a preceding transformation or an initial opportunity to employ one-one correspondence, there was no evidence of the prevalence of a consistent principle. They were almost evenly divided between those who maintained that the top row contained more counters and those who considered the bottom row represented the greater quantity.

In contrast to these results when the children were presented with a task involving the application of the conservation principle to the change from the first to the third situation in Figure XV they produced non-conserving responses. Bryant attributes this alteration in the level of performance to a clash between the conservation principle and the principle that 'longer means more'. The latter is the stronger principle in children in the age range being studied and can be easily applied to the third situation. It was found, however, that when taught that the length principle was inappropriate the four- and five-year-olds readily abandoned it in favour of the more basic conservation principle. The main feature of development is, thus, not the acquisition of conservation but rather learning when it is essential that the conservation principle should take precedence over less reliable quantification principles.

How do these findings affect the use of conservation tests as indicators of the level of children's intellectual development? Rather than totally invalidating the conservation criterion, a parsimonious interpretation of the evidence suggests that the classic Genevan conservation task should be viewed as tapping one aspect of a complex and protracted developmental process. This viewpoint is not seriously at variance with Piaget's more recent pronouncements on the topic of conservation. This is illustrated in the following section from his discussion of the work of Mehler and Bever: 'In general, children expect conservation, but since they cannot know beforehand what will be conserved and what will not be conserved, they have to construct new means of quantification in every new sector of experience. The inadequacy of the means of quantification explains nonconservation, and it is worth noting that nonconservation therefore indicates an effort to analyse and to dissociate variables; very young children and severely mentally retarded subjects pay no attention to these variables, whereas the older, normal children pass through a stage of nonconservation as they reorganize relations which they cannot yet grasp in full' (Piaget, 1968, p. 978).

The remainder of this discussion will be devoted to the presentation of a theoretical account of the development of conservation of quantity which is broadly consistent with the views expressed by Piaget and, also, of the level of complexity necessary to be consistent with recent experimental results. It constitutes the point of departure for the application of information processing analysis to the problems posed by development of quantification processes in which the writer is currently engaged in co-operation with Professor David Klahr of Carnegie-Mellon University (Klahr and Wallace, 1972)

The account to be offered is nativist exactly to the extent admitted by Piaget (1968) when accepting the necessity of an innate point of departure. An innate neurological and organic *functioning* is required to permit the construction of the processes involved in conservation and quantification in general. No '*structural* hereditary programmation' is presumed. Conservation is not regarded as being 'wired in' but emerges as a result of the operation of a 'functional kernel' via 'a series of self-regulations and equilibrations in which even the errors play a functional success-promoting rôle'.

The basic approach involves regarding the child as an information processing system. The main features of the 'functional kernel' are two systemic principles which are considered to be innate and essential in any account of the transition mechanism underlying cognitive development.

(1) The system constantly searches for consistent sequences of events which will enable the elimination of redundant processing. For example, if the outcome of the application of an operator to a particular repeatedly occurring situation is found to be consistent, the system stores the situation-operator-outcome chain in LTM (long term memory) and dispenses with the processing involved in ascertaining the nature of the outcome on each occasion that the operator is applied.

(2) If the system in a particular context fails to detect consistent sequences the basis of search is widened. This is accomplished by widening the range of the variables in the context which are being considered in the search for consistency. In the case of the development of quantity conservation this is accomplished by widening the range of dimensions of the situation under consideration.

These general principles guide the development of conservation rules. If we judge a child to have conservation, then what he 'has' is a set of rules in LTM that enables him to dispense with a requantification and test of two quantities initially judged equal if a perceptual transformation has been applied to one of them. These rules arise from the detection of consistently recurring outcomes of comparison-transformation-comparison sequences. These sequences are noticed, stored in LTM, classified and generalized in a fashion to be outlined below. Ultimately, the outcomes of initial comparisons and transformations are mapped onto one of these stored sequences and the terminal judgement is read off the sequence, rendering a second quantitative comparison unnecessary.

The account of the appearance of conservation is presented in terms of the development and interaction of three quantification operators or sub-systems which appear to be employed by all humans in their interaction with the environment. These comprise the subitizing (Q_s), counting (Q_c) and estimation (Q_e) quantification operators. In adults Q_s can usually cope with the quantification of collections of up to six discrete elements. The main evidence in support of its existence has been provided by latency studies which indicate that collections within this numerical range can be quantified with a rapidity that seems to rule out the possibility of counting having taken place (Taves, 1941; Saltzman and Garner, 1948; Jensen, Reese and Reese, 1950). Subitizing has tended to be regarded as a primitive largely perceptually based mode of quantification but consideration of the information processing required in a sufficient Q_s (Klahr and Wallace, 1972) suggests that this description is founded on a serious misconception.

Q_s supplies only cardinal numerical information. It is left to Q_c to deal with the ordinal as well as the cardinal aspects. In counting, a term in the list of number names is assigned in ordered succession to each member of the collection of discrete elements being quantified until the collection is exhausted. The term assigned to the last member of the collection is the number of the collection.

Subitizing and counting deal only with discontinuous quantity. Q_e, in contrast, is chiefly employed in coping with continuous quantity although it can be applied to discontinuous elements. The quantitative values generated by the application of Q_s or Q_c first to an elephant and then to a mouse would be identical. It is Q_e which can generate size analogue (*SA*) symbols recording the quantitative difference between the two animals. In adults Q_e can produce more than one *SA* symbol for attachment to the internal representation of an object. This multiple assignment forms the basis for the effective application of Q_e to collections of discontinuous elements. An estimate of the quantity of objects in a long regularly spaced line, for example can be represented by an *SA* symbol equated with the overall length of the line and an *SA* symbol equated with the distance between each pair of objects.

As indicated above, the nature of conservation and the course of its development are determined by the interrelationships of the child's quantification operators. In the Genevan, Mehler and Bever, and Bryant test situations a child is confronted with two quantities of material and encouraged to establish their relative amount by employing any quantification system which he has at his disposal. One of the quantities is then subjected to a perceptual transformation and the child is asked for a judgement on the relative quantitative situation which results. To exhibit conservation the child, for example, must be able to assert the continuing equality of the two quantities without resorting to a reapplication of a quantifying system to them after the transformation. Possession of equivalence conservation can, thus, be characterized in terms of a quantitative comparison-transformation-quantitative comparison rule. The conserving child is able to respond without carrying out the second quantitative comparison. It is hypothesized that this is to be attributed to the detection of consistently recurring outcomes of comparison-transformation-comparison sequences. This permits the storage in LTM of initial comparison outcome-transformation-terminal comparison outcome rules. These provide the basis for future relative quantitative judgements. If the outcome of an initial quantitative comparison and the nature of a transformation which follows it can be mapped onto one of the stored rules a relative quantitative judgement on the terminal situation can be read off the rule, thus rendering a second quantitative comparison unnecessary. It will be noted that this account of equivalence conservation rests heavily on the first of the two systemic assumptions outlined at the outset. The particular initial comparison outcome-transformation-terminal comparison outcome rules necessary to underpin equivalence conservation are presented in Table 27.

The above discussion has been couched in terms of quantitative comparison and quantitative judgement. These general labels were employed to indicate that the account of conservation offered is regarded as being independent of the Q used in carrying out the comparisons and reaching the judgements. In other words, the fundamental criterion for the possession of what Piaget would call 'operational' conservation is that the rules included in Table 27 should be employed in making terminal judgements when any of the three basic Q's is the mode of quantification being applied. Since there are marked differences between the Q's this raises the related developmental questions of how the rules are first detected and how they become a common feature of the application of all three Q's.

It is hypothesized that the answer to the first question lies in the orbit of Q_s. The empirical evidence (Descoeudres, 1946) supports the view that Q_s and Q_e are in operation prior to Q_c and that they probably develop concurrently. Despite their concurrent development the two Q's are far from being equal in their potential for the detection of the rules. Q_s is well suited to this activity since it does not introduce any inconsistency into the situation which prevents the detection of consistent sequences. If the quantities of material

TABLE 27: *Rules necessary for equivalence conservation*

INITIAL RELATION	TRANSFORMATION	FINAL RELATION
Q $x = y$	$T_p\,(y) \to y'$	Q $x = y'$
Q $x = y$	$T_+\,(y) \to y'$	Q $x < y'$
Q $x = y$	$T-\,(y) \to y'$	Q $x > y'$

$$x, y \equiv \text{collections of material}$$
$$y' \equiv \text{collection } y \text{ after a transformation}$$
$$\underset{=,\,>,\,<}{Q\ Q\ Q} \equiv \text{same quantity, greater quantity, smaller quantity}$$
$$T\pm \equiv \text{addition/subtraction}$$
$$T_p \equiv \text{perceptual transformation (i.e., non} - T\pm)$$

being dealt with are discontinuous and lie within a child's subitizing range Q_s will reliably produce quantitative symbols which will give rise to the terminal comparison outcomes listed in Table 27 and, thus, expedite the search for consistency. The Q_e, in contrast, at the same developmental level is a source of so much inconsistency that, if it was the only available quantification operator, the detection of the consistent sequences would be impossible. The reasons for this assertion will be presented below.

The assignment of an important part in the development of conservation to Q_s appears plausible in the context of children's everyday experience. As Bunt (1951) has pointed out, in the course of play experiences and daily activities there is ample opportunity for children to employ subitizing to detect the consistent effects of addition, subtraction and perceptual transformations on small quantities of discrete items such as the other members of their family, shoes, cutlery and so on. 'This experience, gained at first with small numbers of relatively large objects, is gradually extended to large numbers of smaller objects.' Bunt's statement raises the second of the two questions posed above. If the consistent sequences are first detected via the operations of Q_s how do they also become a feature of the functioning of the other two Q's. An answer to this question will be sought for Q_c first and then Q_e will be considered.

Q_c resembles Q_s in that if dealing with discontinuous materials, it will facilitate the discovery of consistent sequences by reliably generating quantitative symbols which will give rise to the terminal comparison outcomes listed in Table 27. It is, thus, possible that the rules are detected in the functioning of Q_c quite independently of their discovery in the context of Q_s. It would, however, be more consistent with the general principle of the elimination of redundancy wherever possible if the system, having detected the consistent sequences in using Q_s, then investigated their applicability to Q_c and Q_e. This proposal is supported by the extreme improbability of independent detection of the consistent sequences in the operations of Q_e. The reliability and consistency characteristic of the fully developed Q_c would render the establishment of the appropriateness of the rules to its functioning a relatively straightforward process.

Before proceeding to Q_e a few remarks will be inserted parenthetically about one-one correspondence. This is most appropriately viewed as a quantification technique closely related to Q_s and developing concurrently with it rather than as a fourth quantification operator in its own right. Since a full justification of this assertion would require a detailed account of the hypothesized course of development of Q_s only an outline of the argument can be offered in the confines of the present discussion.

At the outset of the development of Q_s, if confronted with two identical objects the child represents the situation internally by setting up two identical lists each carrying the values which describe the objects. This mode of operation clearly involves a considerable degree of redundancy and the system, accordingly, adopts an alternative form of representation. In dealing with identical objects only a single list comprising all of the values of the objects is set up. The other objects are represented by empty lists attached to the fully detailed list and labelled as being identical to it. The labelled, empty lists constitute a model collection (Dantzig, 1954) for the type of objects being dealt with. With increasing experience of dealing with a particular type of object several such model collections each representing a possible collection are constructed and stored in LTM. A similar process occurs for other types of objects which the system has to deal with regularly. As a result the system is in the position of having a number of subitizing lists representing the same range of cardinal numbers but tied by labelling to specific classes of objects.

The emergence of the next phase in the refinement of Q_s is, once again, to be attributed to the removal of redundancy. The number of redundant subitizing lists is steadily reduced by 'broadening' the labels to permit the use of single ranges of subitizing lists in coping with several classes or categories. A fairly advanced point in this process is illustrated in the Thimshian language of a British Columbian tribe. It comprises seven distinct sets of number words one of which is used in dealing with flat objects, one with round objects, another for long objects and so on. In our own society this movement away from several subitizing systems linked to specific, concrete classes is eventually complete and gives rise to a single, abstract system. The basis for the operation of the Q_s is thus, a list of lists. Each of the sub-lists represents a model collection and contains a number of 'general object' symbols. In the vast majority of adults the subitizing list comprises six sub-lists which contain from one to six symbols respectively.

When Q_s is in operation, the quantification process consists of the sequential comparison of the list of symbols which constitutes the internal representation of the collection being quantified with each of the sub-lists on the subitizing list. If a match is obtained with one of the sub-lists the collection is assigned the quantitative symbol (number name) which is attached to the appropriate sub-list. The sequential nature of the process is consistent with the experimental data indicating a linear increase in latency when subjects are asked to enumerate collections of dots in the 1–6 range (Saltzman and Garner, 1948).

One-one correspondence resembles Q_s in being purely concerned with cardinal numerical information but differs in that it is only concerned with relative not absolute quantification judgements. The technique of using one-one correspondence in which each object in one collection is compared with an object in the other is in process terms identical to the comparison of a collection with a sub-list which is central to Q_s. In effect, each of the collections being set in one-one correspondence is being used as a model collection for the quantification of the other.

On the basis of the theoretical argument deployed above it would be predicted that, since they share many common processes, the one-one correspondence technique should develop concurrently with the subitizing Q and, in terms of the numerical level at which it can be successfully employed, perhaps quicker due to its relative nature and no internal representation of model collections being required.

Although it produces only relative quantification judgements it is conceivable that the conservation rules might be detected, independently of Q_s, during applications of the one-one correspondence technique to two collections of discrete elements within the subitizing numerical range. It appears unlikely, however, that the one-one correspondence technique alone is sufficient to permit the discovery that rules hold good for collections beyond the subitizing range. Although establishing initial quantitative equality is straightforward if two large collections are arranged in corresponding rows, using one-one correspondence becomes an extremely difficult and error prone technique to employ in making the terminal judgement after a perceptual transformation has destroyed the initial correspondence. It is in just such a situation that Q_c proves its worth.

Q_e develops concurrently with Q_s and is geared to dealing with continuous quantity or collections of discontinuous elements viewed as continuous quantities. As already indicated its initial mode of operation renders the detection of the consistent sequences under-lying the rules virtually impossible. Not only does this preclude the independent discovery of the conservation rules in the functioning of Q_e but it prevents the establishment of the applicability to it of the rules derived from the operations of Q_s.

As Halford (1970) has indicated the main source of inconsistency is that the quantitative symbols generated for comparison by Q_e are based on only one dimension of the situation. This is illustrated in the classic non-conservation responses obtained with the Piagetian equivalence conservation task. Some of the children carry out a terminal comparison of quantitative symbols derived from the lengths of the two collections being compared. Others compare symbols representing the density or distance between the elements of the collections. The early appearance in development of such unidi-mensional quantification by Q_e is attested to by Descoeudres (1946). In a task requiring the construction of a row of objects equal in quantity to a row already constructed by the experimenter he reports that the younger children pay less attention to the number to be reproduced than to the space to be occupied by the row of elements. 'A boy of 3:6 years, for example, who had to reproduce a line of six objects placed the first one and the last one then filled in the space separating them with all of the objects he had saying "It stretches to there, doesn't it?" He had replaced discontinuous quantity with continuous quantity.'

Unidimensional quantification prevents the detection of consistent sequences since no consistent relations between perceptual, addition or subtraction transformations and the results of subsequent quantitative comparisons of the rows are obtained. This is, of course, due to the effect of variations in the dimension of the rows which is ignored during the quantification. Appropriate alterations in the ignored dimension can produce any of the three possible outcomes (more, less or equal) under any of the transformations. In contrast, if both dimensions are included in the quantification process consistent relationships emerge between the transformations and subsequent judgement outcomes.

What underlies the shift of Q_e from a single to a two dimensional mode of working? As indicated above, it is hypothesized that in accordance with the general principle of eliminating redundancy the system investigates the applicability to Q_e of the rules discovered in using Q_s. Independent of the redundancy elimination principle there is striking empirical evidence that the preservation of consistency and agreement between the judgmental outcomes of the $Q's$ operates as an important goal. The intriguing examples of the expedients to which children will resort to obtain consistency between the outcomes of Q_e and Q_c provided by Inhelder and Sinclair (1969) have already been described (p. 108–9).

Attempts to apply the conservation rules to Q_e and to preserve agreement between its outcomes and those of the other $Q's$ are doomed to failure due to its unidimensional basis. It is at this juncture in development that the second systemic assumption outlined above becomes relevant. Confronted with the failed goal of detecting consistent sequences it is suggested that the system seems to remove the difficulty by widening the range of the variables in the context being considered. This tactic gives rise to the quantification of the second dimension and, consequently, to the detection of the sequences and success in the application of the conservation rules to the operations of Q_e.

When the applicability to Q_c and Q_e of the rules detected in the functioning of Q_s has been established the child has attained the criterion proposed for 'operational' conservation. The conservation rules will be employed in making terminal judgements when any of the three basic $Q's$ is the mode of quantification being applied. The adoption of this criterion has important implications. It leaves considerable room for individual variations in the course of the development of conservation. This emphasis on individual variation is consistent with a number of empirical findings. As indicated above, Gréco (1962), for example, reports that some of his subjects when undergoing equivalence conservation trials with two rows of discontinuous elements continue to give classic non-conservation responses on the terminal quantitative judgements but when questioned on the numerosity of the terminal collections are able to respond correctly that 'You have six and I have six' or 'There were five before'. This distinction between 'quotité' and 'quantité' can be interpreted in terms of our criterion as stemming from subjects who are employing the conservation rules in making terminal judgements when Q_c is in operation but whose Q_e is still functioning on an unidimensional and, thus, inconsistent basis.

What interpretation of the recent experimental evidence can be advanced on the basis of the account offered of the development of conservation of quantity? Three features of the proposed theory seem to be particularly relevant. They comprise the existence of variations in the developmental level of the three Q's, the system's tactic of applying two Q's to the same situation and seeking to preserve consistency and agreement between their judgemental outcomes, and the occurrence of switching from Q to Q in the course of a quantification task. A fine example of switching has been provided by Descoeudres (1946). This, once again, arose from the children's performance on the task requiring the construction of a row of objects equal in quantity to a row already constructed by the experimenter. A subject aged 3:6 years, asked to reproduce a row of four objects put three in his row, paused and asked the experimenter, 'There are still some aren't there?', and then made his row up to five. This behaviour is consistent with the child reaching the limit of his subitizing competence at three and switching to Q_e to complete the task.

In the case of the Mehler and Bever experiments the results of the replication studies have produced a confused situation in which the data points that a sufficient theory would have to fit are unclear. Numerous procedural variations in the studies have contributed to the complex picture presented by the data. The theory outlined above, however, suggests that some of the complexity may be attributable to a cognitive—developmental rather than a procedural source. As Figure XV indicates the basic experimental situation used in these studies is of a type likely to produce a complex interaction between the three Q's. Quantitative equivalence between the two rows of counters in the initial situation could be established on the basis of Q_s, one-one correspondence, Q_c or Q_e operating on one or two dimensions. This is followed by a difficult, double transformation combining a perceptual change (T_p) with addition (T_+). The resulting situation includes a row that is beyond the numerical range of Q_s in the vast majority of children in the two to four years age range, and, also, exceeds their counting competence. Even if operating on two dimensions of the final situation there is no guarantee that Q_e will produce the correct judgement. Success can only be certain if the system possesses *and employs* a Q in which the conservation rules have been adopted. In view of the prevalance of double application and switching of Q's this, in turn, is only sure if 'operational' conservation has been achieved and the rules are applied in the functioning of all three quantification operators.

The current situation with regard to Bryant's findings is still comparatively clearcut since, at the time of writing, the details necessary for the replication of his experiments are not yet available. In terms of the suggested theory, the general success of even Bryant's youngest subjects in coping with the transformation of the first situation in Figure XV to the second is attributed to the application of conservation rules possessed by Q_s in a situation in which a switch to Q_c or Q_e after the perceptual transformation is unlikely. The initial quantitative comparison, as Bryant asserts, is accomplished via one-one correspondence. Due to the close connection between this approach and Q_s the conservation rules attached to Q_s are mobilized and applied to the situation. The resulting judgement becomes the child's final response since the numerical level of the rows of counters is beyond the competence of Q_c and Q_e does not produce a unique result. Density appears to be the most probable single dimension of the second situation to which Q_e could be applied. No unique outcome would result since this situation is an example of what Bryant (1971b) calls an 'indeterminate display'. It does not give rise to a definite quantitative judgement, as a scan of the upper and lower rows indicates that both are 'more dense' in part. In contrast, when the first situation in Figure XV is transformed to the third, the application of Q_e and the adoption of the outcome as the final response is much more frequent since it yields an unambiguous result on either the length or density dimensions. The high frequency of non-conserving responses indicates that in the third situation length is the preferred dimension for the operation of Q_e.

It will be recalled that Bryant succeeded in eliciting conservation responses from his subjects in spite of the first to third situation transformation by teaching them that the length principle is an inappropriate judgemental basis. This technique is effective because it discourages the children from using Q_e and, consequently, removes the main distinction between the outcome of the first to third and the first to second situation transformations. The apparent importance of the counting activity elicited by both of the acceleration techniques in the present study (see p. 122–125) can be partly explained in a similar fashion. The adoption of an approach involving counting or recounting after the situation has been transformed discourages the use of Q_e. It, also, facilitates generalization of the application of the conservation rules to Q_c or their independent discovery in the operations of Q_c.

In conclusion it should be pointed out that a training technique aimed solely at decreasing the frequency with which Q_e is employed in making quantitative judgements may improve children's conservation performance in the type of test situations described but is not sufficient to produce 'operational' conservation. This requires that the conservation rules be applied in the operations of all three Q's. For this objective to be achieved Q_e must be permitted to function in order that the system may shift from one to two dimensional working. With this accomplished, further exercise of Q_e is necessary to permit detection of the consistent sequences and, consequently, discovery of the applicability of the conservation rules.

REFERENCES[1]

ANNETT, M. (1959). 'The classification of four common class concepts by children and adults', *Brit. J. Educ. Psychol.*, **29**.

ATTNEAVE, F. (1959). *Applications of Information Theory to Psychology*. New York: Holt, Rinehart & Winston.

AZUMA, H. (1965). Report of study conducted by Faculty of Education, University of Tokyo, included in private communication to the writer.

BARTLETT, F. C. (1958). *Thinking*. London: Allen & Unwin.

BEILIN, H. (1965). 'Learning and operational convergence in logical thought development', *J. Exper. Child Psychol.*, **2**, 317–39.

BEILIN, H. (1968). 'Cognitive capacities of young children: a replication', *Science*, **162**, 920–1.

BERLYNE, D. E. (1960). *Conflict, Arousal and Curiosity*. New York: McGraw-Hill.

BERLYNE, D. E. (1965). *Structure and Direction in Thinking*. New York: Wiley.

BERTALANFFY, L. VON (1960). 'Comments on Professor Piaget's paper'. In: TANNER, J. M. and INHELDER, B., eds. *Discussions on Child Development, Vol. IV*. London: Tavistock.

BEVER, T. G., MEHLER, J. and EPSTEIN, J. (1968). 'What children do in spite of what they know', *Science*, **162**, 921–4.

BIRCH, H. G. and LEFFORD, A. (1963). 'Intersensory development in children', *Monogr. Soc. Res. Child Dev.*, **28**, No. 5.

BRAINE, M. D. S. (1959). 'The ontogeny of certain logical operations: Piaget's formulations examined by non-verbal methods', *Psychol. Monogr.*, **73**, 5.

BRAINE, M. D. S. (1962). 'Piaget on reasoning; a methodological critique and alternative proposals'. In: KESSEN, W. and KUHLMAN, C., eds. 'Thought in the young child', *Child Dev. Monogr.*, **27**, 2, 41–61.

BRAINE, M. D. S. (1964). 'Development of a grasp of transitivity of length: a reply to Smedslund', *Child Dev.*, **35**, 799–810.

BRAINE, M. D. S. and SHANKS, BETTY L. (1965). 'The development of conservation of size', *J. Verbal Learning & Verbal Behav.*, **4**, 227–42.

BRIMER, M. A. (1967). *The Classification of Qualitative Data*. Unpublished document. University of Bristol, School of Education.

BRUNER, J. S. (1964). 'The course of cognitive growth', *Amer. Psychologist*, **19**, 1–15.

BRUNER, J. S., GOODNOW, JACQUELINE, J. and AUSTIN, G. (1956). *A Study of Thinking*. New York: Wiley.

BRUNER, J. S., OLVER, ROSE and GREENFIELD, PATRICIA M. (1966). *Studies in Cognitive Growth*. New York: Wiley.

[1]References relating to Appendix B appear as a separate section at the end of this list.

BUNT, L. N. H. (1951). *The Development of Ideas of Number and Quantity According to Piaget*. Groningen: Wolter.

CELÉRIER, G. (1972). 'Some information processing tendencies of recent experiments in cognitive learning: Part B'. In: FARNHAM-DIGGORY, S., ed. *Information Processing in Children*. New York: Academic Press.

CHURCHILL, E. M. (1958). 'The number concepts of the young child', *Leeds Univ. Res. & Stud.*, **17**, 34–49, and **18**, 28–46.

DIENES, Z. P. (1959). *Concept Formation and Personality*. Leicester: University Press.

DIENES, Z. P. (1965). 'Mathematics in primary education', *International Studies in Education* (UNESCO Institute for Education), Hamburg, 33–4.

DODWELL, P. C. (1960). 'Children's understanding of number and related concepts', *Canad. J. Psychol.*, **14**, 191–205.

ELKIND, D. (1961). 'Quantity conceptions in junior and senior high school students', *Child Dev.*, **32**, 551–60.

ERNST, G. and NEWELL, A. (1969). 'GPS: A Study in Generality and Problem Solving'. New York: Academic Press.

FERRIER, W. M. (1962). *The New Cage*. Four Way Number Picture Readers, Book 2. Leeds: Arnold.

FLAVELL, J. H. (1963). *The Developmental Psychology of Jean Piaget*. New York: Van Nostrand.

FLAVELL, J. H. (1971). 'Stage-related properties of cognitive development'. *Cognitive Psychol.*, **2**.

FLAVELL, J. H. and WOHLWILL, J. F. (1969). 'Formal and functional aspects of cognitive development'. In: ELKIND, D. and FLAVELL, J. H., eds. *Studies in Cognitive Development*. New York: Oxford University Press.

FRANK, F. (1964). See: 'The course of cognitive growth', by BRUNER, J. S. *Amer. Psychologist*, **19**, 1, 6–7.

FURTH, H. G. (1966). *Thinking Without Language, Psychological Implications of Deafness*. New York: Free Press.

GAGNÉ, R. M. (1968). 'Contributions of learning to human development', *Psychol. Rev.*, **75**, 177–91.

GAL'PERIN, P. YA and TALYZINA, N. F. (1961). 'Formation of elementary geometrical concepts and their dependence on directed participation by the pupils'. In: O'CONNOR, N., ed. *Recent Soviet Psychology*, 247–72. London: Pergamon.

GELLERMANN, L. W. (1933). 'Chance orders of alternating stimuli in visual discrimination experiments', *Ped. Sem.*, **42**, 206–8.

GONZALEZ, R. C. and ROSS, S. (1958). 'The basis of solution by children of the intermediate-size problem', *Amer. J. Psychol.*, **71**, 742–6.

GRÉCO, P. (1962). 'Quotité et quantité'. In: PIAGET, J., ed. *Structures Numeriques Elementaires*. Paris: Presses Universitaires de France (Etudes d'Épistemologie Génétique, 13).

GREGG, L. W. and SIMON, H. A. (1967). 'Process models and stochastic theories of simple concept formation', *J. Math. Psychol.*, **4**, 246–76.

DE GROOT, A. D. (1965). *Thought and Choice in Chess*. The Hague: Mouton.

GRUEN, G. E. (1965). 'Experience affecting the development of number conservation in children', *Child Dev.*, **36**, 963–79.

HALL, V. C. and KINGSLEY, R. (1968). 'Conservation and equilibration theory', *J. Genet. Psychol.*, **113**, 195–213.

HARLOW, H. F. (1959). 'Learning set and error factor theory'. In: KOCH, S., ed. *Psychology: a Study of a Science, Vol. II*, 492–537. New York: McGraw-Hill.

HUMPHREY, G. (1963). *Thinking*. New York: Wiley.

INHELDER, BARBEL (1965). 'Operational thought and symbolic imagery'. In: MUSSEN, P. H., ed. 'European research in cognitive development'. *Monogrs. Soc. Research in Child Develop.* Serial No. 100, **30**, No. 2, 4–18.

INHELDER, BARBEL (1972). 'Information processing tendencies of recent experiments in cognitive learning'. In: FARNHAM-DIGGORY, S., ed. *Information Processing in Children*. New York: Academic Press.

INHELDER, BARBEL, BOVET, MAGALI, SINCLAIR, HERMINE and SMOCK, C. D. (1966). 'On cognitive development', *American Psychologist*, **2**, 160–4.

INHELDER, BARBEL and SINCLAIR, HERMINE (1969). 'Learning cognitive structures'. In: MUSSEN, P., LANGER, J. and COVINGTON, M., eds. *Trends and Issues in Developmental Psychology*. New York: Holt, Rinehart & Winston.

ITO, Y. and HATANO, G. (1963). 'An experimental education of number conservation', *Japanese Psychological Research*, **5**, 4, 161–70.

JEEVES, M. A. (1968). 'Experiments on structured thinking', *Austral. J. Psychol.*, **20**, 93–110.

KENDLER, H. H. and VINEBERG, R. (1964). 'The acquisition of compound concepts as a function of previous training'.

KESSEN, W. (1962). 'Stage and structure in the study of children'. In: KESSEN, W. and KUHLMAN, C., eds. 'Thought in the Young Child'. *Monographs Soc. Res. in Child Develop.*, **27**, 2, 65–86.

KINGSLEY, R. and HALL, V. C. (1967). 'Training conservation through the use of learning sets'. *Child Develop.*, **38**, 1111–26.

KISS, G. R. (1968). 'Words, associations and networks'. *J. Verbal Learning and Verbal Beh.*, **7**, 703–13.

KISS, G. R. (1969). 'Steps towards a model of word selection'. In: MELTZER, B. and MICHIE, D., eds. *Machine Intelligence 4*. Edinburgh: The University Press.

KLAHR, D. and WALLACE, J. G. (1970a). 'An information processing analysis of some Piagetian experimental tasks', *Cognitive Psychol.*, **1**, 358–87.

KLAHR, D. and WALLACE, J. G. (1970b). 'The development of serial completion strategies: an information processing analysis', *Brit. J. Psychol.*, **61**, 243–57.

KLAHR, D. and WALLACE, J. G. (1972). 'Class Inclusion Processes'. In: FARNHAM-DIGGORY, S., ed. *Information Processing in Children*. New York: Academic Press.

KOFSKEY, ELLEN (1966). 'A scalogram study of classificatory development', *Child Dev.*, **37**, 191–204.

LAURENDEAU, MONIQUE and PINARD, A. (1962). *La Pensée Causale*, Paris: Presses Universitaires de France.

LAURENDEAU, MONIQUE and PINARD, A. (1966). 'Reflexions sur l'apprentissage des structures logiques'. In: BRESSON, F. and DE MONTMOLLIN, M., eds. *Psychologie et Epistemologie Génétique*. Paris: Dunod.

LOEVINGER, J. (1947). 'A systematic approach to the construction and evaluation of tests of ability', *Psychol. Monogr.*, **61**, 4 (whole No. 285).

LUNZER, E. A. (1970). 'Effectiveness of short-term instruction in conservation'. Abstracts of BPS Education Section Annual Conference, 44–7.
LURIA, A. R. (1969). *The Mind of a Mnemonist*. London: Cape.

MAXWELL, A. E. (1961). *Analysing Qualitative Data*. London: Methuen.
MCNEILL, D. (1970). *The Development of Language*. New York: Harper & Row.
MEHLER, J. and BEVER, T. G. (1967). 'Cognitive capacity of very young children'. *Science*, **158**, 141–2.
MURRAY, J. P. and YOUNISS, J. (1968). 'Achievement of inferential transitivity and its relation to serial ordering'. *Child Dev.*, **39**, 1259–68.

NEWELL, A. and SIMON, H. A. (1961). 'Computer simulation of human thinking'. *Science*, **134**, 2011–17.
NEWELL, A. and SIMON, H. A. (1971). *Human Problem Solving*. New York: Prentice-Hall.

OBUKHOVA, L. F. (1966). 'Experimental formation of representations of invariantness in five- and six-year-old children'. In: *Symposium 24: Concept Formation and Inner Action*, XVIII. International Congress of Psychology, Moscow, 103–8.
OLÉRON, P. (1961). 'L'acquisition des conservations et le langage', *Enfance*, 201–19.
OSTERRIETH, P. A. (1956). 'Les stades du développement selon d'autres écoles de psychologie'. In: OSTERRIETH, *et al. Le Probleme des Stades en Psychologie de l'Enfant*, 43–9. Paris: Presses Universitaires de France.

PAIGE, J. M. and SIMON, H. A. (1966). 'Cognitive processes in solving algebra word problems'. In: KLEINMUNTZ, B., ed. *Problem Solving: Research, Method and Theory*. New York: Wiley.
PASCUAL-LEONE, J. and SMITH, J. (1969). 'The encoding and decoding of symbols by children: a new experimental paradigm and a neo-Piagetian model', *J. Exp. Child Psychol.*, **8**, 328–55.
PASCUAL-LEONE, J. (1970). 'A mathematical model for the transition rule in Piaget's developmental stages', *Acta Psychologica*, **32**, 301–45.
PIAGET, J. (1926). *La Presentation du Monde chez L'Enfant*. Paris: Alcan.
PIAGET, J. (1941). 'Le mécanisme du développement mental et les lois du groupement des operations', *Arch. Psychol.* (Geneve), **28**, 215–85.
PIAGET, J. (1952). *The Origin of Intelligence in the Child*. New York: International Universities Press.
PIAGET, J. (1954). *The Construction of Reality in the Child*. New York: Basic Books.
PIAGET, J. (1956). 'Les stades du développement selon d'autres écoles de psychologie'. In: OSTERREITH, P. A., *et al.*, *Le Problème des Stades en Psychologie de L'Enfant*, 43–9. Paris: Presses Universitaires de France.
PIAGET, J. (1957). 'Logique et équilibre dans les comportements du sujet'. In: APOSTEL, L., MANDELBROT, B. and PIAGET, J., *Logique et Equilibre, Etudes, D'Epistémologie Génétique*, **2**, 27–113.
PIAGET, J. (1959). 'Apprentissage et connaissance: II'. In: GOUSTARD, K., GRÉCO, P., MATALON, B. and PIAGET, J., 'La Logique des Apprentissages'. *Etudes d'Epistémologie Génétique*, **10**, 159–88.
PIAGET, J. (1960). In: TANNER, J. M. and INHELDER, B., eds. *Discussions on Child Development*, **IV**, 3–27, 77–83. London: Tavistock.

REITMAN, W. R. (1965). *Cognition and Thought*. New York: Wiley.
RENWICK, E. M. (1963). *Children Learning Mathematics*. Stockwell: Ilfracombe.

References

ROTHENBERG, BARBARA B. and OROST, JEAN H. (1969). 'The training of conservation of number in young children', *Child Dev.*, **40**, 707–26.

SCHRODER, H. M., DRIVER, M. and STREUFERT, S. (1967). *Human Information Processing: Individuals and Groups Functioning in Complex Social Situations.* London: Holt, Rinehart & Winston.

SIGEL, I. E., ROEPER, ANNEMARIE and HOOPER, F. H. (1966). 'A training procedure for acquisition of Piaget's conservation of quantity: a pilot study and its replication', *Brit. J. Educ. Psychol.*, **36**, 301–11.

SIGEL, I. E. (1969). 'The Piagetian system and the world of education'. In: ELKIND, D. and FLAVELL, J. H., eds. *Studies in Cognitive Development.* New York: Oxford University Press.

SINCLAIR-DE ZWART, HERMINE (1967). *Acquisition du Langage et Développement de la Pensée.* Paris: Dunod.

SIMON, H. A. (1963). 'An Information Processing Theory of Intellectual Development'. In: KESSEN, W. and KUHLMAN, C., eds. *Thought in the Young Child.* Lakebluff, Illinois: Child Development Publications.

SLOBIN, D. I. and WELSH, C. A. (1967). 'Elicited imitation as a research tool in developmental psycholinguistics'. Unpublished paper, Department of Psychology, University of California (Berkeley).

SMEDSLUND, J. (1959). 'Apprentissage des notions de la conservation et de la transitivité du poids'. In: MORF, A., SMEDSLUND, J., VINH-BANG and WOHLSILL, J. F., 'L'Apprentissage des Structures Logiques', *Etudes d'Epistémologie Génétique*, **9**, 85–124.

SMEDSLUND, J. (1961). 'The acquisition of conservation of substance and weight in children', *Scand. J. Psychol.*, 2.

SMEDSLUND, J. (1963a). 'Patterns of experience and the acquisition of conservation of length'.

SMEDSLUND, J. (1963b). 'Development of concrete transitivity of length in children', *Child Dev.*, **34**, 389–405.

SMEDSLUND, J. (1964). 'Concrete reasoning: a study of intellectual development', *Child Dev. Monogr.*, **29**, 2.

SMEDSLUND, J. (1966a). 'Les origines sociales de la décentration'. In: BRESSON, F. and DE MONTMOLLIN, M., eds. *Psychologie et Epistémologie Génétique.* Paris: Dunod.

SMEDSLUND, J. (1966b). 'Microanalysis of concrete reasoning I. The difficulty of some combinations of addition and subtraction of one unit', *Scand. J. Psychol.*, **7**, 145–56.

SMEDSLUND, J. (1966c). 'Microanalysis of concrete reasoning II. The effect of number transformations and non-redundant elements, and some variations in procedure', *Scand. J. Psychol.*, **7**, 157–63.

SMEDSLUND, J. (1966d). 'Microanalysis of concrete reasoning III. Theoretical overview', *Scand. J. Psychol.*, **7**, 164–7.

SMEDSLUND, J. (1968). 'Conservation and resistance to extinction: a comment on Hall and Simpson's article', *Merrill-Palmer Quarterly*, **14**, 211–4.

SMEDSLUND, J. (1969). 'Psychological diagnostics', *Psychol. Bull.*, **71**, 237–48.

SMITH, I. D. (1968). 'The effects of training procedures upon the acquisition of conservation of weight', *Child Dev.*, **39**, 515–26.

SONSTROEM, A. McK. (1965). In: Fifth Annual Report of Harvard University Center for Cognitive Studies, 51–4.

STAATS, A. W. (1968). *Learning, Language and Cognition.* New York: Holt, Rinehart & Winston.

TERRELL, G. (1959). 'Manipulatory motivation in children', *J. Comp. Physiol. Psychol.*, **52**, 705–9.

UZGIRIS, INA (1964). 'Situational generality of conservation'. *Child Dev.*, **35**, 831–42.

VINH-BANG (1957). 'Elaboration d'une échelle de développement du raisonnement'. In: Proceedings of 15th International Congress of Psychology, Brussels.

WALLACE, J. G. (1965). *Concept Growth and the Education of the Child.* Slough: NFER.

WALLACE, J. G. (1967). 'An inquiry into the development of concepts of number in young children involving a comparison of verbal and non-verbal methods of assessment and acceleration'. Unpublished PhD Dissertation, Dept. of Psychology, University of Bristol.

WALLACE, J. G. and LEIGH-LUCAS, L. (1970). 'The acquisition and "extinction" of conservation of weight', *Durham Res. Rev.*, **24**, 441–8.

WALLACH, L. and SPROTT, R. L. (1964). 'Inducing number conservation in children', *Child Dev.*, **35**, 1057–71.

WALLACH, LISE, WALL, A. J. and ANDERSON, LORNA (1967). 'Number conservation: the roles of reversibility, addition-subtraction and misleading perceptual cues', *Child Dev.*, **38**, 425–42.

WHITE, S. H. (1963). 'Learning'. In: STEVENSON, H. W., *Child Psychology*, Part I, 62nd Yearbook, NSSE.

WILLIAMS, A. A. (1958). 'Number readiness', *Educ. Rev.*, **11**, 310–45.

WOHLWILL, J. F. (1960). 'A study of the development of the number concept by scalogram analysis', *J. Genet. Psychol.*, **97**, 345–77.

WOHLWILL, J. F. (1966a). 'Readiness, transfer of learning and the development of cognitive structures'. Paper presented at Annual Conference of Canada Psychol. Ass.

WOHLWILL, J. F. (1966b). 'Piaget's theory of the development of intelligence in the concrete operations period'. In: GARRISON, M., ed. 'Cognitive models and development in mental retardation'. *American Mental Def. Monogr. Suppl.*, **70**, 57–83.

WOHLWILL, J. F. and LOWE, R. C. (1962). 'Experimental analysis of the development of the conservation of number', *Child Dev.*, **3**, 152–67.

ZAZZO, R. (1960). 'Comments on Professor Piaget's paper'. In: TANNER, J. M. and INHELDER, B., eds. *Discussions on Child Development*, Vol. IV. London: Tavistock.

ZIMILES, H. (1963). 'A note on Piaget's concept of conservation', *Child Dev.*, **34**, 691–5.

ADDITIONAL REFERENCES RELATING TO APPENDIX B

ACHENBACH, T. M. (1969). ' "Conservation" below age three: fact or artefact?' *Proceedings of the 77th Annual Convention of the American Psychological Assoc.*, **4**, 275–6.

BRYANT, P. E. (1971a). Experiments described in the *Observer*, 22nd August, 1.

BRYANT, P. E. (1971b). 'Cognitive development', *British Medical Bulletin*, **27**, 200–5.

CALHOUN, L. G. (1971). 'Number conservation in very young children: the effect of age and mode of responding', *Child Dev.*, **42**, 561–72.

DANTZIG, T. (1954). *Number: The Language of Science*, 4th edit. revised. New York: Macmillan.

DESCOEUDRES, A. (1946). *Le Développement de L'Enfant de Deux à Sept Ans* 3rd edit. Neuchatel: Delachaux & Niestlé.

HALFORD, G. S. (1970). 'A theory of the acquisition of conservation'. *Psychological Rev.*, **77**, 4, 302–16.

JENSEN, E. M., REESE, E. P. and REESE, T. W. (1950). 'The subitizing and counting of visually presented fields of dots', *J. Psychol.*, **30**, 363–92.

KLAHR, D. and WALLACE, J. G. (1972). 'Quantification processes in the development of conservation'. To be presented at the XXth International Congress of Psychology, Tokyo.

ROTHENBERG, B. and COURTNEY, R. (1968). 'Conservation of number in very young children: a replication of and a comparison with Mehler and Bever's study', *J. Psychol.*, **70**, 205–12.

SALTZMAN, I. J. and GARNER, W. R. (1948). 'Reaction time as a measure of span for attention', *J. Psychol.*, **25**, 227–41.

TAVES, E. H. (1941). 'Two mechanisms for the perception of visual numerousness', *Arch. Psychol.*, **37**, 1–47.

AUTHOR INDEX

SUBJECT INDEX

CHRIST CHURCH COLLEGE
CANTERBURY

This book must be returned (or renewed) on or
before the date last marked

11 JAN 1975

13 MAY 1975

14 OCT 1975

20 JAN 1977

11 DEC 1978

DEC 1979

980

80

21. JUN. 1997

– 6 MAY 2005

C61180

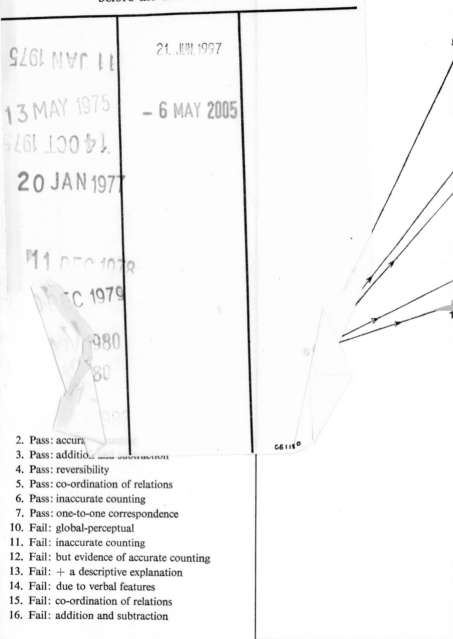

...lustrating the develop...
...ost-test data (see Cha...

2. Pass: accur...
3. Pass: addition and subtraction
4. Pass: reversibility
5. Pass: co-ordination of relations
6. Pass: inaccurate counting
7. Pass: one-to-one correspondence
10. Fail: global-perceptual
11. Fail: inaccurate counting
12. Fail: but evidence of accurate counting
13. Fail: + a descriptive explanation
14. Fail: due to verbal features
15. Fail: co-ordination of relations
16. Fail: addition and subtraction